TWIN RESEARCH 3
Part C
Epidemiological and Clinical Studies

PROGRESS IN CLINICAL AND BIOLOGICAL RESEARCH

Series Editors
Nathan Back
George J. Brewer

Vincent P. Eijsvoogel
Robert Grover
Kurt Hirschhorn

Seymour S. Kety
Sidney Udenfriend
Jonathan W. Uhr

RECENT TITLES

See pages 281 – 282 for previous titles in this series.

TWIN RESEARCH 3

Proceedings of the Third International
Congress on Twin Studies
June 16 – 20, 1980
Jerusalem

Part C
Epidemiological and Clinical Studies

Editors

Luigi Gedda
The Gregor Mendel Institute of
Medical Genetics and Twin Studies
Rome

Paolo Parisi
The Gregor Mendel Institute of
Medical Genetics and Twin Studies
Rome

Walter E. Nance
Department of Human Genetics
Medical College of Virginia
Richmond, Virginia

Alan R. Liss, Inc., New York

Address all Inquiries to the Publisher
Alan R. Liss, Inc., 150 Fifth Avenue, New York, NY 10011

Copyright © 1981 Alan R. Liss, Inc.

Printed in the United States of America.

Library of Congress Cataloging in Publication Data

International Congress on Twin Studies (3rd : 1980 :
    Jerusalem)
    Twin research 3.

    (Progress in clinical and biological research ;
v. 69)
    Includes indexes.
    Contents: pt. A. Twin biology and multiple
pregnancy — pt. B. Intelligence, personality, and
development — pt. C. Epidemiological and clinical
studies.
    1. Pregnancy, Multiple — Congresses. 2. Twins —
Congresses. 3. Twins — Psychology — Congresses.
4. Diseases in twins — Congresses.   I. Gedda, Luigi.
II. Parisi, Paolo. III. Nance, Walter E. IV. Title.
V. Series. [DNLM: 1. Research — Congresses. 2. Twins —
Congresses. W1 PR668E v. 69 / WQ 235 I59 1980a]
RG567.I57 1980   610'.88045   81-12376
                                    AACR2

3 Volume Set ISBN 0-8451-0069-6
Part C Epidemiological and Clinical Studies ISBN 0-8451-0160-9

Contents

Contributors to Part C

Sheree Andersen [187]
Department of Medical Biophysics and Computing, LDS Hospital, The University of Utah, Salt Lake City, UT 84143

Jacob E. Bearman [13]
Epidemiology Unit, Ben-Gurion University of the Negev, Be'er Sheva, 84120 Israel

Kåre Berg [117, 163]
Institute of Medical Genetics, University of Oslo, Oslo, Norway

W. Carl Breckenridge [149]
Department of Biochemistry, Faculty of Medicine, Dalhousie University, Halifax, Nova Scotia, B3H 4H7, Canada

G. Brenci [9, 169, 247]
The Gregor Mendel Institute of Medical Genetics and Twin Studies, Piazza Galeno 5, 00161 Rome, Italy

Joseph Brocteur [239]
Laboratory of Blood Groups and Transfusion, University of Liège, Liège, Belgium

Kenneth S. Brown [97]
Laboratory of Developmental Biology and Anomalies, National Institute of Dental Research, Bethesda, MD 20205

Philip R.J. Burch [179]
Department of Medical Physics, University of Leeds, The General Infirmary, Leeds, LS1 3EK, England

Dorit Carmelli [187]
Department of Medical Biophysics and Computing, LDS Hospital, The University of Utah, Salt Lake City, Utah 84143

Joe C. Christian [149]
Department of Medical Genetics, Indiana University School of Medicine, Indianapolis, IN 46223

C.A. Clifford [47, 77]
Department of Psychology, Institute of Psychiatry, De Crespigny Park, London, SE5 8AF, England

J. Craig [89]
Department of Pharmacology, University of Sydney, Sydney, NSW 2006, Australia

A.B. Das-Chaudhuri [231]
Department of Anthropology, University of Hamburg, Hamburg, Federal Republic of Germany

The boldface number in brackets following each contributor's name indicates the opening page number of that author's paper.

Elisabeth Defrise-Gussenhoven [239]
Centrum of Biomathematics, Free University of Brussels, (V.U.B.)
Brussels 1050, Belgium

C. Di Fusco [247]
The Gregor Mendel Institute of Medical Genetics and Twin Studies,
Piazza Galeno 5, 00161 Rome, Italy

Richard R. Fabsitz [97]
Epidemiology Branch, National Heart, Lung, and Blood Institute,
Bethesda, MD 20205

Manning Feinleib [97, 149]
Epidemiology Branch, National Heart, Lung, and Blood Institute,
Bethesda, MD 20205

Gary D. Friedman [17]
Department of Medical Methods Research, Kaiser-Permanente Medical
Care Program, Oakland, CA 94611

D.W. Fulker [47]
Department of Psychology, Institute of Psychiatry, De Crespigny Park,
London, SE5 8AF, England

R.J. Garrison [149]
Epidemiology and Biometry Program, Division of Heart and Vascular
Diseases, National Heart, Lung, and Blood Institute, Bethesda, MD
20205

L. Gedda [9, 169, 247]
The Gregor Mendel Institute of Medical Genetics and Twin Studies,
Piazza Galeno 5, 00161 Rome, Italy

J.B. Gibson [89]
Department of Population Biology, Research School of Biological
Sciences, Australian National University, PO Box 475, Canberra City,
ACT 2601, Australia

Donald W. Goodwin [71]
Department of Psychiatry, University of Kansas Medical Center, 39th
and Rainbow, Kansas City, KS 66103

H.M.D. Gurling [47, 77]
Department of Psychiatry, Institute of Psychiatry, De Crespigny Park,
London, SE5 8AF, England

Donald Guthrie [105]
Department of Psychiatry and Biobehavioral Sciences, University of
California, Los Angeles, CA 90024

Arvid Heiberg [163]
Institute of Medical Genetics, University of Oslo, Oslo, Norway

Niels V. Holm [211]
Institute of Clinical Genetics and the Danish Twin Register, Odense
University, DK-5000 Odense, Denmark

Bernadette Hoste [239]
Laboratory of Blood Groups and Transfusion, University of Liège,
Liège, Belgium

Zdenek Hrubec [1]
Medical Follow-up Agency, National Academy of Sciences-National
Research Council, Washington, DC 20418

Helen B. Hubert [97]
Epidemiology Branch, National Heart, Lung, and Blood Institute, Bethesda, MD 20205

Stephen B. Hulley [17]
Department of Epidemiology and International Health, University of California, San Francisco, CA 94143

Lillian Ingster-Moore [149]
Epidemiology and Biometry Program, Division of Heart and Vascular Diseases, National Heart, Lung, and Blood Institute, Bethesda, MD 20205

Lissy F. Jarvik [105]
Department of Psychiatry and Biobehavioral Sciences, University of California, Los Angeles, CA 90024

Jaakko Kaprio [23, 37, 139, 217]
Department of Public Health Science, University of Helsinki, 00290 Helsinki 29, Finland

Mary-Claire King [17]
Department of Biomedical and Environmental Health Sciences, University of California, Berkeley, CA 94720

Arthur L. Klatsky [17]
Department of Medicine, Kaiser-Permanente Medical Care Program, Oakland, CA 94611

Gerhard Koch [201]
Institut für Humangenetik und Anthropologie, Hartmannstrasse 105, 8520 Erlangen, Federal Republic of Germany

Markku Koskenvuo [23, 37, 139, 217]
Department of Public Health Science, University of Helsinki, 00290 Helsinki 29, Finland

Einar Kringlen [131]
Institute of Behavioral Sciences In Medicine, University of Oslo, Sognsvannv 9, Oslo 3, Norway

Heimo Langinvainio [23, 139]
Department of Public Health Science, University of Helsinki, 00290 Helsinki 29, Finland

F.A. Lints [225]
Department of Genetics, University of Louvain, 2. Place Croix-du-Sud, 1348 Louvain-la-Neuve, Belgium

Edward H. Liston [105]
Department of Psychiatry and Biobehavioral Sciences, University of California, Los Angeles, CA 90024

Per Magnus [163]
Institute of Medical Genetics, University of Oslo, Oslo, Norway

N.G. Martin [89]
Department of Population Biology, Research School of Biological Sciences, Australian National University, PO Box 475, Canberra City, ACT 2601, Australia

Yvette Michotte [239]
Department of Analytical Chemistry and Bromatology, Free University of Brussels, (V.U.B.), Brussels 1050, Belgium

Masaki Munaka [259]
Department of Biometrics, Research Institute of Nuclear Medicine and Biology, University of Hiroshima, Hiroshima City, Japan

R.M. Murray [47, 77]
Department of Psychiatry, Institute of Psychiatry, De Crespigny Park, London, SE5 8AF, England

Walter E. Nance [163]
Department of Human Genetics, Medical College of Virginia, Richmond, VA 23298

A. Noto [247]
The Gregor Mendel Institute of Medical Genetics and Twin Studies, Piazza Galeno 5, 00161 Rome, Italy

J.G. Oakeshott [89]
Department of Population Biology, Research School of Biological Sciences, Australian National University, PO Box 475, Canberra City, ACT 2601, Australia

Naomasa Okamoto [259, 271]
Department of Genticopathology, Research Institute of Nuclear Medicine and Biology, University of Hiroshima, Hiroshima City, Japan

Hajime Okita [271]
Department of Internal Medicine, Research Institute of Nuclear Medicine and Biology, University of Hiroshima, Hiroshima City, Japan

Paolo Parisi [225]
The Gregor Mendel Institute of Medical Genetics and Twin Studies, Piazza Galeno 5, 00161 Rome, Italy

Nancy Pedersen [53]
Institute of Behavioral Genetics, University of Colorado, Boulder, CO 80309

J. Perl [89]
Department of Pharmacology, University of Sydney, Sydney, NSW 2006, Australia

Eero Pukkala [217]
Finnish Cancer Registry, Helsinki, Finland

Matti Romo [139]
Department of Public Health Science, University of Helsinki, 00290 Helsinki 29, Finland

E. Roselli [247]
The Gregor Mendel Institute of Medical Genetics and Twin Studies, Piazza Galeno 5, 00161 Rome, Italy

C. Rossi [9]
Department of Mathematics, University of Lecce, Lecce, Italy

Seppo Sarna [37, 139]
Department of Public Health Science, University of Helsinki, 00290 Helsinki 29, Finland

Yukio Satow [271]
Department of Geneticopathology, Research Institute of Nuclear Medicine and Biology, University of Hiroshima, Hiroshima City, Japan

Marc A. Schuckit [61]
Department of Psychiatry, University of California, San Diego, and Alcoholism Treatment Program, Veterans Administration Hospital, 3350 La Jolla Village Drive, San Diego, CA 92161

J. Theodore Schwartz [249]
Bureau of Medical Services, Health Services Administration, USPHS, Room 1125, 6525 Belcrest Road, West Hyattsville, MD 20782

John H. Simpson [105]
Department of Psychiatry and Biobehavioral Sciences, University of California, Los Angeles, CA 90024

G.A. Starmer [89]
Department of Pharmacology, University of Sydney, Sydney, NSW 2006, Australia

Charles Susanne [239]
Center of Anthropogenetics, Free University of Brussels, (V.U.B.), Brussels 1050, Belgium

Lauri Tarkkonen [23]
Department of Public Health Science, University of Helsinki, 00290 Helsinki 29, Finland

Lyly Teppo [217]
Finnish Cancer Registry, Helsinki, Finland

Irene Uchida [149]
Department of Pediatrics and Pathology, McMaster University, Hamilton, Ontario, Canada

Hiroshi Ueoka [259]
Department of Biometrics, Research Institute of Nuclear Medicine and Biology, University of Hiroshima, Hiroshima City, Japan

Shoji Watanabe [259]
Department of Epidemiology and Social Medicine, Research Institute of Nuclear Medicine and Biology, University of Hiroshima, Hiroshima City, Japan

A.V. Wilks [89]
Department of Population Biology, Research School of Biological Sciences, Australian National University, PO Box 475, Canberra City, ACT 2601, Australia

R. Ziparo [9]
The Gregor Mendel Institute of Medical Genetics and Twin Studies, Piazza Galeno 5, 00161 Rome, Italy

Twin Research 3

Contents of Part A: Twin Biology and Multiple Pregnancy

Contents of Part B: Intelligence, Personality, and Development

TWIN RESEARCH IN DEVELOPMENTAL STUDIES AND TEMPERAMENT

Preface

The Third International Congress on Twin Studies, held in Jerusalem in June 1980, was a successful event because of its site and because of the number and quality of contributors, as reflected in these proceedings. But its relevance and success were perhaps also partly due to its taking place at a particular stage in the evolution of human biological sciences. The latter, and medicine among them, can no longer do without the lead offered them by genetics, since the study of the individual needs to be approached within the context of the generational tissue. Without genetics, it is impossible to understand what takes place in the phenotype, or to forecast what will occur in the offspring.

The boom in genetics can be compared to that of nuclear physics. In fact, the study of nonliving matter requires the understanding of nuclear forces, just as the study of living matter requires that of gene forces. The energy of the gene is the force behind any gene information, and the interweaving of the primary gene products is the loom on which the generational tissue is produced, from which life and its variability depend. Our understanding of these processes, as deep as it may be, is still comparable to what one gathers looking through a keyhole. The study of twins, with its many modern refinements, can frequently offer a broader understanding of the genetic times and processes involved in the human design, both at the physical and the psychological level.

Any research into human biology can draw water from this well, as is made clear by the variety of the contributions to these proceedings, and of those already published in the 30 years of life of the journal I established in 1952, *Acta Geneticae Medicae et Gemellologiae* (the proceedings of the First International Congress on Twin Studies, held in Rome in 1974, were published in Volume 25 of this journal in 1976), as well as by the increasing membership and impact of the International Society for Twin Studies. This has been largely the result of a truly collaborative effort, to which many have contributed, from many countries and various areas of interest. They cannot all be mentioned but I should like to at least acknowledge the efforts of Gordon Allen, organizer of the Second International Congress on Twin Studies held in Washington in 1977 (the proceedings of which were published by Alan R. Liss, Inc. in 1978 in three volumes entitled *Twin Research,* edited by Walter Nance with coeditors Gordon Allen and Paolo Parisi), and Ian MacGillivray, organizer of the Aberdeen Workshop in 1979, respectively Past President and President of our International Society, as well as those of Walter Nance and Paolo Parisi, the coeditors of these proceedings.

Luigi Gedda

Twin Research 3: Epidemiological
and Clinical Studies, pages 1 — 7

Methodologic Problems in Matched-Pair Studies Using Twins

Zdenek Hrubec

*Medical Follow-Up Agency, National Academy of Sciences — National
Research Council, Washington, DC*

Twin studies either estimate the heritability of a particular quantitative characteristic or qualitative trait, or they try to remove genetic effects from an assessment of the relationship between other characteristics or traits. For example, using twins, we can study the heritability of cough. Alternatively, we can study the relationship between cigarette smoking and cough in twin pairs so that possible genetic effects are negated. These two kinds of questions can be explored in the same body of data, but the methods used and the problems that attend them are distinctly different.

No attempt will be made here to deal with methods of estimating heritability. The problem of controlling heredity in comparisons of other factors can be considered as a special application of the methodology of matched-pair comparisons. The latter topic has produced a vast literature, but little of it has been formulated specifically in terms of twins.

The concept of a matched-pair comparison is that pairs of similar individuals are assembled who differ on a recognized experience, measurement, or trait. These discordant pair members are then compared on another, target, measurement or trait that may be simultaneous with, follow, or predate the one that formed the basis of the original pairing. For example, twin pairs with one member a smoker and another member a nonsmoker could be compared on the following target characteristics: a) the prevalence of cough determined at the same time as the smoking, to be done only if there had not been much prior cough-related mortality; b) survival at some future time, long after smoking status was determined; c) success in grade school determined from data recorded before the subject had any smoking experience. In compiling the matching pairs, we consider covariables or characteristics that are known or suspected of being related to the target characteristic. Study pairs may be selected so that the members are equal for these covariables of interest. For example, we could select pairs of twins of the same or similar body weight. Or we could match on some other characteristics and carry information on body weight as a covariable into the analysis of the data.

When the two members of the discordant pairs are twins, they have been matched by nature. If monozygotic (MZ) they are exactly comparable on all genetic determinants. Dizygotic (DZ) twins are not matched exactly, but are about as similar genetically as brothers or sisters. For all twins, pair members are of the same age. Because they shared the same uterine and early childhood environment, discordant twins are probably matched on many factors, the importance of which may be unrecognized and perhaps not demonstrable. These factors can neither be matched explicitly nor be included in a refined analysis as covariables. In a matched-pair analysis using twins, one hopes to reduce biases due to such covariables.

Ideally, twin pair discordance is created by an investigator's intervention. He will randomly expose one twin to an experimental condition as his cotwin serves as a comparison subject. In this approach, differences between pair members other than those due to the experimental condition, on average, are shared equally by the experimental and the comparison group. If there is no treatment effect, the random assignment will usually produce only small variations in the observed endpoints. It is possible to calculate the probability that the observed difference between the groups in the target variable or endpoint results only from the random assignment. If that difference is large, the probability that it results from random assignment is low, and we then conclude that the difference is due to the experimental condition and not the assignment of subjects.

Because twin pair members tend to be similar on many variables that differ widely among unrelated individuals, by studying twins even small treatment effects may be detected. A larger number of pairs of unrelated individuals assigned at random would generally be needed to demonstrate the same effect.

If the twins assigned at random to treatments are MZ twins, all genetic factors will be controlled in the comparison. If there is gene-environment interaction, that is, if some genotypes react to a given treatment differently from other genotypes, then the matched comparison is valid only for the distribution of genotypes studied. Sampling a different distribution of genotypes may lead to different conclusions about the effect of the experimental treatment.

Experiments with damaging or painful exposures may not be carried out on human subjects, and we may want to study conditions that cannot be created experimentally. We then have to find twin paris in whom discordance for the condition of interest occurred naturally, through accident, or by the pair members' own choice. Examples are diseases of unknown etiology, like multiple sclerosis; environmental exposures, like that to asbestos; or self-induced exposures, like smoking. The index, or exposed individuals, form one group and their nonexposed cotwins the other. Statistical evaluation can again be made to state the probability that the difference observed arose by chance assignment of subjects. However, since subjects were not randomized to begin with, this computation merely provides an analogy that describes what we could expect if the process creating the discordance did operate at random. In relying on such probability statements we assume that variables not specifically included in the analysis, but related to the outcome, divide between the study groups as they would with random assignment.

If there are covariables that are related both to the target variable and to the variable for which discordance was established, the twin pair comparison will be biased. When information on the biasing covariable is available, the bias can either be corrected in the analysis of the data or it can be avoided by an appropriate selection of pairs concordant for the biasing covariable, but discordant for the primary variable.

To illustrate these points, Figure 1 presents data on the prevalence of cough reported on a questionnaire by reports of tobacco smoking, by reports of heavy alcohol drinking and the percentage of heavy drinkers by smoking. The subjects are 4,377 male twin pairs in the National Research Council Twin Registry with both members returning a questionnaire. The left vertical bars compare 16, as the percentage reporting cough among individual cigarette smokers, with 4 and 3 as the percentages, respectively, among those not smoking cigarettes and not smoking anything at all. The percentage among those who never smoked is almost the same as among non-cigarette smokers. The numbers of respondents are shown below the bars. It is worth noting that the percentage of reported cough was highest among those smoking the most cigarettes.

The middle bars show that cough is related to heavy alcohol drinking. Among the heavy drinkers, 16% reported cough, and among those who were not heavy drinkers, 8% did so.

The bars on the right show that cigarette smokers more often reported heavy drinking than non-cigarette smokers, who in turn reported heavy drinking more often than those who never smoked. This suggests that some of the original four-fold difference in the prevalence of cough with cigarette smoking may be due to the higher percentage of drinkers among smokers than among nonsmokers.

Let us now suppose that the questionnaire had not asked about drinking and we knew nothing about it. Because we suspect that smoking may be related to many covariables, we choose to do a matched twin pair analysis, particularly one in which pairs discordant for cigarette smoking are compared. We now need to define smoking discordance. One definition, which should show the effect of tobacco smoking most clearly, is one that compares extreme groups, that is, heavy cigarette smokers, with those who never smoked. In this sample of World War II veterans, cigarette smokers consumed an average of 23 cigarettes per day in 1968. Thus, comparing twin pairs with one member a cigarette smoker and the other a nonsmoker seems a suitable definition of smoking discordance.

The left side of Figure 2 again shows how the percentage of heavy drinkers distributes by smoking status, as we saw before in Figure 1. The right side shows how the percentage of heavy drinkers distributes in pairs where both twins smoked cigarettes, one twin smoked cigarettes and the other never smoked, and where both never smoked. If we knew nothing about drinking we could not show this,

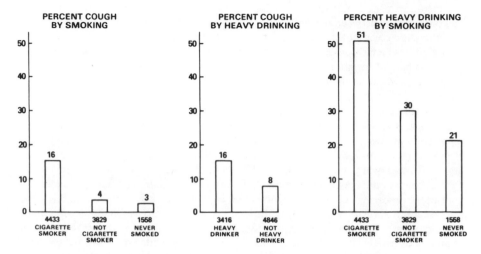

Fig. 1. Percent Cough and Percent Heavy Drinking—Individuals.

but among the cigarette smokers matched to those who never smoked, the percentage of heavy drinkers, 46%, is only slightly less than among all cigarette smokers; and among the matching nonsmokers it is 24%, almost the same as among all individuals who never smoked. So, under this discordance definition, the matched twin pairs are really not more comparable on drinking than individual cigarette smokers and nonsmokers. Another difficulty is that there has been a considerable reduction in sample size to only 359 pairs. In this sample of twin veterans, there are few individuals who never smoked but whose twin brothers reported smoking cigarettes.

Another matching is possible that improves matters. We can include a much bigger fraction of the sample by defining smoking discordance as one twin smoking more cigarettes than the other. Those who never smoked, former smokers, or light cigar and pipe smokers can be retained as the "low" smokers in comparison to their cotwins who smoked cigarettes. The results of that classification are shown in Figure 3. For comparison, shown on the left are the same percentages as were shown in Figure 2 for the pairs in which cigarette smokers were matched to twins who never smoked. Under the new definition of smoking discordance, shown on the right, the members of discordant pairs who smoked more cigarettes had a mean of 25 cigarettes per day and the low-smoking members had a mean of eight cigarettes per day, a mean difference of 18 cigarettes per day. This comparison includes 1,204 pairs with both twins reporting smoking cigarettes, but in different amounts, for whom the mean difference was 14 cigarettes per day.

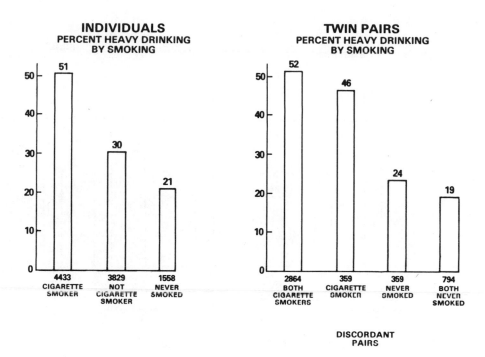

Fig. 2.   Percent Heavy Drinking by Smoking.

In this second matching, among the lower cigarette-smoking twins in the discordant pairs, 40% are heavy drinkers, a bigger percentage than among non-cigarette smoking pairs, among whom it is 27%, or individual non-cigarette smokers, among whom it is 30%. Thus, this matching makes the study groups more comparable on their drinking experience than the comparison of individuals. The percentage of heavy drinkers among the pairs with both twins smoking an equal number of cigarettes is 51%, the same as among all individual cigarette smokers.

From what we have seen in Figures 1 to 3, we can carry out a matched-pair analysis that considers both the distribution of smoking and of drinking between twin pair members. Figure 4 shows the same 2,419 smoking-discordant pairs shown in Figure 3, but distributed by a definition of drinking discordance. The outside comparisons consist of pairs with similar heavy drinking reported by both twins and none reported by either twin. In each case, the smoking members of these pairs have a risk of cough about twice that of the nonsmoking members. On the inside left, those who smoke and drink more have a risk of 4.7 times that of their cotwins who do less of both, and on the inside right the heavier smokers who

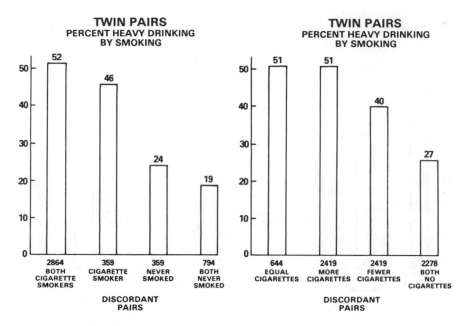

Fig. 3.   Percent Heavy Drinking by Smoking.

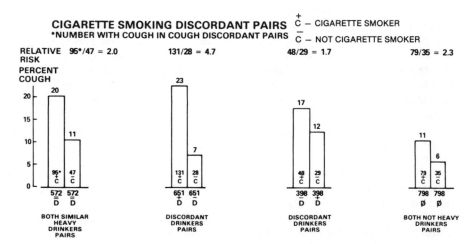

Fig. 4.   Percent Cough by Heavy Drinking Concordance of Pair.

drink less have 1.7 times more cough than their cotwins who smoke less but drink more. These risks are estimated as the ratio of the number of twin pair members discordant for cough given in the body of the bars.

The above exercise makes clear that appropriate definition of a matching pair, or twin pair discordance, is critical. Extreme discordances will reduce sample size and result in highly selected samples that may be biased. It is encouraging that, in this example at least, the matched-pair analysis without considering the alcohol drinking covariable provided about the same answer as when drinking was considered. For MZ twins, genetic factors would, of course, be matched, and a comparison of MZ and DZ smoking-discordant twins might provide evidence of such an effect. In this application, the analysis of data on individuals, adjusted for the drinking covariable, seemed to work as well as the matched-pair analysis. However, we do not know what all the covariables are that have been controlled in the matched-pair comparison, and we may, in fact, have both reduced bias and gained considerable efficiency.

Twin Research 3: Epidemiological
and Clinical Studies, pages 9 — 11

Twin Azygotic Test: An Application to Italian Twin Data

L. Gedda, C. Rossi, G. Brenci, and R. Ziparo
*The Mendel Institute, Rome (L.G., G.B.), Institute of Mathematics,
University of Lecce (C.R.) and Institute of Physiology, University of Rome
(R.Z.)*

INTRODUCTION

In a previous paper [1] we proposed a "twin azygotic test" to estimate gene frequencies on the basis of twin data drawn from vital statistics. We will now deal with an application of the test to Italian twin data on the basis of the posterior distribution of the two random quantities, p = gene proportion and m = probability that a twin pair be monozygotic.

To simplify calculation we consider uniform prior distribution and a point estimation given by the mode ($\bar{m}$, $\bar{p}$) of the posterior bivariate distribution.

MATHEMATICAL MODEL

Consider an autosomal diallelic trait determined, in the absence of dominance, by two alleles, a_1 and a_2, with frequencies p and $q = 1-p$. Calling x, y, and z the phenotypes corresponding to the three genotypes, a_{11}, a_{12}, and a_{22}, respectively, and assuming that the twin condition introduces no further factor of variability, the following probability distribution of phenotypes in a twin population is obtained:

$$f_{xx} = mp^2 + \tfrac{1}{4} dp^2 (1+p^2) \qquad f_{xy} = dp^2q(1+q)$$

$$f_{yy} = 2mpq + dpq(1 + pq) \qquad f_{xz} = \tfrac{1}{2} dp^2q^2 \qquad (1)$$

$$f_{zz} = mq^2 + \tfrac{1}{4} dq^2 (1 + q^2) \qquad f_{yz} = dpq^2(1 + q)$$

where m is the conditional probability that a twin pair is monozygotic and $d = 1-m$ is the probability that it is dizygotic.

We can denote by **a** the random vector **a** $<=>$ (a_{xx}, a_{yy}, a_{zz}, a_{xy}, a_{xz}, a_{yz}), the components of which are the observed absolute frequencies of twin pairs, xx, yy, zz, xy, xz, and yz, respectively. If we introduce the prior probability density of parameters p, m, which can be considered independent random variables:

$$\Phi_{p,m}(p, m) = \Phi_1(p)\, \Phi_2(m)$$

we can calculate the posterior probability density of the parameters, given a realization of vector **a**, during a given time unit:

$$\Phi_{p,m}(p,m/\mathbf{a} = \mathbf{h}) = k_4 f_{p,m}(p,m/\mathbf{a} = \mathbf{h}) \qquad [2]$$

$$\text{where } k_4 = \left[\int_0^1 \int_0^1 f_{p,m}(p,m/\mathbf{a} = \mathbf{h})\, dp\, dm\right]^{-1} \text{ and}$$

$$f_{p,m}(p,m/\mathbf{a} = \mathbf{h}) = \left[mp^2 + \tfrac{1}{4} dp^2(1 + p^2)\right]^{h_1} \left[2mpq + dpq(1 + pq)\right]^{h_2}$$

$$\left[mq^2 + \tfrac{1}{4} dq^2(1 + q^2)\right]^{h_3} \left[dp^2 q(1 + p)\right]^{h_4} \left[\tfrac{1}{2} dp^2 q^2\right]^{h_5} \left[dpq^2(1 + q)\right]^{h_6}$$

We can now consider the point estimations given by the joint or marginal modes of the posterior joint or marginal densities. This way of calculating point estimations for p and m is equivalent to the classic maximum likelihood estimation, since we have uniform prior densities for p and m. On the contrary, Bayesian point estimations are quite different from the classic ones.

APPLICATION

In the present application we deal with traits given by two alleles with dominance, the posterior probability density must be replaced by the following expression:

$$\Phi_{p,m}(p,m/h_1, h_2, h_3, h_4, h_5, h_6) = k_4\, f_{p,m}(p,m/h_1, h_2, h_3, h_4, h_5, h_6)$$

with:

$$f_{p,m}(p,m/h_1, h_2, h_3, h_4, h_5, h_6) = (f_{xx} + f_{yy} + f_{xy})^{h_1+h_2+h_4}(f_{xz} + f_{yz})^{h_5+h_6} f_{zz}^{h_3}$$

where $h_1 + h_2 + h_4$ is the absolute frequency of twin pairs with two healthy individuals $h_5 + h_6$ is the absolute frequency of twin pairs with a healthy individual and an ill individual and h_3 is the absolute frequency of twin pairs with two ill individuals.

For Italian twin data related to anencephaly and cleft palate we have, respectively:

1) $h_1 + h_2 + h_4 = 44894$ $h_5 + h_6 = 15$ $h_3 = 0$

and

2) $h_1 + h_2 + h_4 = 44892$ $h_5 + h_6 = 14$ $h_3 = 3$

To eliminate possible noise over the estimation of m given by dominance, we get a preestimation for such parameter on the basis of other twin data. We could obtain for m the following preestimation: $\bar{m} = 0.29$ ($\bar{d} = 0.71$). Replacing such values in (2) and choosing a uniform prior density for p, we get the following point estimations:

1) $\bar{p} = 3/100$

2) $\bar{p} = 3/100$

Using least-squares method for estimating p we get the same results.

REFERENCES

1. Gedda L, Rossi C, Brenci G: Twin azygotic test for the study of hereditary qualitative traits in twin population. Acta Genet Med Gemellol 28:15–19, 1979.

Twin Research 3: Epidemiological
and Clinical Studies, pages 13—16
© 1981 Alan R. Liss, Inc., 150 Fifth Avenue, New York, NY 10011

Twin Studies: Are Sequential Methods Useful?

Jacob E. Bearman

Epidemiology Unit, Ben-Gurion University of the Negev, Be'er-Sheva, Israel

INTRODUCTION

When data become available sequentially, for example in twin studies and/or in clinical trials of a proposed new therapy against conventional treatment, in pairs of subjects whose responses are to be compared, there exists the possibility of using the data more efficiently than by using "classical" statistical analysis. Specifically, this means the possibility of requiring only a fraction of the number of subjects in order to arrive at a decision concerning which is the better of the two treatments.

The method is "Sequential Analysis", and was developed by the late Abraham Wald [4] in the early part of the 1940's. It should be immediately mentioned that others have contributed materially to extending the work of Wald. In medical applications, an important name is Peter Armitage [1] and, more recently, O'Neill and Anello [3] have proposed the use of the sequential approach to the design of matched-pair case-control studies in epidemiology.

"SAVING" OBSERVATIONS: HEURISTIC APPROACH

The idea of "saving" observations can be understood in the light of an oversimplified example, described first using the "classical" method. Suppose, using currently accepted surgical methods, a very serious surgical procedure has a very high incidence of complications. Further, an innovation is developed that is believed to improve the prognosis of success, and its implementation will result in cutting the complication rate at least in half. A clinical trial is to be conducted using the new device to determine the resulting relative frequency of complication, an all-or-none phenomenon; for the sake of simplicity, comparison will be made to the previous complication rate, which is known.

For the "classical" method of planning and analysing the trial, let us assume that a sample of 50 patients is required to distinguish the anticipated reduction in complication rate, if it truly exists (with a very low probability, β, of failing to detect such a reduction), as well as to identify the failure to lower the complication rate, if such is truly the case (except for another very low probability, call it α). Simply: If the innovation actually is good, we wish to say it is bad with very low probability and, if it is not good, we want to claim success with low probability. Suppose further that, among the 50 patients who are to undergo the surgery in the trial, if 32 or more of them recover with no intervening complications, then we decide that the innovation is accomplishing its goal. It is, of course, tacitly assumed that the patients entering the trial randomly represent all candidates for the surgery.

The salient feature is that, in the "classical" method of designing and carrying out the trial, one would operate on all 50 patients (or, if in a comparative trial, on all 50 *pairs* of patients) and not examine the results (ie, "break the code" as to which patient of the pair had the innovation used and which didn't) until all the results had been assembled. The beauty of Wald's Sequential Probability Ratio Test (SPRT) is that he said, in effect, what is obvious to every one of you: "Wait! If the data are collected sequentially, ie, the data from one patient (or pair of patients) are available before the next arrives for surgery, you may be doing more 'testing' than you need to do." Very simply if, for example, the first 32 pieces of data show that the innovation is good, why go on? His insight went even further; there is only a tiny probability of obtaining 31 of the first 32 as successes if the innovation is *not* good; and a larger probability, but still very small, of 30 successes among the first 32; etc, or even of obtaining *all* of the first 9 or 10 as successes, if the innovation is not truly an improvement. The SPRT takes into account all the configurations of outcomes in the order in which they might arise, and allows us to make a decision (after a certain minimum number) after each datum is evaluated as "successful" or not, retaining the same risks as with the "classical" method, α and β, of coming to the wrong conclusion. The SPRT, compared to the "classical" test, *using the same α and β*, will arrive at a conclusion, on average, with approximately one-half the number of patients needed for the "classical" method — sometimes more, sometimes less. This kind of "savings," of course, has strong ethical overtones when sequential analysis is possible, particularly in view of the fact that, if the results indicate a marked difference between responses in the different treatment groups, the trial will end relatively rapidly.

In matched-pair comparisons of two treatments, the two treatments essentially "run a race" in each pair. If both patients are "successess" or if both are "failures," then the race ends in a tie. As with other matched-pair studies, in the sequential clinical trial it is only non-ties (where one therapy succeeds and the other fails) that contribute information as to which treatment is superior. Even though unknown at the start, if one therapy is far better than the other, the better one will "win" many more than half the "races" and the decision concerning its superiority comes quickly. Again, as with all matched-pair studies, it is necessary that the two treatments be randomly assigned within each pair in order that the probability calculations be strictly justified.

A CLINICAL TRIAL AS AN EXAMPLE

Such was the case with the clinical trial of magnesium-ion supplement to "usual best therapy" versus "usual best therapy" alone in the treatment of very young children (mean age just a little over 3 years) who were suffering severe protein malnutrition disease (kwashiorkor) [2]. It appeared advisable to carry out the study as a matched-pair study; and since there were only two hospital beds available for the reseach, a new pair of patients could not be entered into the trial until bed space was available, ie, until the information on the previous pair was completed. Sequential analysis of the data was obvious. The trial was designed to distinguish a cure rate of 65% or more (for magnesium supplement) as compared to 35% or less (for the unsupplemented standard treatment) versus indifference to a cure rate of 55% or less (magnesium) as compared to 45% or more (standard therapy).

The study was performed as a double-masked, placebo-controlled, matched-pair, sequential trial, with random allocation (within each pair) of intramuscularly injected 50% magnesium sulfate heptahydrate or isotonic sodium chloride, both in addition to the standard treatment. The only designed difference in patient care was in allocation of the magnesium or placebo. The α and β were both taken to be 0.05. Patients were matched on severity of disease, either severe or critical.

Method of Analysis

In a sequential trial, the decision to stop or continue after any pair depends on the results so far obtained. The method of analysis, completely suppressing the background mathematics and the numerical calculations, can be described graphically. On the upper-right quadrant of an (x,y) coordinate system, the calculations provide two parallel lines running generally lower-left toward upper-right; the upper line intersects the vertical axis above the origin, and the lower line intersects the horizontal axis to the right of the origin. The scale on the horizontal axis measures the number of (not tied) pairs; the vertical axis's scale is the number of those pairs in which the magnesium-treatment was preferred. As the results of each (not tied) pair are known, starting with the first at the origin, we move one square to the *right*; if the placebo was the preferred treatment in the pair, stop; however, if the magnesium was the preferred treatment, also move *up* one square. Then wait for the results of the next (not tied) pair, and proceed.

This analysis provides a progression generally to the right if the placebo is usually preferred; and there is a progression "to the northeast" if the magnesium is continually preferred. If the upper line is touched or crossed, then the decision is reached that the magnesium treatment is superior to the placebo; if the lower line is touched or crossed, the placebo is superior; as long as the "track" remains *between* the two lines, no decision is reached and another pair is tested. In our study, had the first nine (non tied) pairs all shown the magnesium to be preferred, the upper line would have been attained, and the decision reached that magnesium was the superior treatment. For such a decision to be reached in case the placebo was preferred in any pair(s), an *additional* 3 pairs were required *in which magnesium was preferred,* for each time that the placebo had been preferred.

For a corresponding "classical," fixed sample-size study, the estimated sample size was over 50 pairs. We required 26 total pairs (of whom the patients were critically ill in 18 pairs, and seriously ill in 8 pairs). If clinical signs suggestive of patient deterioration developed despite an adequate trial of the treatment, then the drug being used for that patient was declared a "treatment failure," the code was broken for the investigating physician by the hospital pharmacist, and, if indicated in the opinion of the physician, magnesium was administered. However, the paired drug was declared "preferred" *only* if its code was *not* required to be broken *and* that patient went on to recover.

Results in the Clinical Trial

Among the 26 pairs there were 9 "ties." In two of these, both patients were apparently not so severely ill and both recovered with no code broken. In the other seven both were so critically ill that both died. Among the remaining 17 (not tied) pairs, magnesium was preferred in 15 and the placebo in 2. The study drug was declared a failure 25 times (ie, the code was broken) and was found to be magnesium on 4 of those occasions and placebo 21 times.

Severe magnesium defiency is associated with, among other things, depressed or inverted T-waves in the ECG. ECG tracings of placebo-treated patients, before and after the code was broken, show the rapid conversion of the T-wave to normal. Similarly, tracings of magnesium-treated patients, before and after administration of the drug, show the same kind of changes. Pictures of the patient after treatment, whether originally assigned to magnesium or whether the patient received magnesium only following treatment failure of originally assigned placebo, are difficult to identify with pictures of the same patient on admission to the study.

DISCUSSION AND CONCLUSIONS

This study, in my opinion, exhibits the advantage of the sequential method, *when it is applicable.* In addition, on average, sequential experimentation and analysis will arrive at a decision with savings in the sample size required over "classical" fixed-sample-size design. This savings is provided without any sacrifice in protection against errors in the decision, ie, with the same probabilities of being in error, α and β. If one of the two treatments is far superior to the other, then the potential for savings in sample size is further enhanced.

APPLICATION TO TWIN STUDIES

If twin studies are proper candidates for "classical" matched-pair design and analysis, and if the pairs present themselves sequentially, then there appears to me no reason to rule against the sequential method for analyzing the data. But it must be emphasized that, for *any* of the known methods of statistical analysis to be applicable, random assignment of "treatment" within pairs is essential. But this is also the situation with all case-control studies. It is *not* my intent to criticize any studies in which such randomization is absent. My only intent is to suggest great caution in drawing conclusions from such studies, and to point out that the fact that this requirement cannot be guaranteed in many instances of case-control studies is only one of many factors that make epidemiology a very difficult affair.

REFERENCES
1. Armitage P: "Sequential Medical Trials," 2nd Ed. New York: John Wiley and Sons, 1975.
2. Caddell JL: Studies in protein calorie malnutrition: II. A double-blind clinical trial to assess magnesium therapy. N Engl J Med 276:535–540, 1967.
3. O'Neill RT, Anello C: Case-control studies: A sequential approach. Am J Epidemiol 108:415–424, 1978.
4. Wald A: "Sequential Analysis," New York: John Wiley and Sons, 1947.

Twin Research 3: Epidemiological
and Clinical Studies, pages 17 — 22
© 1981 Alan R. Liss, Inc., 150 Fifth Avenue, New York, NY 10011

Characteristics of Smoking-Discordant Monozygotic Twins

Gary D. Friedman, Mary-Claire King, Arthur L. Klatsky, Stephen B. Hulley

Department of Medical Methods Research (G.D.F.) and Department of Medicine, Kaiser-Permanente Medical Care Program, Oakland, California, (A.L.K.), University of California, Berkeley, (M.-C.K.), and Department of Epidemiology and International Health, University of California, San Francisco (S.B.H.)

Compared to their nonsmoking counterparts, cigarette smokers in smoking-discordant monozygotic (MZ) twins show less increase in the occurrence of clinical coronary heart disease (CHD) than do smokers in the general population [2, 8]. Although the numbers of twins studied have been few so far, these findings have been cited as evidence against the view that cigarette smoking is a causative factor in the development of CHD [10].

Even if the relative similarity in CHD occurrence is confirmed by additional data from smoking-discordant MZ twins, the question still arises as to whether this rules out cigarette smoking as a causative factor or whether some other characteristics of these genetically matched study subjects might explain the similarity.

The present study examines a number of characteristics of smoking-discordant MZ twins, many of which are pertinent to the relation of cigarette smoking to CHD.

MATERIALS AND METHODS

The Kaiser-Permanente Twin Registry contains over 8,000 pairs of twins who (or whose parents) volunteered their participation in a program of medical research on twins [5]. All age groups and a diverse racial and socioeconomic spectrum are represented. Most of the participants have been subscribers to the Kaiser Foundation Health Plan in northern California. About once a year a newsletter is mailed to all participating twins, informing them of the progress of the program and presenting other medical facts of interest to twins.

Supported by the Council for Tobacco Research, USA, grant no. 985, and the National Heart, Lung, and Blood Institute, grant no. 5-RO1-HL21971.

TABLE 1. Questionnaire Response and Numbers of Cigarette Smoking-Discordant Pairs by Sex and Zygosity

	Female pairs		Male pairs	
	MZ	DZ	MZ	DZ
Target group[a]	1,047	1,185	695	755
Number responding:				
only one twin	271	389	234	277
both twins	451	387	186	138
Smoking discordant:[b]				
based on self-report	42	66	6	15
both agree (subset of those based on self-report)	33	58	5	14

[a]Breakdown of target group by sex and zygosity is an estimate based on proportions in each category from an earlier census.
[b]Each pair contained a cigarette smoker and a nonsmoker. Excludes cigar, pipe, or past cigarette smoking from nonsmokers but not from smokers.

In 1977 and 1978 a large health questionnaire was mailed to all twins aged 18 years and over. After the first mailing in June 1977, a reminder postcard was sent in October 1977 to nonresponding same-sex twins. A further plea for completion was included in our January 1978 newsletter. Since this was sent by first class mail we learned of many new addresses and discovered that many twins had moved and had not yet received the questionnaire or reminder postcard, which had been sent by bulk mail. The final mailing was completed largely in February 1978. We then telephoned as many as possible of the nonresponding cotwins of twins who had responded, reminding them to complete the questionnaire. Of all questionnaires received, about 60% were received by October 1977, 22% more by February 1978, and the final 18% by October 1978. Table 1 shows the numbers of same-sex pairs who responded. The response rate for individual twins ranged from 37% to 56%, and for complete pairs, from 18% to 43%; the highest response rates were in the female MZ twins.

Each twin was asked about his or her own smoking habits and those of his or her cotwin. Table 1 shows the numbers of twins discordant for *current* cigarette smoking in each sex and zygosity group. By definition, the nonsmoker in the pair could not have been either a pipe, cigar, or former cigarette smoker. For this study we required that both twins agree about the smoking habits of each twin because even the small amount of misclassification error expected from the responses of individual twins can seriously dilute the differences between trait-discordant pairs [4]. As shown in Table 1 this requirement substantially reduced the number of eligible pairs. The twins of primary interest were MZ and there were too few males, ie, five pairs, for meaningful information. Even the 33 eligible female MZ pairs represent a relatively small sample but they were necessarily the subjects of the analyses to be described. All additional data reported here were derived from the same questionnaire.

In a comparative study of questionnaire responses vs determination of multiple genetic markers in blood specimens, we [9] have found that self-reported MZ sta-

TABLE 2. Comparison of the Smoking Habits of Smokers in Smoking-Discordant Female MZ Pairs (Discordant Smokers) With Those of Smokers in all Other Female MZ Pairs

	Discordant smokers (N = 33)	All other smokers (N = 205)	P*
Median age (yrs)			
in 1977	40.0	40.5	> 0.90
when started smoking	22.1	19.7	< 0.05
Quantity ≥ 1 pack/day	27%	49%	< 0.05
Low-tar cigarettes	58%	40%	< 0.05
Ever tried to stop	85%	74%	~ 0.20
Inhale	97%	90%	~ 0.40
Filtered cigarettes	94%	93%	> 0.90

*Based on χ^2 test with Yates correction (applied for comparisons of medians to numbers above and below the overall median).

tus of twins in this registry is almost always (85 of 87) confirmed. Recently 11 of the 33 pairs participated in one of our examination programs that provided extensive testing of genetic markers in blood. All 11 pairs were found to be MZ. Thus we feel confident that all or nearly all of the self-reported MZ twins studied here are in fact MZ.

RESULTS

Smoking Habits

The 33 cigarette smokers in the smoking-discordant pairs, hereafter termed "discordant smokers" for brevity, were first compared with the 205 other MZ female cigarette smokers (Table 2). Large and statistically significant differences were noted in some measures of smoking intensity. Discordant smokers were much less likely to smoke at least one pack per day and to smoke low-tar cigarettes. Their median age of starting smoking was over two years greater; median ages of the two groups in 1977 were similar. Differences not statistically significant were found for the percentage who had ever tried to stop smoking, percentage who inhaled, and percentage using filtered cigarettes.

Other Exposures

Additional comparisons were between the discordant smokers and their non-smoking cotwins (Table 3). Because of small numbers, none of the differences to be described were statistically significant except as specified. The smokers were more apt regularly to drink alcohol, coffee, and cola, and less apt to drink tea. They were more apt to smoke marijuana, take estrogens, and to "like to add plenty of salt" to their food. There was no difference in the number who had ever used oral contraceptives or who reported exposure to any occupational hazard, and tranquilizer use was reported less often by the smokers.

It is generally accepted that the strength of associations in studies involving matched pairs, such as twins, is best estimated by the ratio of pairs discordant for the characteristic under consideration [3]. As can be seen in the right column of

TABLE 3. Comparison of Cigarette Smokers With Nonsmokers in 33 Smoking-Discordant MZ Pairs With Respect to Other Exposures

	Number reporting the exposure		Ratio of numbers of dis-
	Smokers	Nonsmokers	cordant pairs[a]
Any occupational hazard	13	13	6/6
Alcohol, 1 + drinks/month	21	18	8/4
Alcohol, 1 + drinks/day	8	5	5/2
Coffee, 1 + cups/day	27	20	8/2
Tea, 1 + cups/day	4	9	2/7
Cola, 1 + glass/day	7	3	4/1
Marijuana, any current use	6	4	4/2
Estrogens	13	10	8/6
Oral contraceptives, ever	20	20	2/2
Tranquilizers	1	4	1/3
Like to add plenty of salt	8	4	6/2

[a]Number of pairs with characteristic present only in the smoker/number of pairs with characteristic present only in the nonsmoker.

TABLE 4. Comparison of Cigarette Smokers With Nonsmokers in 33 Smoking-Discordant MZ Pairs With Respect to Other Characteristics

	Number reporting the characteristic		Ratio of numbers of dis-
	Smokers	Nonsmokers	cordant pairs[a]
Not presently married	9	8	5/4
At least 1 year of college	19	22	1/4
Leisure time exercise, moderate or more	17	22	3/9
Physical fitness is very important to me	21	27	2/10[b]
Left-handed	5	3	5/3
Mean height (cm)	163.8	163.1	P ~ 0.15
Mean weight (kg)	59.0	61.3	P < 0.05

[a]Number of pairs with characteristic present only in the smoker/number of pairs with characteristic present only in the nonsmoker.
[b]Two nonsmokers, cotwins of smokers answering "yes," did not answer.

Table 3, all of the characteristics described above as being more or less frequent in the smokers, except for estrogen use, showed a discordant-pair ratio of at least 2, implying a substantial degree of association.

Other Characteristics

The nonsmoking twins tended to have more formal education, to exercise more in their leisure time, and to be more concerned with physical fitness (Table 4). There was almost no difference in the number who were currently married. The smokers were slightly taller and leaner on the average. The differences in mean weight was statistically significant (P < 0.05). Interestingly, left-handedness was somewhat more frequent among the smokers.

DISCUSSION

Although the number of twin pairs that could be studied was small, these data suggest that genetically identical smoking-discordant twins are not matched for other characteristics, some of which have been shown to be relevant to the development of CHD. This observation has important implications concerning the value of the so-called cotwin control study design in identifying associations between an environmental exposure and a disease. It is sometimes assumed that MZ twins discordant for an exposure under consideration represent nearly ideal subjects for assessing the effects of this exposure because they have the same heredity and generally share the same early environment. This would certainly apply to experimental studies in which the exposure is assigned randomly by the investigator to one member of each pair. This was the original recommendation for use of the cotwin control method [7]. In observational studies, however, one must ask, as did Buck [1], how individuals so well matched in other respects became discordant for the exposure of concern and, further, whether they differ in other characteristics related to the disease or outcome under consideration. These questions must be answered for MZ twins just as they must be answered for any subjects of observational epidemiologic studies. MZ twins contribute complete genetic matching and some environmental matching to observational studies, which may be very valuable indeed. But they do not assure comparability in all important characteristics. As stated by Cederlöf et al, "Genetic control is not sufficient . . . if it does not at the same time afford control of environmental factors . . . ." [2 p 16].

With regard to CHD, our data suggest that the discordant smokers are leaner and consume more alcohol than their nonsmoking cotwins. While these traits are associated with a lower risk of CHD, smokers also tended to be less educated and reported less exercise and concern about physical fitness, consistent with higher risk. Our findings are similar to those of Cederlöf et al [2], who showed, however, that the smoker-nonsmoker differences were less in their smoking-discordant MZ twins that in their group as a whole. These differences between discordant smokers and their nonsmoking cotwins are generally in the same direction as differences between smokers and nonsmokers that have been observed in general population samples [6]. (A notable exception is our and Cederlöf's [2] failure to find a difference in oral contraceptive use.) Thus these differences do not appear to explain why, compared to corresponding nonsmokers, discordant smokers show less excess risk of CHD than do smokers in the general population.

Our findings concerning smoking intensity may provide at least a partial explanation. On average, discordant smokers smoked fewer and lower-tar cigarettes and started smoking later than other smokers. Thus, if smoking is a cause of CHD, less CHD would be expected in discordant smokers than in all smokers. In addition, unless carefully avoided, the dilution effect of misclassification [4] would further attenuate an apparent association of smoking and CHD among smoking-discordant twins. It is therefore clear that there are at least these two aspects of smoking-discordant MZ twins that work against the finding of an association between smoking and a disease. These biases must be taken into account in evaluating the findings of twin studies of smoking and health.

CONCLUSIONS

Data on a limited number of smoking-discordant female MZ twins suggest that, even with genetic identity, twins who differ in one characteristic may differ in other characteristics relevant to the outcome under consideration. In our study group, cigarette smokers who have an MZ nonsmoking cotwin tended to start smoking later and to smoke fewer cigarettes than other cigarette smokers; this may explain, in part, the smaller difference in CHD occurrence between smokers and nonsmokers within smoking-discordant twins than between smokers and nonsmokers in the general population.

ACKNOWLEDGMENTS

Establishment of the Kaiser-Permanente Twin Registry and the development and mailing of the questionnaires was supported by grant no. 985 from the Council for Tobacco Research – U.S.A. Recent studies of cardiovascular disease, including the present analyses, were supported by grant no. 5-RO1-HL21971 from the National Heart, Lung, and Blood Institute. Agnes Lewis, Kenneth Weaver, and Gary Lee made major contributions to the collection and analysis of these questionnaire data.

REFERENCES

1. Buck C: Re: "A potential pitfall in studying trait-discordant twins." Am J Epidemiol 106:342, 1977.
2. Cederlöf R, Friberg L, Lundman T: The interactions of smoking, environment, and heredity and their implications for disease etiology: A report of epidemiological studies on the Swedish twin registries. Acta Med Scand Suppl 612, 1977.
3. Fleiss JL: Statistical methods for rates and proportions. New York: John Wiley & Sons, pp 72–75, 1973.
4. Friedman GD: A potential pitfall in studying trait-discordant twins. Am J Epidemiol 105:291–295, 1977.
5. Friedman GD, Lewis AL: The Kaiser-Permanente Twin Registry. In Nance WE (ed): "Twin Research: Biology and Epidemiology." New York: Alan R. Liss, 1978, pp 173–177.
6. Friedman GD, Siegelaub AB, Dales LG, Seltzer CC: Characteristics predictive of coronary heart disease in ex-smokers before they stopped smoking: Comparison with persistent smokers and nonsmokers. J Chron Dis 32:175–190, 1979.
7. Gesell A: The method of co-twin control. Science 95:446, 1942.
8. Hrubec Z, Cederlöf R, Friberg L: Background of angina pectoris: Social and environmental factors in relation to smoking. Am J Epidemiol 103:16–29, 1976.
9. King M-C, Friedman GD, Lattanzio D, Rodgers G, Lewis AM, Dupuy ME, Williams H: Diagnosis of twin zygosity by self-assessment and by genetic analysis. Acta Genet Med Gemellol (in press).
10. Seltzer CC: Smoking and cardiovascular disease. Am Heart J 90:125–126, 1975.

Twin Research 3: Epidemiological
and Clinical Studies, pages 23 — 35
© 1981 Alan R. Liss, Inc., 150 Fifth Avenue, New York, NY 10011

Structural Analysis of Smoking, Alcohol Use, and Personality Factors in MZ and DZ Twin Pair Relationships

Heimo Langinvainio, Jaakko Kaprio, Markku Koskenvuo, and Lauri Tarkkonen
Department of Public Health Science, University of Helsinki

INTRODUCTION

Psychosocial, familial, and genetic factors affect alcohol use and its relationships to other substance abuses. Alcohol-use discordant twin pairs can permit elucidation of the environmental determinants of alcohol use and of its correlates to psychosocial factors.

While monozygotic (MZ) twins have identical genes, and therefore discordance is, in principle, due to environmental factors, dizygotic (DZ) twins are genetically full sibs but are of the same age and often share the same rearing environment to greater extent than singleton sibs of different ages.

The comparability of the two types of twins, MZ and DZ, has been questioned from a number of aspects. Prenatal influences on twins of either type are dissimilar [25] and variation by chorion type occurs [5]. Also, other influences special to twin types exist [8] that have led many investigators to question the validity of results from twin studies. Despite shortcomings, twin studies offer many advantages unavailable in other data sets in humans [23]. Therefore, to be able to utilize twin data, it is necessary to ensure carefully the comparability of the data of twins of either type and of singletons, both when making comparisons between twin types and when generalizing to the singleton population from twin data. Also, if in the two twin types the relationships between the phenomena under study are comparable, it is more likely that inferences made from MZ trait-discordant pairs on the environmental determinants of that trait are more likely to be valid. In other words, internal validity of the data used is enhanced.

This study has been supported by a grant from the Council for Tobacco Research, U.S.A. The authors would like to thank Timo Alanko M. Soc. Sc., for encouragement during the preparation of the paper, and Heli Rita, M. Soc. Sc. for programming assistance.

Tests for the comparison of data on single variables from twin data have been proposed. After testing of twin means, testing of total variances can be performed to compare variability by twin type [7].

The purpose of this paper was to extend the testing of twin type comparability to a multivariate situation. The smoking characteristics, alcohol use patterns, and personality factors of MZ and DZ twin pairs concordant and discordant for frequent heavy alcohol use were described. The effect of constraining covariance relationships in individuals of either twin type was tested to estimate comparability of pairwise structures. Also, the covariance relationships in individual twins were compared to those of singletons. For such analyses, the general model for the estimation of linear structural equation systems by maximum likelihood methods (LISREL IV) [12] was applied to data from the Finnish Twin Registry. Finally, multivariate analysis results from alcohol-use discordant pairs are presented.

MATERIALS AND METHODS
The Study Materials

The study population was part of the Finnish Twin Registry [14]. A postal questionnaire study was carried out in 1975 to measure various health-related variables. The questionnaire was mailed to all Finnish adult same-sexed twin pairs with both members alive in 1975. The overall response rate was 89%. Zygosity was determined by the questionnaire method and was validated by blood testing [26]. The registry also contains singletons gathered during the compilation process. The compilation process and baseline characteristics of the questionnaire study have been documented in detail, including univariate distributions for the variables described below [15–17]. (Note: These may be obtained from the authors.) Responses from 1,919 male twin pairs and 807 singleton men aged 20–29 were used in this study. This age group was chosen so that somatic and psychosocial effects due to smoking- and alcohol-associated morbidity would be minimized.

Measurement of Study Variables

Various aspects of alcohol use were assessed. The number of days per month during which spirits, wines, and beer were used, as well as the amount consumed on average per month in each category was recorded. Heavy drinking, defined as the consumption of at least five bottles of beer, a bottle of wine, or half a bottle of spirits on the same occasion at least once a month was used as the discordance criterion. The total amount consumed on average per month was expressed as grams of alcohol/month.

A current cigarette smoker was defined as one who had ever smoked more than 5–10 packs of cigarettes and who smoked daily or almost daily. Also the year of starting and stopping smoking and the average amount smoked daily were asked.

Extroversion and neuroticism were measured using a 19-item abbreviated form of the Eysenck Personality Inventory [9]. A four-item life-satisfaction scale [1] and a four-item scale measuring experienced stress of daily activities were also used.

ANALYTICAL APPROACH

Initial Data Analysis

Initial data analysis consisted of the description of the study variables. First, the means were analyzed in individual twins of both MZ and DZ pairs according to the concordance status of the pair with respect to heavy use of alcohol (Table 1). There were no significant differences between mean levels of study variables by twin type for concordant twin pairs (217 MZ and 422 DZ negatively concordant, and 189 MZ and 422 DZ positively concordant pairs). For discordant twin pairs (169 MZ and 500 DZ pairs), however, DZ twins were at significantly different mean levels from MZ twins; that is, DZ cotwins of a discordant pair differed more from each other than discordant MZ cotwins even when the same discordance criteria were used. This finding was found for both alcohol and cigarette-smoking variables.

When heavy-drinking and light-drinking singletons were compared (Table 2), the heavy-drinking members smoked highly significantly more and had higher mean scores on the extraversion and neuroticism scales ($P < 0.001$).

The mean differences of study variables in discordant twin pairs by zygosity were, as expected, highly significant for alcohol-use variables (Table 3). The twin exhibiting heavy alcohol behavior also smoked more and had smoked for a longer time in both MZ and DZ pairs. In the personality scales, MZ and DZ pairs behaved differently. MZ heavy-drinking twins were significantly more neurotic than their light-drinking cotwin ($P < 0.05$) and more dissatisfied ($P < 0.01$). DZ heavy-drinking twins were, however, both more extraverted and more neurotic ($P < 0.05$).

The Structural Comparability Analysis Model

Structural analyses were carried out using the LISREL model [12]. LISREL is a general method for estimating the unknown coefficients in a set of linear structural equations, including variables containing measurement errors and assuming reciprocal causation between unmeasured variables. The method can be used for the statistical description and testing of covariance structures in several populations. Also, a pooled covariance matrix can be estimated and the difference between two or more observed covariance matrices can be tested [12].

The variables involved in the model are divided into x independent observed variables and y dependent observed variables. A measurement model of x variables and y variables is specified, defining the relationship of the x variables to the latent variable(s) ξ and of the y variables to the latent variable(s) η. The structural relationship between the latent variables ξ and η are given by partial regression coefficients. Measurement errors can be included in the model or omitted as desired. The model is specified by the following measurement equations:
$x = \Lambda_x \xi + \delta$ and $y = \Lambda \eta + \epsilon$ and the structural equation:
$\beta \eta = \Gamma \xi + \zeta$, where Λ_x and Λ_T are the coefficient matrices for the measurement models of x and y; δ and ϵ are their corresponding measurement errors.

In the structural equations model, β is the matrix of b(i) coefficients, which describe the interrelationships of the variables η, while the elements g(i) of the matrix Γ describe the relationship of the η and ξ variables. The elements of the matrix ζ are errors of the model.

TABLE 1. Mean Values of Study Variables in Individuals by Zygosity and Concordance Status With Respect to Heavy Alcohol Use

Variable		Negatively Concordant	Discordant		Positively Concordant
			Neg	Pos	
Grams alcohol	MZ	140	256	478	705
per month	DZ	142	201**	566*	684
Current	MZ	25	47	55	67
smokers (%)	DZ	24	39	58	64
Years smoked	MZ	2.4	4.6	5.3	5.5
	DZ	2.2	4.6	5.3	5.7
Cigarettes/	MZ	5.0	9.9	12.0	12.6
day	DZ	5.0	8.3**	11.9	13.3
Stress of	MZ	13.1	12.7	12.4	12.8
daily activities[a]	DZ	13.1	13.0	12.9	12.7
Extraversion	MZ	4.4	4.5	4.6	4.8
	DZ	4.3	4.4	4.8	4.7
Neuroticism	MZ	3.5	4.0	4.4	4.5
	DZ	3.5	4.0	4.3	4.6
Dissatisfaction	MZ	8.4	8.1	9.1	9.0
	DZ	8.4	8.4	8.7	9.1

[a]Small score for stress of daily activities indicates greater stress.
* $P < 0.05$
** $P < 0.01$
*** $P < 0.001$

TABLE 2. Mean Values of Study Variables in Singleton Men Aged 20–29 With Respect to Heavy Alcohol Use

Variable	Light drinkers	Heavy drinkers	P value
Grams alcohol per month	177	777	***
Years smoked	3.5	6.1	***
Cigarettes/day	7.1	12.4	***
Current smokers (%)	31.8	56.8	***
Stress of daily activities	12.6	12.3	NS
Extraversion	4.0	5.0	***
Neuroticism	3.8	4.7	***
Dissatisfaction	8.6	9.1	NS
Number	397	410	

The structural analysis model is defined by eight parameter matrices: Λ_T and Λ_x, the coefficients of the measurement model; β and Γ, the coefficients of the structural equations; the covariance matrices, $cov(\xi) = \Phi$, $cov(\zeta) = \Psi$; and the covariances of the measurement errors, $cov(\delta) = \Theta_\delta$ and $cov(\epsilon) = \Theta_\epsilon$.

Any of the parameters can be fixed by prior knowledge or assumptions or it can be estimated from the data. If the numbers of parameters (t) estimated from the data do not exceed the degrees of freedom of the model, the goodness-of-fit of the model can be tested by a chi-square test. The degrees of freedom of the model depend on the number of measured variables in the data.

TABLE 3. Mean Intrapair Differences[a] of Study Variables by Zygosity in Twin Pairs Discordant With Respect to Heavy Alcohol Use

Variable	MZ pairs	P value[b]	DZ pairs	P value[b]
Grams alcohol per month	223	***	367	***
Frequency of beer drinking				
days per month	2.3	***	2.8	***
Years smoked	0.63	**	1.5	***
Cigarettes/day	2.0	**	3.5	***
Stress of daily activities	-0.27	NS	-0.12	NS
Extraversion	0.14	NS	0.38	*
Neuroticism	0.42	*	0.36	*
Dissatisfaction	1.0	***	0.25	NS

[a] Mean difference of heavy-drinking-member value minus light-drinking value.
[b] Matched pair t-test.

When there are p x-variables and q y-variables, then the degrees of freedom are given as df $= (p+q)(p+q+1)/2 - t$ [12]. The covariance matrix of x and y can be described by means of the eight-parameter matrices, and if the fit of the model is fair, the model can be assumed to describe the data in a sufficient manner. The value of the chi-square is also a function of the number of observations.

By comparing the fit of different models to each other, models can be ranked and tested against each other. If the change in chi-square between two models relative to the change in degrees of freedom is significant, it can be said that the fit of the newer model is statistically significantly better than the fit of the previous model. Thus the effect of taking into account various dependencies and relationships at either fixed or free levels can be evaluated. This method also permits the evaluation of the comparability of data sets from two different populations, be they of different twin types or differ with respect to some behavioral characteristic or disease. Constraints on the parameters can be set also over the groups and the effect of such constraints evaluated by computing the change in fit after removal of the constraints.

Empirical Model Fitting

Various twin and singleton group covariance structures were compared by alternatively freeing or constraining parameters in individuals. Changes in total fit and parameters or intrapair relationships were then evaluated.

To study the covariance structures in the twin pairs, two structural analysis models were defined (one for individuals as the observation unit, the other for pairs as the observation unit permitting assessment of intrapair relationships).

The basic model that was used is shown in Figure 1. The model was tested for the individual twins belonging to both MZ and DZ pairs as well as for singletons. The model was defined to be as simple as possible, and model-fitting to minimize chi-square, ie, to seek absolute fit to the data, was not performed. Emphasis was placed on examining the changes in fit between models for different data sets. Smoking was defined as one latent independent variable and the four personality scores formed the second independent latent variable. Exploratory factor analysis of the personality variables indicated that one common factor per individual could

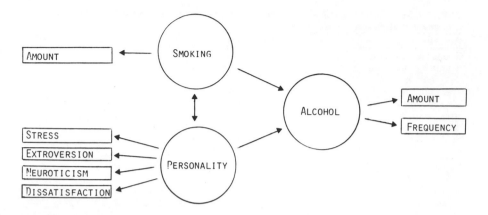

Fig. 1. Structural analysis model for smoking, personality factors, and alcohol use in individuals with relationships between observed and latent variables and relationships of latent variables shown.

be formed using the four scales of measurement available. The neuroticism scale had the largest factor loading on the new factor. The two other large loadings were from the scale on the stress of daily activities and the life dissatisfaction scale. The extraversion scale had the smallest loading. The dependent latent variable was formed by two measures of alcohol use (amount consumed and frequency of alcohol consumption). An intercorrelation between smoking and personality was allowed and measurement errors are associated with all observed variables and the latent dependent variable, η.

The significance of the change in fit of models of individuals was evaluated by computing the change in chi-square for two group analyses when constraints on the measurement model and structural model were imposed, but measurement errors were left free over groups.

The change in chi-square between the two analysis types was evaluated between the following groups of individuals disregarding their status for heavy alcohol use: singletons vs twins, singletons vs MZ twins, singletons vs DZ twins, and DZ twins vs MZ twins. All changes in chi-square were nonsignificant, indicating that the covariance structures of individual men did not vary significantly between groups.

Next, pair concordance status was considered (Tables 4 and 5). MZ and DZ cotwins of concordant pairs were first compared. The second part of the tables shows the results of the comparison within twin type, of the effect of belonging to a discordant vs a concordant pair, when heavy-drinking status is the same. Finally, the heavy-drinking members are compared to light-drinking members of discordant pairs within twin type. Variation in the values of the separate coefficients in the structural model according to twin type, concordance status of the pair and heavy drinking behavior was found (Table 4). The path coefficient between the

TABLE 4. Structural Analyses of Smoking and Personality Factors in Relation to Alcohol Use in Individual Twins by Concordance Status of Heavy Drinking and Zygosity

Analysis Group[a]			Coefficients between latent variables		
Conc	Zyg	HD	Smoking–alcohol	Personality–alcohol	Smoking–personality
N	MZ	–	0.261 ***	0.104	0.097
N	DZ	–	0.198 ***	–0.102	0.045
P	MZ	+	0.173 **	0.113	0.185 *
P	DZ	+	0.253 ***	0.088	0.178 **
D	MZ	–	0.069	0.117	–0.005
D	DZ	–	0.105 *	0.026	–0.004
D	MZ	+	0.398 ***	0.118	–0.009
D	DZ	+	0.181 ***	0.136 **	0.061

[a] Conc = concordance status of the twin pair with respect to heavy alcohol use : N = negatively concordant, P = positively concordant, D = discordant pairs.
HD = status with respect to heavy drinking behaviour: + heavy drinker, –not heavy drinker.
Zyg = zygosity of the twin pair.

TABLE 5. Structural Analyses of Smoking and Personality Factors in Relation to Alcohol Use in Individual Twins by Concordance Status of Heavy Drinking and Zygosity

Analysis Type						2-Group Model Chi-Square Value[a]		Change In
Group 1			Group 2			Free Model	Constrained Model	Chi-Square
Conc	Zyg	HD	Conc	Zyg	HD	(DF = 26)	(DF = 32)	+ P value
N	MZ	–	N	DZ	–	58.81	65.90	7.09 NS
P	MZ	+	P	DZ	+	38.88	43.11	4.33 NS
N	MZ	–	D	MZ	–	47.17	51.88	4.71 NS
N	DZ	–	D	DZ	–	63.79	68.06	4.27 NS
D	MZ	+	P	MZ	+	22.83	28.05	5.22 NS
D	DZ	+	P	DZ	+	62.64	69.40	6.86 NS
D	MZ	–	D	MZ	+	26.44	33.77	7.33 NS
D	DZ	–	D	DZ	+	72.30	78.50	6.20 NS

[a]Free model: no constraints over groups.
Constrained model: relationship of latent variables to original variables (Λ_x and Λ_T matrices) and between latent variables (Γ matrix) constrained to be equal over groups.

smoking and alcohol latent variables was high in all groups except for the light-drinking members of discordant pairs. The relationship between the personality and alcohol variables was weak in all but heavy-drinking members of discordant members. The smoking–personality correlation coefficient was strong and statistically significant in members of positively concordant pairs. Despite the variation in individual coefficients in various groups, the change in chi-square between groups in the free and constrained models was nonsignificant (Table 5).

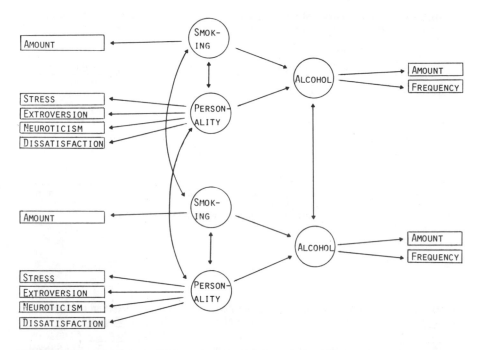

Fig 2. Structural analysis model for twin pairs showing relationships in twins and between twins for latent variables.

After the basic model had been developed and analyzed, it was extended to a pairwise analysis (Fig. 2). In addition to the basic relationships for individuals, intrapair relationships between the latent variables were considered. In this model, this intrapair relationship can be considered to correspond to intraclass correlations for smoking, personality, and alcohol. The analysis was carried out by comparing, for example, two groups (MZ and DZ pairs) in two separate analyses: 1) individual relationships free, and 2) individual relationships constrained to be equal but free.

Relationships in MZ and DZ pairs negatively (Table 6) and positively (Table 7) concordant for heavy alcohol use were compared. The strongest intrapair dependencies were found in the negatively concordant groups, with slightly weaker relationships in the positively concordant groups. The changes from one model to another were greatest for MZ intraclass correlation for alcohol use in light-drinking pairs. Yet changes in overall fit were nonsignificant in both analyses.

Using this model, heavy-drinking discordant pairs and the relationship of heavy- to light-drinking twins in MZ and DZ pairs were examined. The parameters in light-drinking individuals of both groups and in heavy-drinking individuals were

TABLE 6. Changes in Overall Fit and in Latent Variable Correlations Between Free and Constrained Model in MZ and DZ Pairs Negatively Concordant for Heavy Alcohol Use

A.

Free model	$X^2 = 404.33$	df = 149
Constrained model	$X^2 = 415.25$	df = 159
Difference	$X^2 = 10.92$	df = 10 P > 0.05

B.

Intraclass correlations Latent Variable(s)	Free model		Constrained model	
	MZ	DZ	MZ	DZ
Smoking	0.65	0.34	0.66	0.34
Personality	0.78	0.35	0.79	0.33
Alcohol use	0.91	0.32	0.78	0.31

TABLE 7. Changes in Overall Fit and in Latent Variable Correlations Between Free and Constrained Model in MZ and DZ Pairs Positively Concordant for Heavy Alcohol Use

A.

Free model	$X^2 = 313.03$	df = 149
Constrained model	$X^2 = 322.77$	df = 159
Difference	$X^2 = 9.74$	df = 10 P > 0.05

B.

Intraclass correlations Latent Variable(s)	Free model		Constrained model	
	MZ	DZ	MZ	DZ
Smoking	0.52	0.29	0.56	0.28
Personality	0.65	0.30	0.67	0.30
Alcohol use	0.44	0.14	0.44	0.13

separately constrained to be equal. In the discordant pair analysis (Table 8), the intraclass correlation for alcohol use was nil, and the other intraclass correlations were also weaker than in the concordant groups.

Multivariate Analysis of Discordant Pair Differences

After evaluating the comparability of the discordant pairs in MZ and DZ pairs in different ways, a matched-pair logistic model was applied to the discordant pair data to enable evaluation of the relative roles of the variables as well as their statistical significance. The logistic analyses were carried out by the conditional likelihood method [11], and parameters and model fit were estimated by standard maximum likelihood methods [2]. In the MZ pairs, the overall model fit was satisfactory and two variables had statistically significant estimates—smoking and life dissatisfaction. The pattern for DZ pairs was similar to that found in the univariate analysis of differences, ie, estimates for smoking and both extroversion and neuroticism were statistically significant (Table 9).

DISCUSSION

Methods of data analysis and the interpretation of results from twin studies have been quite varied, with no special established standards [13]. Recent reviews of analysis methods point toward a gradual agreement on the basic methods of analysis

TABLE 8. Changes in Overall Fit and in Latent Variable Correlations and Path Coefficients Between Free and Constrained Model in MZ and DZ Pairs Discordant for Heavy Alcohol Use

A.

Free model	$X^2 = 283.11$		df = 142
Constrained model	$X^2 = 291.13$		df = 159
Difference	$X^2 = 4.02$		df = 12 P > 0.05

B. Correlations for intrapair relationships

Latent	Free model		Constrained model	
Variable(s)	MZ	DZ	MZ	DZ
Smoking	0.53	0.29	0.50	0.29
Personality	0.66	0.19	0.68	0.19
Alcohol use	0.00	0.03	0.02	0.12

C. Path coefficients for intervariable relationships in individuals by concordance status

Path	Concordance status	Free model		Constrained model
		MZ	DZ	
Smoking–	Neg	0.026	0.024	0.117 **
alcohol	Pos	0.393 ***	0.205 ***	0.258***
Personality–	Neg	0.034	0.002	0.041
alcohol	Pos	0.095	0.140 **	0.171**

TABLE 9. Matched-Pair Multiple Logistical Analysis of Alcohol-Use-Discordant Twin Pairs

	MZ pairs (N = 169)			DZ pairs (N = 500)		
Variable	Estimate	standard error	P value	Estimate	standard error	P value
Amount smoked	0.044	0.021	*	0.056	0.010	***
Stress of daily activities	0.007	0.064	NS	0.007	0.034	NS
Extroversion	0.102	0.072	NS	0.077	0.030	**
Neuroticism	0.070	0.070	NS	0.067	0.033	*
Dissatisfaction	0.152	0.055	**	0.035	0.029	NS
Goodness-of-fit test	X^2_{164} =	174.0		X^2_{495} =	505.3	

[7]. Also, data from twin populations have been used often without sufficient regard to representativeness, adequate sampling techniques, and comparability of variables [22]. Although such aspects may not be relevant in some studies, they are of great importance in epidemiological studies, when quantitative measures (prevalence, incidence, relative risk, etc) are reported.

The analysis of comparability of variables by twin type is here extended to the analysis of pairs discordant or concordant for a trait. A univariate approach of this kind has been the nonexposed twin (NET) analyses of Cederlöf et al [6]. They compared, for instance, the nonsmoking cotwins of smoking twins and twins of pairs concordant for nonsmoking with respect to psychosocial factors and alcohol use. A basic assumption in this method is naturally the comparability of the two types of nonsmoking twin with respect to the possible effect-modifying variables. Although the mean levels of study variables may be different between groups according to concordance status and trait discordance, this does not necessarily imply that the covariance structures are different in the different groups.

Multivariate methods in twin studies were used by Bock and Vandenberg [3] to identify independent genetic components of mental ability tests. Multivariate modeling has been performed by Fulker [10] to partition genetic and environmental effects from twin data. Marshall and Knox [19] present a parametrizable model, which can account for effects before and after cleavage of the zygote, when data on the zygosity of individual twin pairs are unknown.

The method used here is demonstrative of one approach to the analysis of twin data, particularly when studying trait-discordant twins. Despite the finding of differences in means, the covariance structures of groups of individuals were comparable. The overall changes in fit when comparing groups of individuals were nonsignificant, suggesting that a null hypothesis of comparability of covariance structures between the groups could not be rejected. Similarly, the covariance structures of MZ and DZ pairs of any concordance status seemed to be comparable, as the changes in fit between models were also nonsignificant.

The power of this method to detect differences between groups has not been evaluated. Martin et al [20] studied the power of the classical twin method. Although the size of twin sample utilized here suffices for many estimates using the classical twin method, the subdivision by trait discordance in addition to using data on zygosity may have yielded too small groups, particularly of trait-discordant MZ pairs, for sufficient analysis.

The analysis of covariance structures to assess comparability of groups by twin type and/or concordance status is a useful method of extending the analysis of twin data in a multivariate approach. Although methodological development is no doubt needed, further information needed for epidemiological studies is yielded by studying the relationships between variables in addition to the study of means and mean differences.

Partanen et al [24], in their study on adult same-sexed male twin pairs, found very weak correlations between personality factors and alcohol use factors, but a strong dependency of alcohol use and smoking. In alcohol-use discordant pairs, 75% of the MZ heavy-drinking members smoked vs 62% in the DZ alcohol-use discordant pairs. Myrhed [21] found a history of greater cigarette smoking in high alcohol consumer twins of pairs discordant for alcohol consumption. The finding was statistically significant in DZ but not MZ pairs. These findings on smoking in alcohol-discordant pairs agree with the results of this study.

In studies on the national Swedish Twin Registry, the known relationship between alcohol consumption and cigarette smoking was also observed in individual twins [6]. Also neuroticism, extraversion, and experienced stress were more common among smokers than nonsmokers. In other studies of the Swedish Twin Registry, Lorich and Cederlöf [18] compared drinkers and nondrinkers with respect to their psychosocial environment. As individuals, drinkers experienced more stress and insomnia than nondrinkers irrespective of smoking status. Within discordant pairs, stress and insomnia did not differ by drinking status in either MZ or DZ pairs. NET-analysis, however, indicated that DZ cotwins of drinking twins experienced more stress than cotwins in concordant pairs.

Borg et al [4] studied 63 middle-aged, alcohol-discordant male twin pairs. They found no obvious differences in the use of psychotropic drugs and in the occurrence of psychiatric symptoms. Thus the association of alcohol use with psychological factors would seem to be found for normal traits, but not for signs of psychopathology.

In this study the differences between heavy- and light-drinking individuals were most clear-cut in singletons. They differed in the mean smoking levels, and the extraversion and neuroticism scores. The same result was obtained in DZ twin pairs discordant for heavy alcohol use. In discordant MZ pairs, however, the smoking differences were observed but the personality factor differences were seen in the neuroticism and life dissatisfaction scales, suggesting that the basis of discordance in MZ twins may differ from that in DZ pairs and singletons. The proportion of discordant pairs was 29% in MZ and 37% in DZ pairs, less than the expected value, but classification errors have probably affected the pairs likewise.

The multivariate analysis of differences in MZ and DZ discordant pairs confirmed the results from the univariate analyses, the relative significance of neuroticism in MZ pairs becoming weaker and statistically nonsignificant. Smoking, neuroticism, and life dissatisfaction, independent of genetic factors, seem to be indicators of processes leading to heavy alcohol use.

REFERENCES

1. Allardt E: About dimensions on welfare an explanatory analysis of the comparative Scandinavian survey. University of Helsinki, Research Group of Comparative Sociology. Research Reports No. 1, Helsinki, 1973.
2. Baker RJ, Nelder JA: Generalised linear interactive modelling (GLIM) system. Numerical algorithms group, Oxford, 1978.
3. Bock RD, Vandenberg SG: Components of Heritable Variation in Mental Test Scores. In Vandenberg SG (ed): "Progress in Human Behavior Genetics." Baltimore: Johns Hopkins Press, 1968, pp 233–260.
4. Borg S, Fyrö B, Myrhed M: Psychosocial factors in alcohol-discordant twins. Br J Addict 74:189–198, 1979.
5. Bulmer MG: "The Biology of Twinning in Man." London: Oxford University Press, 1970.
6. Cederlöf R, Friberg L, Lundman T: The interactions of smoking environment and heredity and their implications for disease etiology. Acta Med Scand Suppl 612, 1977.
7. Christian JC: Testing twin means and estimating genetic variance. Basic methodology for the analysis of quantitative twin data. Acta Genet Med Gemellol 28:35–40, 1979.
8. Elston RC, Boklage CE: An examination of fundamental assumptions of the twin method. In Nance WE (ed): "Twin Research: Psychology and Methodology." New York: Alan R. Liss, 1978, pp 189–199.
9. Floderus B: Psycho-social factors in relation to coronary heart disease and associated risk factors. Nord Hyg T Suppl 6, 1974.
10. Fulker DW: Multivariate extensions of a biometrical model of twin data. In Nance WE (ed): "Twin Research: Psychology and Methodology." New York: Alan R. Liss, 1978, pp 217–236.
11. Holford TR, White C, Kelsey JL: Multivariate analysis for matched case-controlled studies. Am J Epidemiol 107:245–256, 1978.
12. Jöreskog KG, Sörbom D: LISREL IV. A General Computer Estimation of Linear Structural Equation Systems by Maximum Likelihood Methods. Uppsala, 1978.
13. Kang KW, Christian JC, Morton JA: Heritability estimates. Acta Genet Med Gemellol 27:39–44, 1978.

14. Kaprio J, Sarna S, Koskenvuo M. Rantasalo I: The Finnish Twin Registry: Formation and compilation, questionnaire study, zygosity determination procedures and research program. Prog Clin Biol Res 24B:179–184, 1978.
15. Kaprio J, Sarna S, Koskenvuo M, Rantasalo I: Baseline characteristics of the Finnish Twin Registry: Section II: History of symptoms and illnesses, use of drugs, physical characteristics, smoking, alcohol and physical activity. Publications of the Department of Public Health Science M37, Helsinki, 1978.
16. Kaprio J, Koskenvuo M, Artimo M, Sarna S, Rantasalo I: Baseline characteristics of the Finnish Twin Registry: Section I: Materials, methods, representativeness, and results for variables special to twin studies. Publications of the Department of Public Health Science M47, Helsinki, 1979.
17. Koskenvuo M, Langinvainio H, Kaprio J, Rantasalo I, Sarna S: The Finnish Twin Registry: Baseline characteristics, Section III: Occupational and psychosocial factors. Publication of the Department of Public Health Science M49, Helsinki, 1979.
18. Lorich V, Cederlöf R: The alcohol habit and its environmental and diseasee correlates. In Nance WE (ed): "Twin Research: Clinical Studies." New York: Alan R. Liss, 1978, pp 63–69.
19. Marshall T, Knox EG: Disease concordance and sex similarity in twins. J Epidemiol Comm Health 34:1–8, 1980.
20. Martin NG, Eaves LJ, Kearsey MJ, Davies P: The power of the classical twin study. Heredity 40:97–116, 1978.
21. Myrhed M: Alcohol consumption in relation to factors associated with ischemic heart disease: A co-twin control study. Acta Med Scand Suppl 567, 1974.
22. Nance WE, Corey LA, Boughman JA: "Monozygotic Twin Kinships. A New Design for Genetic and Epidemiologic Research in Genetic Epidemiology." NE Morton, CS Chung (eds): New York: Academic Press, 1978, pp 88–114.
23. Nance WE: "The role of twin studies in human quantitative genetics. In Steinberg A, Bearn A, Motulsky A, Childs B (eds): "Progress in Medical Genetics 3." Philadelphia: WB Saunders, 1979, pp 73–107.
24. Partanen J, Bruun K, Markkanen T: Inheritance of drinking behavior. A study of intelligence, personality and use of alcohol of adult twins. The Finnish Foundation for Alcohol Studies, 1966.
25. Price B: Primary biases in twin studies. Am J Hum Genet 2:293–352, 1950.
26. Sarna S, Kaprio J, Sistonen P, Koskenvuo M: Diagnosis of twin zygosity by mailed questionnaire. Hum Hered 28:241–254, 1978.

Twin Research 3: Epidemiological
and Clinical Studies, pages 37—46
© 1981 Alan R. Liss, Inc., 150 Fifth Avenue, New York, NY 10011

Cigarette Smoking, Use of Alcohol, and Leisure-Time Physical Activity Among Same-Sexed Adult Male Twins

Jaakko Kaprio, Markku Koskenvuo, and Seppo Sarna
Department of Public Health Science, University of Helsinki

INTRODUCTION

Smoking, alcohol use, and physical activity have been much studied as risk factors of disease. Smoking and alcohol have been commonly linked with both total mortality risk and specific causes of death [1, 17, 23, 24]. Physical activity would seem to protect from certain specific diseases, particularly coronary heart disease [16, 20, 26].

These three factors, however, are not independent of each other and the correlation between smoking and alcohol use is well known [11, 27]. The study of interactions among various health risk behavior patterns is therefore necessary. In the formation of health behavior patterns and their manifestation in adult life, familial and possibly genetic factors are of importance. Because these factors are interrelated, the finding of higher concordance rates in twin studies for diseases that are known to be related to smoking, alcohol use, or physical inactivity may be explained by the higher association of the risk factors and not necessarily by a genetic or familial influence on the disease itself.

The purpose of this chapter is to present the relationships of cigarette smoking, alcohol use, and leisure-time physical activity among adult men in a Finnish population study of twins. Combinations of these factors will be considered, and the relationship of the factors to each other in relation to the twin pair situation will also be examined.

MATERIALS AND METHODS

The Finnish Twin Registry consists of those same-sexed twin pairs with both members alive in 1967 and born before 1958. The material was compiled from the Finnish Central Population Register computer files by selecting as twin candidates those pairs of persons with the same date of birth, the same surname of birth and the same community of birth. This procedure yielded also twin candidate pairs that were singletons matched for these variables. To clarify twinship and zygosity, and to measure baseline characteristics of the material, a questionnaire was mailed in 1975 to all those pairs with both members alive at that date. A response rate of 89% was obtained for the twins, and the nontwins could be distinguished from the material using their responses and further clarification from the local population registries. The final material consisted of 16,269 twin pairs. The compilation process of the registry has been described elsewhere [8]. Univariate and pairwise results for the variables of the questionnaire study have been documented earlier [9, 10, 14].

Twin zygosity was determined by examining the response of both members of the twin pair to questions on similarity of appearance and confusion by strangers during childhood. A set of decision roles was used to classify the twin pairs as monozygotic (MZ), undetermined, or dizygotic (DZ). Some 93% of all respondent pairs could be correctly classified with a very small probability of misclassification (1.7%) as verified by using blood tests [21]. In this study, responses from 1537 MZ and 3507 DZ male pairs aged 18 and over were analyzed (Table 1).

A cigarette smoker was defined as a person who had smoked at least 5–10 packs of cigarettes in his whole life and had smoked daily or nearly daily. Persons not satisfying these criteria were determined to be nonsmokers. Smokers were then classified as current smokers or ex-smokers depending on whether they smoked at present or not. The amount currently or last smoked and the age of starting and stopping smoking were also asked. Because the number of regular cigar- and pipe-smokers was small (2.5% and 4.0% respectively), these variables were not included in the smoking analyses presented in this chapter.

Alcohol use was queried by asking the amount of beer, wine, and spirits consumed on average per week or month as well as the frequency of their use. The average current consumption was transformed to give the amount in grams of alcohol per month. Also it was queried whether alcohol use had been greater previously then at present. Heavy drinking was asked for by whether at least once a month on the same occasion at least five bottles of beer, a bottle of wine, or a half-bottle of spirits was consumed.

Leisure-time physical activity was measured by the individual's subjective opinion of the amount of physical activity currently engaged in, its intensity and duration, and number of years of physical activity engaged in the adult life. The intensity score for physical activity was based on three questions related to sweating and breathlessness and the self-rated intensity of the leisure-time physical activity compared to walking, jogging, or running. For the duration score, the number of minutes on one leisure-time physical activity session and the number of such sessions per week were also asked for. The intensity and duration scores were multiplied together to obtain an activity score.

For these variables on alcohol, smoking, and physical activity, questionnaire results from the twins considered as individuals (with one member of each pair being included) were used. Three factor analyses were carried out (one on each variable group) to yield a condensed score for each variable group. The factor loadings in the principal components model of the raw variables, their communality

TABLE 1. Age Distribution of Study Series

Age group	No. of pairs by zygosity	
(years)	MZ	DZ
18–29	731	1,628
30–39	351	812
40–49	191	563
50–59	137	300
60+	127	204
Total	1,537	3,507

TABLE 2. Factor Analysis of Individual Risk Variables; Cigarette Smoking, Use of Alcohol, and Physical Activity

Factor analysis for alcohol use variables	Factor loading	Communality estimate
Beer drinking frequency	0.658	0.527
Wine drinking frequency	0.539	0.481
Spirit drinking frequency	0.705	0.560
Heavy drinking once/month	0.600	0.486
Earlier drunk more	0.074	0.091
Current grams/month	0.787	0.560
Eigenvalue for factor = 2.21		
Factor analysis for cigarette smoking variables		
Years smoked	0.793	0.688
Cigarettes smoked per day	0.847	0.776
Current smoker	0.756	0.647
Ever smoker	0.881	0.776
Eigenvalue for factor = 2.70		
Factor analysis for leisure-time physical activity variables		
Physical activity on work journey	0.089	0.152
Subjective opinion of own physical activity	0.768	0.632
Intensity score for physical activity	0.649	0.601
Duration score for physical activity	0.824	0.813
Activity score for physical activity	0.897	0.813
Years of physical training in adulthood	0.468	0.404
Eigenvalue for factor = 2.72		

estimates, and the eigenvalues of the factors are shown in Table 2. These factor scores were used as the basis for the univariate analyses in individuals and pairs.

To examine whether the study material could be differentiated into various constellations according to the study variables, a cluster analysis was carried out. The cluster analysis was carried out using as variables three factors obtained by factor analysis of all study variables in the same analysis. This was done to obtain uncorrelated variables for the cluster analysis, as this procedure yields more stable results than when correlated variables are used. The cluster analyses were repeated with different numbers of clusters set and different random starts until a stable pattern was obtained. Eight clusters were found to be stable in group–regroup situations with over 90% of members remaining in the same cluster from one analysis to another. Because the cluster analysis was performed on a random sample, 799 members (all from different pairs) of the whole series, the classification of the study series into the obtained clusters was done using a multiple discriminant analysis where the analysis model was constructed using the three factors and their grouping result.

The effect of intrapair contact on response pattern of individuals to the mailed questionnaire was studied by examining the relationship of variables measuring contact frequency between the twins to the use of alcohol, smoking habits, and leisure-time physical activity (Table 3). Fairly weak correlations were found, indicating that the level of risk factors was only slightly dependent on the amount of intrapair contact. The highest correlation was 0.15 for cigarette smoking and cohabitation status, ie. twins living apart smoked more than twins living together.

RESULTS

The age-specific mean standardized scores for the cigarette smoking, alcohol, and leisure-time physical activity factor are shown in Figure 1. The physical activity factor means were almost constant over age, but there was a decrease with age in the alcohol consumption factor score after an initial rise. For the smoking factor, there was a steady increase with age until 50–54 years, after which a slight decrease occurred. All variations are at most half a standard deviation from the mean. Because of the observed age trends, the results of all further analyses were age-adjusted.

The correlation coefficients between the factors in the whole series are shown in Table 4. A high correlation ($r = 0.32$) was found between the cigarette smoking and use of alcohol factors. Small negative correlations existed for the physical activity and cigarette smoking factors and, on the other hand, for physical activity and use of alcohol factors.

The intraclass correlations for the factor scores were computed by age and zygosity (Table 5). It can be seen that, for nearly all age groups, the differences of MZ and DZ correlations are statistically significant, as are also the differences of total intraclass correlations of all three factors. For physical activity, there is a decrease in intraclass correlations with age for both MZ and DZ pairs, but the heritability estimates remain fairly stable over age, whereas for cigarette smoking and alcohol use, heritability estimates are low in those older than 60.

For the cluster analysis, Table 6 shows the mean standard scores with respect to deviations about the total mean of each factor. For the cigarette and alcohol factors there were four clusters both above and below the mean, whereas in the physical activity factor there are five clusters below the mean and only three above. There were three large clusters, four clusters of intermediate size, and one small cluster. Table 7 shows the characteristics of each cluster in relation to original variables and the mean ages of the members of the cluster. Analysis of variance indicated that the mean ages of the clusters differed significantly from each other (P < 0.001).

TABLE 3. Correlations Between Risk Factor Scores and Measures of Intrapair Contact (All Men Aged 18+)

	Living apart	Age at separation	Infrequency of contact
Alcohol use	0.073	−0.048	0.029
Cigarette smoking	0.150	0.017	0.140
Physical activity	−0.045	0.033	−0.034

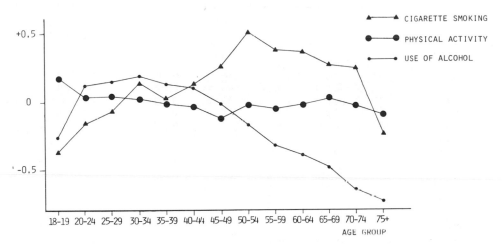

Fig. 1. Mean standardized factor scores for cigarette smoking, physical activity and use of alcohol in men aged 18+ by age group (Mean = 0, SD = 1).

TABLE 4: Intercorrelations of Factor Scores in Men Aged 18+

	Physical activity	Alcohol use
Alcohol use	−0.020	
Cigarette smoking	−0.138	0.322

The largest cluster, with 25.9% of the total sample, contained no current smokers and had below average leisure-time physical activity, and with an alcohol consumption of slightly over 80 grams per month. The subjects of the second cluster, 21.7% of the sample, were nearly 8 years older than the overall mean and smoked more than average, with almost 65% current smokers, smoking an average of 15.5 cigarettes a day. The physical activity was below mean and so was alcohol consumption at 121 grams a month. The third large cluster, containing 19.1% of the sample, was only slightly below mean age and was in smoking characteristics fairly similar to the previous cluster. This cluster had the least physical activity (0.4 hours per week) and above average alcohol consumption, with 72% replying that heavy drinking occurred at least once a month.

The largest medium-size cluster, with 9.7% of the sample, was slightly below the mean age, with nearly 80% current smokers, the physical activity below mean, but greatly increased alcohol consumption with almost 1,200 grams of alcohol per month. The second medium-size cluster (8.9% in size) was of average age, containing 55% current smokers, with a slightly below average alcohol con-

TABLE 5. Intraclass Correlations for Risk Factor Scores of Alcohol Use, Physical Activity, and Cigarette Smoking (Men Aged 18 and Over)

Age group	Intraclass correlation		Heritability 2 (rMZ-rDZ)	P value for rMA-rDZ
	r MZ	r DZ		
Cigarette smoking				
18-29	0.709	0.434	0.550	***
30-39	0.673	0.382	0.582	***
40-49	0.539	0.388	0.302	NS
50-59	0.583	0.377	0.412	*
60+	0.346	0.288	0.116	NS
Total	0.644	0.418	0.452	***
Use of alcohol				
18-29	0.579	0.339	0.480	***
30-39	0.527	0.204	0.646	***
40-49	0.356	0.170	0.372	**
50-59	0.437	0.140	0.594	**
60+	0.225	0.213	0.024	NS
Total	0.536	0.279	0.514	***
Physical activity				
18-29	0.638	0.319	0.638	***
30-39	0.477	0.218	0.518	***
40-49	0.323	0.108	0.430	**
50-59	0.300	0.139	0.322	NS
60+	0.332	0.012	0.620	**
Total	0.569	0.257	0.624	***

* $P < 0.05$
** $P < 0.01$
*** $P < 0.001$

TABLE 6. Distribution of Factor Risk Scores by Risk Cluster

Cluster	Mean risk scores (in SD)			Size (% of total)
	Cigarette smoking	Physical activity	Alcohol use	
1	−1.02	−0.24	−0.56	25.89
2	0.81	−0.37	−0.69	21.69
3	0.62	−0.40	0.36	19.10
4	0.63	−0.13	1.79	9.74
5	0.69	1.03	−0.06	8.91
6	−1.17	−0.13	0.99	8.27
7	−0.39	2.64	−0.26	6.07
8	−0.41	0.43	5.47	0.44
Total	0.03	0.01	0.03	100.00

TABLE 7. Relationship of Cluster Analysis Results to Original Variables

Variable	Cluster							
	1	2	3	4	5	6	7	8
Beer drinking days	1.20	1.80	5.33	10.90	4.35	7.51	4.43	18.10
Wine drinking days	0.64	0.66	1.66	3.31	2.03	2.84	1.43	11.30
Spirits drinking days	0.84	1.00	3.55	6.77	2.90	4.86	2.13	14.40
% with heavy drinking	6.00	8.40	71.70	96.60	46.60	54.60	36.10	100.00
% with previous more	7.50	35.30	17.40	25.00	36.00	18.20	16.40	50.00
Mean monthly consumption	82.40	121.00	452.00	1,166.00	312.00	542.00	255.00	4,782.00
Ever smokers: years smoked	2.00	19.80	11.90	13.70	14.30	1.00	6.00	9.00
Ever smokers: amount daily smoking	2.50	15.50	15.60	18.90	16.20	2.50	13.20	17.30
% current smoker	0.00	64.70	63.80	79.60	54.70	0.00	13.10	50.00
% ever smoker	0.50	100.00	100.00	100.00	100.00	1.30	36.10	50.00
Own physical activity	2.39	2.08	2.07	2.32	3.48	2.54	4.21	2.10
Physical activity intensity	3.34	2.59	2.76	3.52	5.42	4.10	7.16	3.51
Physical activity duration	1.11	0.77	0.44	0.92	3.11	0.80	5.65	5.71
Physical activity intensity • duration	3.48	1.44	1.48	4.00	12.54	3.83	42.80	27.81
Physical activity as adult	1.70	1.40	1.53	1.94	2.75	1.94	3.39	1.42
Age	33.40	41.80	32.20	31.70	35.80	32.30	27.90	31.50

sumption and greatly increased physical activity (three hours per week). The subjects of the third medium-size cluster were nonsmokers, but alcohol consumption was clearly above average, and the physical activity only slightly below average. The last medium-size cluster, with 6.1% of respondents, was physically very active (5.7 hours per week) with only 15.1% current smokers and alcohol consumption below average. The smallest cluster comprised only 0.4% of the study series and differed markedly from the other clusters. It consisted of 56 men, half of whom were current smokers, and below mean age. Their physical activity was above average, but their most distinguishing feature was an extremely high alcohol consumption. Each member of this cluster reported that an episode of heavy drinking occurred at least once a month. Spirits were consumed on 14 days per month on average and mean alcohol monthly consumption was 4,800 grams.

The distribution of pairs by zygosity in the various factor clusters described previously is shown in Table 8. The observed proportions of twins in the same cluster for MZ and DZ pairs are compared to the expected proportion calculated as the square of the proportional size of the cluster as individuals. Overall, 17.9% of pairs would have both members in the same cluster if the twins in a pair were found at random in the clusters. For MZ pairs the proportion observed was 54.7% and for DZ pairs 44.5%. The ratios of observed-to-expected proportions were 3.1 for MZ pairs and 2.5 for DZ pairs. If the small cluster no. 8 (0.4% of the study series) is excluded, the clusters with observed-to-expected ratios most different from the mean were clusters 6 and 7, which comprised 8.3% and 6.1% of the study series, respectively. Both consist of mainly nonsmokers, but cluster 6 has the second highest mean alcohol use, whereas cluster 7 has the highest physical activity factor score mean. For all clusters, the MZ observed-to-expected ratio is greater than the corresponding DZ ratio, although the ratio difference is overall quite small.

DISCUSSION

Twin studies of cigarette smoking, use of alcohol, and physical activity have been carried out to obtain estimates of the relative roles of environmental and genetic factors in the variation of the traits. Some studies have attempted to explain the relationship of these factors to disease in twin pairs.

Twin studies on alcohol use and components of alcohol abuse have been conducted principally in Scandinavia and the United States. Kaij [7] studied twin pairs with alcohol abuse in Sweden. Jonsson and Nilsson [6] studied alcohol consumption in twin pairs in Sweden. In a study of male twins born in 1920–1929 in Finland and their brothers [18], aspects of alcohol control and use with respect to various psychosocial factors were studied. In studies of alcohol metabolism, the dehydrogenation of alcohol has been found to be under genetic control [25]. In the United States, Loehlin [15] found a heritable component to alcohol use in young adult twins.

The study of heritable components of smoking behavior is complex, and has been attempted in twin [3, 5] and family studies [19]. Earlier studies have indicated a higher concordance for MZ than DZ twins with respect to smoking status and amount smoked [2, 4, 22].

TABLE 8. Distribution of Expected and Observed Concordance Proportion by Cluster

Cluster	Observed MZ %	Observed DZ %	Expected %	Observed/Expected MZ	DZ
1	20.95	18.08	6.70	3.13	2.70
2	12.17	10.18	4.70	2.59	2.17
3	7.87	7.27	3.65	2.16	1.99
4	3.19	2.91	0.95	3.36	3.06
5	2.73	1.51	0.79	3.46	1.91
6	3.77	3.31	0.68	5.54	4.89
7	3.84	1.28	0.37	10.38	3.46
8	0.13	0.00	0.002	65.00	0.00
Total	54.65	44.54	17.85	3.06	2.50

Physical activity as a risk factor for disease has not been much analyzed for its heritable components using twin methods, but physical performance and aspects of muscle metabolism have been studied in relatively small samples of healthy twin pairs [12, 13].

Because the three traits under analysis all presented significant heritable factors ($h^2 = 0.45$–0.62) in univariate analysis, it was important to analyze whether this is due primarily to the intracorrelations between traits and the high heritability of only some components or due to independent heritable factors in all three traits. Both MZ and DZ twin pair members were in the same cluster much more often than expected, but the MZ-DZ overall difference was relatively small, indicating that genetic effects on the levels of the variables in the population are probably relatively small. The highest MZ/DZ ratios of observed to expected clustering rates were in two clusters: A) cluster no. 7, which had persons with a high mean degree of leisure-time physical activity; and B) the very small cluster no. 8, which had a very high mean alcohol use.

It may be indicative that these extremes of behavior are then more likely to be genetically determined, although it must be remembered that the analyses in these clusters are based on relatively small sample sizes compared to the whole study series.

When considering the implications of these results with respect to studies of risk factors of disease, it is probable that some of the increased concordance for disease observed among twin pairs is due to the increased similarity with respect to risk-factor behavior patterns. Similarly, familial aggregation of disease is probably in part due to familial aggregation of smoking, alcohol use, and physical inactivity.

Also, the correlations between risk factors should be considered when analyzing twin data on risk factors for disease. Besides the observed dependencies of smoking, alcohol use, and leisure-time physical activity, other factors such as hypertension, hyperlipemias, and nutritional factors may be correlated to the measured risk factors. Likewise, a multivariate analysis of pairwise risk factors of disease should take into account gene–environment interactions of the risk factors.

The study series is being followed up for morbidity and mortality data and will in future permit analysis of the risk factor data in relation to disease experience.

REFERENCES

1. Brody JA, Mills GS: On considering alcohol as a risk factor in specific diseases. Am J Epidemiol 107:462–466, 1978.
2. Cederlöf R: The twin method in epidemiologic studies on chronic disease. University of Stockholm, 1966.
3. Cederlöf R, Friberg L, Lundman T: The interactions of smoking, environment and heredity and their implications for disease etiology. Acta Med Scand Suppl 612, 1977.
4. Friberg L, Kaij L, Dencker SJ, Jonsson E: Smoking habits of monozygotic and dizygotic twins. Br Med J 1:1090–1092, 1959,
5. Hrubec Z, Cederlöf R, Friberg L: Background of angina pectoris. Social and environmental factors in relation to smoking. Am J Epidemiol 103:16–29, 1976.
6. Jonsson AE, Nilsson T: Alkohol konsumption hos monozygota och dizygota tvillingar. Nord Hyg Tidskr 49:21–25, 1068.
7. Kaij L: Studies on the etiology and sequels of abuse of alcohol. Department of Psychiatry, University of Lund, 1960.
8. Kaprio J, Sarna S, Koskenvuo M, Rantasalo I: Finnish Twin Registry: Formation and compilation, questionnaire study, zygosity determination procedures and research program. Prog Clin Biol Res 24B:179–184, 1978.
9. Kaprio J, Sarna S, Koskenvuo M, Rantasalo I: Baseline characteristics of the Finnish Twin Registry: Section II: History of symptoms and illnesses, use of drugs, physical characteristics, smoking, alcohol and physical activity. Publication of the Department of Public Health Science M37, Helsinki, 1978.
10. Kaprio J, Koskenvuo M, Artimo M, Sarna S, Rantasalo I: Baseline characteristics of the Finnish Twin Registry: Section I: Materials, methods, representativeness, and results for variables special to twin studies. Publication of the Department of Public Health Science M47, Helsinki, 1979.
11. Klatsky AL, Friedman GD, Siegelaub AB, Gerard MJ: Alcohol consumption and blood pressure: Kaiser-Permanante multiphasic health examination data. N Engl J Med 296:1194–1200, 1977.
12. Klissouras V: Heritability of adaptative variations. J Appl Physiol 31:338–341, 1971.
13. Komi P, Karlsson J: Physical performance, skeletal muscle enzyme activity, and fibre types in monozygous and dizygous twins of both sexes. Acta Physiol Scan Suppl 462, 1979.
14. Koskenvuo M, Langinvainio H, Kaprio J, Rantasalo I, Sarna S: The Finnish Twin Registry: Baseline characteristics, Section III: Occupational and psychosocial factors. Publication of the Department of Public Health Science M49, Helsinki, 1979.
15. Loehlin JC: An analysis of alcohol-related questionnaire items from the National Merit Twin Study. Ann NY Acad Sci 197:117–120, 1972.
16. Morris JN, Chave SPW, Adam C, et al: Vigorous exercise in leisure-time and the incidence of coronary heart disease. Lancet 2:333–339, 1973.
17. Ouellet BC, Romeder J-M, Lance J-M: Premature mortality attributable to smoking and hazardous drinking in Canada. Am J Epidemiol 109:451–463, 1979.
18. Partanen J, Bruun K, Markkanen T: "Inheritance of Drinking Behavior." The Finnish Foundation for Alcohol Studies, Helsinki: 1966.
19. Pedersen NL: Familial resemblance for usage of common drugs. Third International Congress on Twin Studies, Jerusalem, 1980.
20. Pfaffenbarger RS, Hale WE: Work activity and coronary heart mortality. N Engl J Med 292:545–550, 1975.
21. Sarna S, Kaprio J, Sistonen P, Koskenvuo M: Diagnosis of twin zygosity by mailed questionnaire. Hum Hered 28:241–254, 1978.
22. Shields J: Monozygotic Twins Brought up Apart and Brought up Together." London: Oxford University Press, 1962.
23. Surgeon General: "Smoking and Health." Washington DC: U.S. Department of Health, Education and Welfare, 1979.
24. Tuyns AJ: Epidemiology of alcohol and cancer. Cancer Res 39:2840–2843, 1979.
25. Vesell ES, Rage JG, Passananti GT: Genetic and environmental factors affecting ethanol metabolism in man. Clin Pharmacol Ther 12:192–201, 1971.
26. Wyndham CH: The role of physical activity in the prevention of ischaemic heart disease. SA Med J 56:7–13, 1979.
27. Yano K, Rhoads GG, Kagan A: Coffee, alcohol and risk of coronary heart disease among Japanese men living in Hawaii. N Engl J Med 297:405–409, 1977.

Twin Research 3: Epidemiological
and Clinical Studies, pages 47 — 52
© 1981 Alan R. Liss, Inc., 150 Fifth Avenue, New York, NY 10011

Preliminary Findings From a Twin Study of Alcohol Use

C.A. Clifford, D.W. Fulker, H.M.D. Gurling, and R.M. Murray
Department of Psychology (C.A.C., D.W.F.), and Department of Psychiatry (H.M.D.G., R.M.M.), Institute of Psychiatry, London

One of the most striking features of alcoholism is its familial nature. As Goodwin [9] has stated, "without known exception, every family study of alcoholism irrespective of country of origin, has shown much higher rates of alcoholism among the relatives of alcoholics than apparently occurs in the general population." The key question, however, is the extent to which this is due to imitation and social factors or to inheritance. Twin studies offer one way of assessing the relative importance of these two sources of variation in drinking behaviour.

The results from previous twin studies show little agreement. The most thorough twin study to date is Partanen et al's [15] in which 902 pairs of male twins, aged between 28 and 37 years, were given an extensive interview concerning their drinking habits and social circumstances. A factor analysis of the drinking data suggested 3 separate factors, Density, Amount, and Loss of Control. The heritability estimate for Density was 0•39 and 0•36 for Amount, suggesting the presence of a genetic influence on drinking behaviour. The Loss of Control factor also had a substantial heritability in younger twins at 0•54, but this dropped to zero in older pairs. Jonsson and Nilsson [12], however, who studied 750 male pairs of twins, found that concordance rates for alcohol consumption were essentially the same for monozygotic (MZ) and dizygotic (DZ) pairs. This suggested little effect of heredity and emphasized the importance of social factors. Cederlöf et al [5] examined 13,000 twin pairs and reported that normal drinking appeared to be subject to little hereditary influence in males. In females, the picture was a little different, with data for excessive drinking indicating higher coincidence rates in MZ than DZ females.

This chapter reports preliminary findings from a questionnaire study of drinking practices in a normal twin population drawn from the Institute of Psychiatry's volunteer twin register in London. The Register contains both male and female, MZ and DZ twins as well as a number of opposite-sex pairs. In common with other volunteer registers, females and MZ twins are overrepresented [13]. The questionnaire used was designed for this study by the authors and has three main objectives. First, to ascertain as far as possible actual alcohol consumption, this being estimated from questions and a weekly drinking diary. Second, to determine the physiological effects of alcohol, for example sickness and dizziness, as well as psychological effects such as increase or decrease in sociability and tension. Many other items were also included concerning depression and anxiety, items relating to alcohol-associated problems and screening items for alcoholism including those from the C.A.G.E. questionnaire of Mayfield et al [14].

The present preliminary report is concerned only with weekly alcohol consumption measures, as recorded in the weekly drinking diary, and five measures of psychological effect. Only MZ and DZ males and females were examined in this analysis since there were large sex differences in the data. Before analysis, we compared the means from our sample for weekly consumption with the population norms of Cartwright et al [4], who used a similar weekly drinking diary, and also with the figures for H.M. Customs and Excise [2] and the Office of Population Censuses and Surveys [1] for all people over the age of 15 years. Fears that our twins might be light drinkers since they were volunteers were not borne out by this comparison (see Table 1). Indeed, the twin sample appears to be drinking somewhat larger amounts of alcohol that the general population, but not appreciably so if we consider that consumption has risen since Cartwright's study was carried out [3].

The method of analysis is that outlined in Fulker et al [8] for fitting genetic and environmental components of variation to between-pair and within-pair mean squares derived from an analysis of variance of the twin data. The analysis of variance uses age as a covariate to make appropriate age corrections for the measures in question. The mean squares for male consumption data can be seen in Table 2, subdivided into "weekly total," drinking from Monday to Thursday, "weekend total," drinking from Friday to Sunday. "Week total" is the total of these two variables. The correlations to the right of the mean squares are clearly substantially larger for MZ pairs than for DZ pairs. In fact, the MZ correlations are approximately twice the DZ correlations, suggesting the importance of genetic influences on alcohol consumption in males.

In view of these correlations, the simplest plausible model was fitted to the data. The model is made up of three parameters: additive genetic variance, VA; variance due to shared family environment of the twins, VCE; and specific environmental variance unique to each individual twin, VSE. The genetic component takes the simplest form possible being that appropriate for a population effectively mating at random with respect to the trait in question. This model has consistently been shown adequate for a wealth of personality variables [eg, 8], although we were not unaware of the possible problems in making the assumption of random mating with respect to alcohol consumption [10]. Expectations for MZ and DZ between and within mean squares are shown below:

	For MZ twins	For DZ Twins
Between pair	VSE + 2VA + 2VCE	VSE + 1•5VA + 2VCE
Within pair	VSE	VSE + 0•5VA

TABLE 1. Weekly Total (cl of Absolute Alcohol)

	Males	Females
Twin study	24.19	8.49
Cartwright		
Camberwell	18.00	4.00
Study		
	15.6*	

*This figure is not separated by sexes and includes everyone in the population over 15 years of age.
H.M. Customs and Excise and Office of Population Censuses and Surveys Figures 1978.

TABLE 2. ANOVA and Genetic and Environmental Estimates of Male Consumption Figures

Items	df	Weekday total MS	Weekday total r	Weekend total MS	Weekend total r	Week total MS	Week total r
MZ, between pair	77	9.44	0.80	8.10	0.74	33.40	0.79
within pair	79	1.02		1.20		3.76	
DZ, between pair	48	4.62	0.41	7.84	0.50	21.23	0.46
within pair	50	1.92		2.57		7.80	
Estimates, VA		2.25 ± 0.96		2.59 ± 1.20		9.02 ± 3.56	
VCE		1.13 ± 1.00		1.09 ± 1.00		4.06 ± 3.63	
VSE		0.99 ± 0.15		1.20 ± 0.19		3.71 ± 0.57	
X_1^2		4.46		0.28		1.29	
P		< 0.05		> 0.50		> 0.20	
VA as a proportion of total (h_N^2)		0.51		0.53		0.54	
VCE as a proportion of total		0.26		0.22		0.24	
VSE as a proportion of total		0.23		0.25		0.22	

The method of estimation is described elsewhere in some detail [7], but in essence we employ a modified least-squares procedure in which estimates are chosen to provide the best fit possible to the data. The function we minimize is a log-likelihood ratio statistic based on the distribution of a set of independent mean squares, and is distributed in large samples as X^2, although the estimates of our parameters are still truly maximum likelihood even in the smallest of samples. If we denote the observed mean squares as M_i and their expectations on the basis of the model as EM_i the function we minimize is:

$$X^2 = \sum_{i=1}^{m} n_1 (\log_e (EM_i/M_i \lambda + M_i/EM_i - 1)$$

where n_i are the degrees of freedom for the mean squares and m is the number of mean squares. The parameters in our model are estimated using this function with the added restriction that each parameter should be non-negative as is logically required of a variance component.

The results of this analysis can be seen in Table 2. Together with the parameter estimates are the X^2 goodness-of-fit values for the model fit and also heritability

TABLE 3. ANOVA and Genetic and Environmental Estimates of Female Consumption Figures

Items	df	Weekday total		Weekend total		Week total	
		MS	r	MS	r	MS	r
MZ, between pair	167	0.89	0.63	1.17	0.60	3.73	0.67
within pair	169	0.19		0.28		0.73	
DZ, between pair	99	0.75	0.02	1.23	0.04	3.56	0.03
within pair	101	0.71		1.12		3.35	
$(1 + b^2)$ VA		0.69 ± 0.11		1.09 ± 0.17		3.43 ± 0.49	
bVA		-0.17 ± 0.05		-0.29 ± 0.08		-0.90 ± 0.24	
VSE		0.19 ± 0.02		0.28 ± 0.03		0.73 ± 0.07	
$b \cong bVA / (1 + b^2 VA)$		-0.25		-0.27		-0.26	
X_1^2		0.075		2.2		1.04	
P		> 0.70		> 0.10		> 0.20	

estimates. In all three cases the model provides an adequate fit and estimates for both VA and VSE are substantially larger than their standard errors, although this is not the case for VCE. This might suggest that the parameter VCE should be dropped from the model. Despite the large standard errors however, VCE itself is large in all cases and not appreciably smaller than VA. When a model was fitted again omitting VCE, unrealistically high heritability estimates were obtained, between 80% and 90%. Our sample of males is so far too small to assess accurately the contribution of shared family environment on male consumption habits, but such data as we have suggest the effect is substantial being in excess of 20%.

Female consumption data can be seen in Table 3, set out as for males in Table 2. The correlations to the right of the mean squares are quite different from those of the males. The DZ correlations are far less than the expected one-half of the MZ correlation and the total variation for DZ pairs is clearly larger than for MZ pairs. These two facts indicate a competition effect or a social modeling process in which one twin's behaviour also affects that of the other [6, 11].

In this particular case the modeling appears to be in a negative direction whereby the consumption of one twin, be it high or low, influences the other twin to drink in the opposite manner.

This competition model is shown in Figure 1. Simply stated, the model postulates that the genotype of twin 1 not only influences the phenotype of twin 1 but also has an indirect effect on the phenotype of twin 2. The estimates from the model-fitting procedure can be seen at the foot of Table 3. As can be seen, the X^2 goodness of fits are all adequate and there is indeed a substantial effect of this competition phenomenon on female drinking patterns. From the very small correlations for consumption in the DZ females we can conclude that if G1 produces a heavy drinking P1 by its direct effect, the indirect effect of G1 will produce an abstemious P2.

Psychological effect measures taken from Persson [16] were also examined. The data, taken from five 5-point scales were concerned with psychological experience after consuming alcohol; for example, an increase or a decrease in self-control.

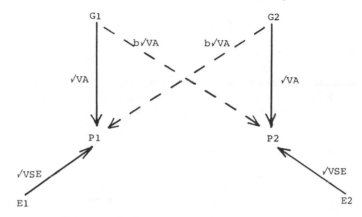

Fig. 1. √VA — Direct genetic effects on phenotype.
  b√VA — Indirect genetic effects of phenotype.
  √ VSE — Specific environmental effects unique to each twin.

TABLE 4. Measures of Psychological Effect of Alcohol: Parameter Estimate From a Two-Parameter Model-Fitting Procedure

Effect	Females			Males		
Pleasant						
VCE	0.51	±	0.11	0.46	±	0.12
VSE	1.22	±	0.10	0.89	±	0.10
X_1^2	1.58		P > 0.20	12.7		P > 0.001
Active						
VCE	0.82	±	0.14	0.44	±	0.15
VSE	0.14	±	0.12	1.15	±	0.14
X_1^2	0.79		P > 0.30	0.024		P > 0.80
Extraversion						
VCE	0.57	±	0.09	0.31	±	0.11
VSE	0.79	±	0.68	0.87	±	0.11
X^2	1.10		P > 0.20	0.20		P < 0.70
Tension						
VCE	0.54	±	0.19	0.23	±	0.10
VSE	0.84	±	0.07	0.89	±	0.11
X^2	0.18		P > 0.70	4.0		P < 0.05
Control						
VCE	0.52	±	0.14	0.19	±	0.18
VSE	1.78	±	0.15	1.83	±	0.22
X^2	1.63		P > 0.20	0.081		P > 0.70

The data clearly showed that in most cases the MZ correlations were no greater than the DZ correlations, suggesting that any within-pair resemblance found was due to shared family environment rather than genetic factors. The model fitted to these data was consequently a two-parameter environmental model involving VCE and VSE but excluding VA. The results are shown in Table 4 and show some good and some poor model fits, probably as a result of sampling variation, since each scale is made up of only one 5-point item. Further analysis of these data in a multivariate fashion will hopefully clarify the issue, but it does seem fairly clear that these measures are largely environmentally determined; that is, familial resemblance is mainly due to shared cultural factors.

To conclude, the preliminary findings of this study suggest a very varied picture of the factors influencing drinking behaviour. Genetic influences seem to be important in alcohol consumption in both males and females, with the added complication of competitive effects in females. However, psychological effects of alcohol appear to be mainly environmentally determined.

REFERENCES

1. Age distribution of the total population of the United Kingdom mid-year estimates. Sources: Office of Population Censuses and Surveys; General Register Office (Scotland); General Register Office (Northern Ireland).
2. Alcoholic drinks. Monthly averages or calendar months. Source: H.M. Customs and Excise.
3. Brewers Society: London: "Brewers Statistical Handbook", 1980.
4. Cartwright AKJ, Shaw SJ, Spratley TA: Designing a comprehensive community response to problems of alcohol abuse. Report to the Department of Health and Social Security by the Maudsley Alcohol Pilot Project. London: MAPP, 1978.
5. Cederlöf R, Friberg L, Lundman T: The interactions of smoking, environment and heredity and their implications for disease aetiology. Acta Med Scand 202/Suppl 612:1.128, 1977.
6. Eaves LJ: A model for sibling effects in man. Heredity 36:205–215, 1976.
7. Fulker DW: Multivariate extensions of a biometrical model of twin data. In Nance WE (ed): "Twin Research: Psychology and Methodology." New York: Alan R. Liss, 1978, pp 217–236.
8. Fulker DW, Eysenck SBG, Zuckerman M: A genetic and environmental analysis of sensation seeking. J Res Personality 14:261–281, 1980.
9. Goodwin DW: Is alcoholism hereditary: A review and critique. Arch Gen Psychiatry 25:545–549, 1971.
10. Jacob T, Favorini A, Meisel S, Anderson C: The alcoholic's spouse, children and family interactions. J Stud Alc 39:1231–1251, 1978.
11. Jinks JL, Fulker DW: Comparison of the biometrical genetical, MAVA, and classical approaches to the analysis of human behaviour. Psychol Bull 73:311–349, 1970.
12. Jonsson E, Nilsson T: Alcoholkonsumtion hos monozygota och dizygota tvillinpar. Nord Hyg Tidskr 49:21–25, 1968.
13. Lykken DT, Tellegen A, De Rubeis R: Volunteer bias in twin research: The rule of two-thirds. Soc Biol 25:1–9, 1978.
14. Mayfield P, McLeod G, Hall P: The Cage questionnaire, validation of a new alcoholism screening instrument. Am J Psychiatry 131:10, 1974.
15. Partanen J, Brunn K, Markkanen T: "Inheritance of Drinking Behavior." Helsinki: The Finnish Foundation for Alcohol Studies, 1966.
16. Persson LO, Sjoberg L, Svensson E: Mood effects of alcohol. Goteborg Psychological Reports No. 4, Vol 8, 1978.

Twin Research 3: Epidemiological
and Clinical Studies, pages 53 — 59
© 1981 Alan R. Liss, Inc., 150 Fifth Avenue, New York, NY 10011

Twin Similarity for Usage of Common Drugs

Nancy Pedersen
*Institute for Behavioral Genetics, University of Colorado, Boulder, and
Department of Environmental Hygiene, The Karolinska Institute,
Stockholm*

Despite the enormous social costs from common, legal drug use and subsequent interest in the etiology of these behaviors, fewer than 20 studies assessing the genetic and environmental sources of variation for common drug use exist in the literature. The majority of these studies report twin concordance rates or heritabilities for smoking status and alcohol use based on samples of twins.

A number of relatively small studies [2, 4, 6, 7, 14, 15] report greater rates of concordance in MZ than in DZ twins for smoking status. Friberg et al [8], Cederlöf et al [1], Crumpacker et al [3], and Kaprio et al [10] have confirmed these results for a variety of definitions of smoking status in Swedish and Finnish twins. Using a path model including twins and their families, Williams et al [16] report a broad-sense heritability coefficient (h_B^2) of 0.51 for ever/never smoking.

Conterio and Chiarelli [2] reported that MZ male Italian twins were not significantly more alike than DZ twins with respect to a drinking/nondrinking dichotomy or a wine drinking/wine nondrinking dichotomy. There were no differences between MZ and DZ concordances for quantity of wine consumed. Concordances reported by Cederlöf et al [1], based on the extensive Swedish Twin Registry, indicate that MZ twins are more concordant than DZ twins for a categorization of grams of alcohol consumed per month. Loehlin [11] reported broad-sense heritability (based on the method of Falconer [5] in which $h_B^2 = 2(t_{MZ} - t_{DZ})$ and t_{MZ} and t_{DZ} are the intraclass correlations for MZ and DZ twins, respectively) for use of wine (0.18), beer (0.10), and spirits (−0.02) from a sample of adolescent American twins. Three studies [10, 12, 13] provide information on alcohol consumption as a quantitative measure. Estimates of heritability from Partanen's [12] sample of male Finnish twins calculated by the present author from intraclass correlations provided were 0.54 for "amount," which measures both amount consumed and duration

Data collected in collaboration with the Department of Environmental Hygiene of the Karolinska Institute and the Swedish National Environmental Protection Board.

Supported by a grant from the Council for Tobacco Research, USA, (CTR-1066).

of drinking during the last reported drinking occasion; 0.58 for "density," a measure of drinking frequency; and 0.16 for "loss of control." The median estimate of heritability for total grams alcohol consumed per month based on correlations of Kaprio et al [10] on male and female Finnish twins of various ages was 0.34. Heritabilities were not significantly different from zero for men older than 54 years and women older than 59 years. Using another statistic for heritability, Perry [13] reports a heritability (H) of 0.56 for amount of alcohol consumed per week. These studies suggest a genetic influence for whether a person is a drinker and, if so, the extent to which he or she drinks.

Only five studies have reported data relevant to genetic influences for coffee and tea consumption [1, 2, 10, 12, 13]. MZ twins are more concordant than DZ twins for heavy consumption of coffee and tea [12] and are also more concordant than DZ twins when quantity consumed is broken into discrete categories [1, 2]. Heritability estimates (h^2) were calculated by the present author for the results of Partanen and for males and females in Kaprio's sample, and found to be 0.46, 0.46, and 0.48, respectively. Perry reported H = 0.49 for coffee use.

Using coincidence statistics, Cederlöf et al [1] and Kaprio et al [10] have examined twin resemblance for tranquilizer and sleeping pill use. For both drugs in both samples, MZ twins are more similar than DZ twins.

From the preceding review, it is apparent that tobacco, alcohol, coffee and tea, and sedative-use behaviors all show some genetic influence. This conclusion is based on heterogeneous studies representing a variety of nationalities, measures, and types of analyses. The present chapter will describe results based on a sample of middle-aged Swedish twins. All habits but smoking status have been quantified. In addition, alcohol use is described in terms of which type of alcoholic beverage is consumed, with a correction for metabolic weight as well as a measure of excessive drinking. The present results also represent an opportunity to assess heritability for sedative use as a continuous variable.

MATERIALS AND METHODS

Sample

The sample comprised 39 MZ male, 36 MZ female, 32 DZ male, and 30 DZ female twin pairs from the Swedish Twin Registry who were participants in a family-of-twins study focused on genetic and environmental factors for smoking behavior. The twins, located with the help of the Department of Environmental Hygiene of the Karolinska Institute and the Swedish National Environmental Protection Board, were born between 1911 and 1935. At the time of the study, all twins were living in either Stockholm or Göteborg, Sweden metropolitan areas. Zygosity diagnosis was determined based on 20 marker loci from blood and saliva. Additional details about the sampling procedures are described by Crumpacker et al [3].

Measures

Subjects participated in group testing sessions at central locations during which they filled out a detailed questionnaire. Quantity–frequency variables for alcohol consumption were derived using the general formula: (grams alcohol per centiliter $\times$ occasions per month $\times$ centiliters per occasion)/(kilograms body weight)$^{0.75}$. Use of this formula provided measures of grams absolute alcohol per month per (kilograms body weight)$^{0.75}$ for beer, wine, and spirits separately. Weight was transformed in this manner to reflect metabolically effective body size [9]. Measures of coffee and tea, tranquilizer, and sleeping pill use are in terms of frequency. Heavy drinking assesses frequency of consuming an excessive quantity of alcohol (more than 6 bottles of beer, 1 bottle of wine, or 1 pint of spirits) on one occasion.

Lifetime tobacco use status was determined during a standardized interview. Subjects who had never smoked, or who had smoked at most a few trial cigarettes, were classified as never-smokers. Subjects who smoked at least 100 cigarettes, 60 cigarillos, 20 cigars, or a 50-gram pack of pipe tobacco in a month or less, or who smoked regularly or socially though in smaller amounts, were classified as ever-smokers. Height and weight were also included in the analyses for comparative purposes. Descriptive statistics for the measures are provided in Table 1.

RESULTS

Means for all the variables are the same in the two zygosity groups, whereas the variances are significantly different for all measures but tranquilizer and sleeping pill use and height. The distributions for all the drug-related measures besides coffee and tea use are highly skewed with a preponderance of zero values, indicating little phenotypic variation.

Intraclass correlations computed using double entry of twins, and estimates of h_B^2, are presented in Table 2. Heritability was calculated by the formula $h_B^2 = 2(t_{MZ} - t_{DZ})$ where t_{MZ} and t_{DZ} refer to the intraclass correlations for MZ and DZ twins, respectively. Results for height and spirits use are within the range of values reported in the literature. However, h_B^2 estimates for weight, coffee and tea use, and smoking status are comparatively high. It is inappropriate to calculate heritability for beer, wine, and sleeping pill use, or for heavy drinking, because DZ correlations are greater than MZ correlations (significantly so for wine use) or the MZ correlation is more than twice the DZ correlation (for heavy drinking). Although the data for females were standardized to those of males, many of the correlations are different for males and females, with female twins most frequently providing less easily interpretable results.

The skewed distributions resemble those of phenotypes such as schizophrenia, which represent the extreme of another behavioral dimension. In these cases, concordances are conventionally calculated after individuals have been diagnosed, based on semiquantitative criteria, as positive or negative for a trait. In this study concordances were computed for the nonnormally distributed variables. Using a median split, cutoff levels for being considered as expressing a trait were 0.230, 0.310, and 0.850 grams alcohol per month per unit weight for beer, wine, and spirits use, respectively. Smoking status was already dichotomized. Heavy drinking and tranquilizer and sleeping pill use were dichotomized into ever versus never categories. The concordances for all pairs are reported in Table 3. For heavy drink-

TABLE 1. Means, Variances, and Sample Sizes for the Measures [a]

Variables		MZ twins	DZ twins
Height in cm	X̄	175.31	175.85
	Var	39.93	44.43
	N	144	120
Weight in kg[b]	X̄	75.46	76.05
	Var	149.92	78.78
	N	150	118
Beer[b]	X̄	2.14	2.11
	Var	13.84	8.71
	N	150	116
Wine[b]	X̄	1.16	1.39
	Var	3.75	6.15
	N	150	118
Spirits[b]	X̄	3.66	5.13
	Var	21.18	50.39
	N	150	118
Coffee and tea[b]	X̄	4.31	4.40
	Var	3.19	5.31
	N	150	120
Heavy drinking[b]	X̄	0.31	0.45
	Var	0.42	0.97
	N	150	120
Tranquilizers[b]	X̄	0.38	0.32
	Var	0.42	0.42
	N	150	118
Sleeping pills[b]	X̄	1.82	0.39
	Var	0.55	0.51
	N	150	120
Smoking status[b]	X̄	1.30	1.67
	Var	0.25	0.24
	N	150	120

[a]Woman's scores were standardized to the men's scores using the equation: new score = (old score − female mean) × male standared deviation/female standard deviation + male mean.
[b]Variances significantly different ($P \leq 0.05$).

ing, tranquilizer use, and smoking status, the MZ twins were more concordant than DZ twins; for spirits and sleeping pill use, there were no differences in concordance rates. In keeping with the correlation results, DZ twins were more concordant than MZ twins for beer and wine consumption.

DISCUSSION

Results from these analyses are problematic: Variances are unequal in the two zygosity groups, and DZ correlations are frequently greater than MZ correlations. These failures to meet basic assumptions of the classic twin model perhaps indicate a lack of representativeness of the twin sample, especially for female twins. Preliminary studies of possible selection bias based on comparison of means [3] demon-

TABLE 2. Intraclass Correlations and h_B^2

Variables	Total sample			Female twins		Male twins	
	t_{MZ}	t_{DZ}	h^{2a}	t_{MZ}	t_{DZ}	t_{MZ}	t_{DZ}
Height	0.78	0.40	0.76	0.78	0.37	0.77	0.42
Weight	0.74	0.29	0.90	0.54	0.07	0.84	0.45
Beer	0.18	0.43	—	0.27	0.28	0.05	0.51
Wine	0.08	0.55	—	−0.02	0.74	0.10	0.20
Spirits	0.44	0.30	0.28	0.47	0.40	0.43	0.24
Coffee and tea	0.57	0.18	0.78	0.61	0.43	0.51	0.07
Heavy drinking	0.68	0.06	>1	1.00	−0.05	0.56	0.15
Tranquilizers	0.29	0.15	0.28	0.28	0.17	0.26	0.12
Sleeping pills	0.25	0.29	—	0.14	0.02	0.33	0.52
Smoking status	0.57	0.15	0.84	0.49	−0.03	0.62	0.27
Number	75	62		36	30	39	32

[a]Calculated using intraclass correlations in the equation $h_B^2 = (t_{MZ} - t_{DZ})$.

TABLE 3. Percentage of Pairs Concordant for Various Drug-Related Measures

Variables	Total twin sample	
	MZ	DZ
Beer	70.7	77.6
Wine	66.7	69.5
Spirits	64.0	67.8
Heavy drinking	94.7	78.3
Tranquilizers	66.7	62.7
Sleeping pills	69.3	65.0
Smoking status	78.7	60.6

strated that this sample did not differ from other twins in the registry who meet the criteria for this study and who indicated willingness to participate, nor from twins meeting the criteria but not responding or responding negatively to recruiting efforts. It is not known, however, how these twins compare to other twins of the same age or to twins in the Twin Registry in general. Furthermore, assessment of similarity for these twins compared to other twins in the registry has not yet been undertaken.

The extremely low similarity of DZ twins for heavy drinking may indicate a competitive interaction between the twins. It is not clear why this type of effect may be acting only for heavy drinking. Interpretations of greater DZ correlations for beer and wine use but not for spirits use are also not readily forthcoming.

In spite of the anomalies, the heritability estimates for height, spirits use, coffee and tea use, tranquilizer use, and smoking status are significantly different from zero and generally similar to heritability estimates based on other twin studies.

Indications of significant involvement of "genetic" factors for variation in tranquilizer use, smoking status, and heavy drinking were further confirmed by the concordance analyses.

Loehlin [11] reported h_B^2 of less than 0.2 for ever/never wine, beer, and spirits use by American adolescents entering college. Even though the current analyses were based on quantitative measures of consumption, the conclusions of very low or no heritability for these measures are similar to Loehlin's results when sampling error is considered. The present results for concordance in wine use are very similar to the results of Conterio and Chiarelli [2].

CONCLUSIONS

In this sample of middle-aged Swedish twins, heritability estimates were 0.28 for spirits use, 0.78 for coffee and tea use, 0.28 for tranquilizer use, and 0.84 for smoking status. It is inappropriate to calculate heritability for beer, wine, and sleeping pill use, or for heavy drinking, because DZ correlations are greater than MZ correlations (significantly so for wine use) or the MZ correlation is more than twice the DZ correlation (for heavy drinking). Results for height and spirits use are within the range of values reported in the literature. However, h_B^2 estimates for weight, coffee and tea use, and smoking status are comparatively high. The failure to meet assumptions of the classical twin method may indicate sampling inconsistencies. However, phenotypic variation for most of the drugs is low in this sample. The majority of the twins consume sedatives and the various alcoholic beverages infrequently or in relatively low quantities. Partitioning already low phenotypic variation into genetic and environmental components may result in spuriously high or low heritability estimates. Twin similarity for usage of common drugs in large samples at a variety of ages should be pursued before further conclusions concerning heritability can be made.

REFERENCES

1. Cederlöf R, Friberg L, Lundman T: The interactions of smoking, environment and heredity and their implications for disease etiology. Acta Med Scand Suppl 612, 1976.
2. Conterio F, Chiarelli B: Study of the inheritance of some daily life habits. Heredity 17:347–359, 1962.
3. Crumpacker DW, Cederlöf R, Friberg L, Kimberling WJ, Sörensen S, Vandenberg SG, Williams JS, McClearn GE, Grevér B, Iyer H, Krier MJ, Pedersen NL, Price RA, Roulette I: A twin methodology for the study of genetic and environmental control of variation in human smoking behavior. Acta Genet Med Gemellol 28:173–195, 1979.
4. Dies R, Honeyman M, Reznikoff M, White C: Personality and smoking patterns in a twin population. Projective Tech Personality Assessment 33:457–463, 1969.
5. Falconer DS: Introduction to quantitative genetics. New York: Ronald Press, 1960.
6. Fisher RA: Lung cancer and cigarettes? Nature 182:180, 1958.
7. Fisher RA: Cancer and smoking. Nature 182:596, 1958.
8. Friberg L, Kaij L, Dencka SJ, Jonsson E: Smoking habits of monozygotic and dizygotic twins. Br Med J 1:1090–1092, 1959.
9. Israel Y, Kalant H, Khanna JK, Orrego H, Phillips MJ, Stewart DJ: Ethanol metabolism, oxygen availability and alcohol induced liver damage. Adv Exp Med Biol 85:343–355, 1977.

10. Kaprio J, Sarna S, Koskenvuo M, Rantasalo I: "The Finnish Twin Registry: Baseline characteristics, Section II." Helsinki: University of Helsinki Press, 1978.
11. Loehlin JC: Analysis of alcohol-related questionnaire items from the National Merit twin study. In Seixas, FA, Omenn GS, Park ED, Eggleston SA (eds): "Nature and Nurture in Alcoholism." Vol. 197, New York: New York Academy of Sciences, 1972.
12. Partanen J, Bruun K, Markkanen T: "Inheritance of Drinking Behavior." Helsinki: The Finnish Foundation for Alcohol Studies, 1966.
13. Perry A: Heredity, personality traits, product attitude, and product consumption — An exploratory study. J Marketing Res 10:376–379, 1973.
14. Raaschou-Nielsen E: Smoking habits in twins. Danish Med Bull 7:82, 1960.
15. Todd GF, Mason JI: Concordance of smoking habits in monozygotic and dizygotic twins. Heredity 13:417–444, 1959.
16. Williams JS, Crumpacker DW, Krier M: Genetic and environmental variance fractions and correlation estimates for smoking behavior in a Swedish population. Unpublished manuscript, 1981.

Twin Research 3: Epidemiological
and Clinical Studies, pages 61 — 70
© 1981 Alan R. Liss, Inc., 150 Fifth Avenue, New York, NY 10011

Twin Studies on Substance Abuse: An Overview

Marc A. Schuckit
*Department of Psychiatry, University of California, San Diego Medical
School, and the Veterans Administration Medical Center, San Diego*

INTRODUCTION

My purpose is to review twin studies from the perspective of substance abuse
with a special emphasis on the most widely studied drug, alcohol. Through this
paper, I hope to raise awareness among twin researchers of substance-related issues
and stimulate future investigations in this area. Then, studies in substance abuse
must be carefully done. The following are a number of factors to be considered.

The Focus of the Study Must Be Clearly Stated

People may decide to use a substance for one set of reasons, experience mild to
moderate temporary drug-related difficulties in their late teens to mid-twenties in
response to other factors, and demonstrate drug abuse for still other reasons.
These factors must be kept in mind in reviewing twin research on substance abuse,
whether it be for decisions to start smoking vs reasons behind a two-pack per day
habit, factors influencing a decision to experiment with drugs vs those responsible
for physiological addiction to opiates, or the reasons behind drinking vs those that
explain alcoholism.

There Are Problems of Definition

The important issue of definition has plagued all behavioral science researchers
(including those studying schizophrenia and depressive disease) and is not unique
to the substance-abuse areas. My bias is to diagnose for the purpose of establishing
prognosis. To meet this goal, criteria must be stated in relatively objective terms
(so that others can use the same rubric) and then have been applied to populations
who are followed over time and shown to demonstrate a relatively homogeneous
course with evidence that the observed syndrome was not just the prodromal phase
of yet another disorder [12]. A good example of this approach has been developed
for alcoholism where the definition that best meets my requirements and that has
most often been applied to populations followed over time is based on life problems. It is therefore my preference to define alcoholism as the occurrence of any
one of a series of major life problems related to alcohol, including a marital sepa-

ration or divorce, *or* multiple arrests, *or* physical evidence that alcohol harmed health, *or* a job loss or layoff related to alcohol [31]. A similar label has been developed for other drugs of abuse [31].

The Genetic Mechanisms Are Diverse

It is conceivable that genetic factors contribute to individual behavior in at least three ways [3]. First, there are a variety of chromosomal abnormalities such as Down's syndrome, Turner's syndrome, and Kleinefelter's syndrome where gross chromosomal abnormalities contribute directly to a variety of behavioral problems. A second mechanism involves mutations of single genes as might be seen in Huntington's chorea, which would profoundly affect mood and behavior. However, as these first two types of genetic influences are relatively rare, it is probable that the major genetic effect on behavioral interactions is mediated through the third avenue, a polygenic type of inheritance where many genes interact with environment to produce a final picture as might be theoretically seen in mathematical abilities or levels of anxiety. Most indirect evidence points toward polygenic types of inheritance as being important in substance abuse problems.

The Associations Are Likely To Be Complex

In looking for an association between genetic factors and traits of any type, it is important to keep in mind that few of these traits are manifested simply or directly [3b]. If the probable mechanism is via multiple genes interacting with environment, and if behavioral syndromes are difficult to define consistently, a genetic factor must be fairly strong before it is clinically identified. It is therefore important to attempt to optimize the chances of observing genetic influences where they exist by studying as homogeneous a population as possible [18]. This is done by utilizing objective criteria and through attempting to study individuals whose behavioral disorder (for example, alcoholism) is a primary syndrome and not just a secondary manifestation of a major preexisting psychiatric disorder such as the antisocial personality of primary affective disorder [12, 29, 30].

Even after all of these steps are followed, the chances of crisply pinpointing a genetic factor are small. This results from a variety of influences including environmental factors that may mediate or alter a clinical course so that it is no longer obvious. In addition, as with diabetes and some of the anemias, it is probable that behavioral disorders may result from a number of different genetic loadings, each with their own environmental precipitants, and that environmental factors alone could produce a picture that closely resembles the genetically influenced disorder (ie, a phenocopy) [18]. Finally, it is very likely that many genetic disorders do not always manifest themselves completely on even a biological level, a phenomenon described as incomplete penetrance.

When all of these factors are combined with the near impossibility of establishing perfect controls in human research (most of such controls would represent potentially harmful and immoral interference with patients' lives), it is probable that the most we can ask of this research is that the results be consistent. In fact, it may be more relevant to look to see whether a variety of studies carried out in different populations with different methodologies reach the same results than to look to any one particular investigation as definitive [27]. As we shall see, despite these problems, the results of twin research in substance use and abuse, especially drinking and alcoholism, are fairly impressive reaching a level of probability equal to that in the affective disorders and schizophrenia [11, 36].

The Type of Twin Approach Must Be Chosen Carefully

Twin research has evolved through a series of stages addressing the issues noted in Table 1. Anecdotal observations of twins served the important function of raising the possibility that biological factors could influence physical functioning and behavior [37]. The remaining uses of twin research are based on attempts to segregate the effects of environment from genetics — always recognizing that the final picture rests with an interaction between both. This takes advantage of the fact that, although all twins are born at the same time and, at least theoretically, therefore share major environmental stressors (thus controlling at least in part for environment), there are two types of twins differing on their level of genetic similarity. Thus the concordance within identical or monozygotic (MZ) twin pairs (sharing 100% of their genes) for genetically influenced factors should be higher than the level of resemblance or similarity for fraternal or dizygotic (DZ) twins sharing only 50% of their genes (the same as any full siblings).

Another use for twin studies is to give an indirect measure of the importance of heredity by observing twin pairs over time in order to determine how sensitive a given factor is to environmental influence — ie, do the twins remain similar on these factors as they grow older? Next, various behavioral or psychologically oriented tasks can be taught members of twin pairs in order to observe similarities or differences between MZ and DZ twins on learning patterns and resulting behaviors. A related approach, called the *cotwin control* method, involves exposing one member of a pair to a learning paradigm or environmental factor, but not the other, to observe how much environment can modify behavior, as developed by Gesell in 1929 [10]. A relevant example would be teaching learning skills such as manual dexterity or reading at an earlier age to only one member of a twin pair and observing both members over time [36, 24].

The remaining approaches are those most frequently used in modern times. Most data regarding drinking practices and alcoholism, as well as use of other substances such as tobacco, compare the level of similarity or concordance for a trait seen within MZ twin pairs with that seen within DZ twin pairs [37]. Finally, a relatively difficult and thus less used approach is to observe similarities or differences within twin pairs who have been separated sometime early in life. These latter two

TABLE 1. Uses of Twin Research

1. To stimulate thinking on genetic traits
2. To observe changes over time
3. To compare MZ vs DZ twins *or* observe separated twins by:
   a) Test of new learning
   b) Cotwin control methods
   c) Observation of concordance on traits

approaches can then be used to generate an estimate of the level of heritability based on the difference between the variance for the trait seen in DZ twins minus the variance noted in MZ pairs divided by the variance of the DZ twins [25].

There Are Biases in Twin Research

As briefly alluded to above, such studies are based on a number of premises, especially the feeling that twin research can adequately control for environment. Of course, no human research completely controls environmental factors, and Table 2 outlines some of the biases involved in twin research. To begin with, factors observed in twins cannot necessarily generalize to the population at large, as twins might differ on their increased rates of infant mortality, lower birth rate, slightly lowered IQ, and their tendency to be the product of women of higher mean age [3]. Even if twins could be compared to the general population, those specific individuals who are involved in an investigation may not be representative of twins in general. For example, as women represent two-thirds of twin pairs studied (but 50% of twins surviving into adulthood), most twin studies use volunteers and thus may study those with abnormal rates of psychopathology. Such sampling techniques raise the possibility of inadvertently selecting MZ twins who are more alike on the trait being studied than would be true of MZ twins in general [22, 37].

Because most behavioral investigations compare the level of similarity or concordance within MZ pairs with that noted for DZ twins, the establishment of zygosity is of key importance. The MZ vs DZ status is usually established by visual observation, anthropomorphic measurements (such as the confirmation of the ear, etc), and the analysis of various serological markers. While some investigators have reported as much as a 60% error rate if observation alone is used [5], others feel that careful observation of appearance and/or use of a questionnaire dealing with the probability that relatives and friends will mistake members of the twin pair can result in a 90% or higher correct establishment of zygosity when results are compared to serological markers [6, 21]. In interpreting results, it also must be recognized that errors in zygosity will tend to blur any differences in concordance between MZ and DZ pairs and decrease the probability of establishing a genetic factor through twin research [37].

Another important bias in twin research is the result of prenatal factors. MZ and DZ pairs may differ in the condition of egg implantation and subsequent positions in utero, their level of shared circulation, and their manner of delivery [23] — all of which are nongenetic factors that could result in differences in level of concordance for a trait in MZ vs DZ pairs. However, there are differences within MZ pairs in utero that could blur MZ-DZ distinctions, including the fact that the first cell of the MZ twins may not have identical amounts of cytoplasmic material and that the circulation for MZ pairs in utero may not be identical, as well as the differential in birthweight that can be seen within MZ twins [37].

Similarly, postnatal rearing environments can bias results. Among those factors that could artificially increase the difference in concordance between MZ and DZ pairs are those that relate to the higher level of physical similarity between MZ individuals. This may result in more mistaken identity than would be true for DZ

TABLE 2. Biases in Twin Reseach

1. Twins are not representative
2. Sampling problems
3. Zygosity determinators
4. Prenatal influences
5. Rearing influences
6. Adult lifestyle

and in the possibility that their physical similarities may result in their parents' more often dressing them alike with the result that people may expect them to act more alike. Also, MZ twins might be expected to spend more time together when they grow up than would be expected for DZ pairs [8, 10]. Biases in the opposite direction, tending to make MZ pairs behave more differently, comes from data showing that parents do evidence different expectations for each member of an MZ twin pair and the fact that environment can never be identical within twin pairs even on such important matters as serious physical illnesses, accidents, the need for surgery, etc [2, 37]. In fact, the similarity in physical appearance can conceivably drive MZ pairs apart when each feels that he must work hard to establish his own identity on level of social interactions, dominance, etc. [15, 16]. While there is little objective evidence on any of these factors, it is interesting to note that twin pairs more concordant for neurotic or personality traits do not show evidence of having been more attached to each other as infants and children [15, 37].

Finally, MZ twin pairs differ from DZ on a variety of factors manifest later in life that could themselves affect behavior. There is some evidence that MZ pairs live longer, are more likely to be concordant on marital status, and more often get together and eat together as adults [8, 37].

In summary, twin research has raised our level of awareness of genetic factors in human behavior and given us an important tool in studying environmental–hereditary interactions. These studies are not perfect as they contain a variety of biases that could tend to increase and/or decrease the probability of establishing a genetic difference between traits noted in MZ versus DZ pairs.

AN INTRODUCTION TO THE GENETICS OF SUBSTANCE ABUSE

One of the goals of this chapter is to place the twin studies in perspective regarding *other* approaches to genetic influences in substance abuse. The most extensive data has been developed for alcoholism. First, it has repeatedly been demonstrated that alcoholism runs strongly in families with approximately one-third of alcoholics reporting alcoholic parents, whereas the same is true for less than 10% of patients with schizophrenia or affective disorder and less than 5% of the general population [7]. Second, animal studies have demonstrated that it is possible to breed strains of rats or mice that prefer relatively dilute alcohol solutions to water and others that will avoid alcohol at all costs, with the two strains differing on taste sensitivity, metabolism of alcohol, and caloric preferences — genetically influenced factors that may be important in human decisions to drink (but may or may not have anything to do with development of alcoholism itself) [11]. Third, genetic marker studies have demonstrated an association between alcoholism and a variety of blood proteins, color blindness, and other known genetic factors — but these findings have been difficult to replicate, perhaps indicating methodological difficulties or implying that different genetic factors may be involved in different populations [11, 14]. Fourth, there is evidence from half-sibling studies [34] and adoption investigations that the children of alcoholics separated from their parents close to birth are at high risk for alcoholism, whether or not they are raised by an alcoholic parent figure and independent of whether they experience a broken home. [4, 11, 13].

Finally, the probability of the importance of genetic factors has justified prospective studies. We are currently engaged in a series of investigations utilizing young men at high risk for the future development of alcoholism vs controls, and twin researchers might consider borrowing some of this methodology [32, 33, 35]. After identifying a group of nonalcoholic young men (ages 21–25) who have first-degree alcoholic relatives, each high-risk individual was matched to a control based on demography and drinking history. Family-history positive and negative matched pairs were then administered a series of personality tests and exposed to alcohol in an attempt to determine whether there were any differences between high and low-risk young men on the metabolism of alcohol, acute reaction to alcohol, and more subacute reactions such as tolerance. Both groups of individuals will be followed longitudinally in order to determine whether these or other predispositions toward chronic consequences of alcohol abuse could mediate a genetic influence in alcoholism. To date, preliminary data indicate that individuals with family histories of alcoholism, when compared to controls, do not differ on their rate of metabolism of ethanol, but do develop significantly higher levels of an intermediary metabolite, acetaldehyde. This in turn could mediate the acute intoxication or, through the formation of tetrahydroisoquinolenes (THQs), affect the level of tolerance or propensity toward physical dependence. In addition, young men with family histories of alcoholism demonstrate higher levels of muscle relaxation during rising blood-alcohol levels, but report less intense intoxication when compared to controls.

A BRIEF INTRODUCTION TO TWIN RESEARCH ON BEHAVIORS RELATED TO SUBSTANCES

There are a variety of psychiatric disorders that might affect alcohol or drug misuse indirectly and which are known to be genetically influenced. These include either unipolar or bipolar affective disorder, both of which are genetically influenced as demonstrated by twin and other research [9, 28, 39]. In the midst of depressions, approximately one-third of patients will increase their alcohol misuse with the same being true for approximately two-thirds of manic patients — in either instance patients could be identified and treated in an alcohol center [30]. Similarly, schizophrenia, a disorder shown to have a probable genetic component [38, 39], is a problem intensified when patients drink heavily — but this would be another instance where alcohol-related problems should be viewed secondary and not necessarily related to any type of genetic propensity toward alcoholism itself [31, 38].

The most relevant data on factors that might indirectly be related to the genetics of alcoholism come from studies of personality. This is important as at least one school of thought believes that personality or coping styles may be important in the development of substance abuse.

In that light, there is indirect evidence that a number of personality attributes are genetically influenced [20]. It is clear that coping mechanisms result from a complex interaction between innate disposition and with the final picture depending upon the person's constitution, the attitude of the rearing parents toward these differences, and the relationship between the twins themselves as well as other factors [3]. The personality data are also consistent with the importance of environment, as even in MZ twins differences in apparent personality style can be noted within the first year of life [3]. Even so, there is evidence of greater concordance on personality test scores for MZ vs DZ twins on poise, traits of neuroticism and/or extroversion, social ease, and IQ. [15, 20, 25, 37].

There is also evidence consistent with the heritability of personality attributes from studies of twins who have been separated at some time during their childhood. These observations are necessarily retrospective and anecdotal, but do demonstrate similarities within separated MZ twins for mannerisms, voice, temperament, sociability, interests, mathematical ability, occupational level, sexual behavior, etc. [24, 37].

In summary, twin studies primarily utilizing comparisons of concordance for MZ vs DZ twins, as well as data on separated MZ twins, are consistent with a genetic influence in a variety of personality traits. Although none of these directly relates to alcoholism, this is useful information in attempting to determine whether a behavioral aberration such as alcoholism might conceivably carry a genetic influence.

TWIN STUDIES ON DRINKING AND ALCOHOLISM

As has been briefly noted before, the twin studies relating to alcohol break down into the majority dealing with drinking practices and one study dealing specifically with alcoholism itself. The data can be marshaled primarily from MZ vs DZ comparisons and anecdotal information on separated twins as summarized in Table 3.

A number of studies have addressed the issue of drinking practices through investigating self-reported behaviors in twins identified through a twin register. Even if the lifetime risk for alcoholism in the general population is 10%, the majority of the variance regarding drinking behavior in these investigations will deal with the 90% or more who are nonalcoholics. Thus these studies, while not necessarily shedding any light directly on alcoholism, have indicated a heightened level of concordance in MZ vs DZ twins for the state of abstinence vs drinking [25], the quantity and/or frequency or amount of drinking [16, 25], and for light drinking vs heavy drinking status [11].

Other investigators have demonstrated that genetic factors might be important in either the absorption [26] or elimination rate of alcohol. Thus at least two investigators have administered alcohol to MZ and DZ twin pairs and demonstrated a

TABLE 3. Twin Studies on Drinking and on Alcoholism

Drinking practices: Heritability for abstinence, quantity, and frequency
Alcohol metabolism: Heritability of 0.41 to 0.98
Alcoholism: MZ Concordance = 58%
           DZ Concordance = 28%

probable high level of heritability for the alcohol elimination rate (0.8–0.98) and acetaldehyde (0.6–0.8) [35, 41]. However, considering how the rate of alcohol metabolism can be affected by the use of other drugs, the usual dietary and drinking habits and smoking history, Kopen points out how such high levels of heritability are unlikely. He relates a study comparing MZ and DZ twins showing a still impressive level of heritability, 0.57 for absorption and 0.46 for elimination of alcohol [19, 40].

There are a series of anecdotal reports of the adult drinking habits of a series of MZ twins separated sometime earlier in life. Because of their retrospective and anecdotal nature, few definite conclusions can be reached and most of these will relate to drinking practices rather than alcoholism, as the former are more frequent. Reviewing the literature, there may be as many as 100 studied cases of separated twins [16, 24, 36] with some feeling given by authors of a level of similarity on whether the separated twins chose to drink, whether they experienced some life problems related to alcohol intake, and in regard to their usual drinking patterns.

Only one known twin study directly addresses the concordance rate for alcoholism in MZ vs DZ twins. Kaij et al studied 174 male twin pairs at least one of whom was registered with an alcohol problem at a temperance board. As many as 90% of the twins were interviewed and zygosity was established by anthropological markers and blood typing [17]. Utilizing relatively crisp criteria for alcoholism, the concordance rate was 58% in MZ twins and 28% in DZ twins.

In summary, there is consistent evidence of a level of heritability in the decision to drink and in the frequency and quantity of alcohol imbibed. The one study dealing directly with alcoholism has also shown a twofold increase in level of concordance for this disorder in MZ vs DZ twins, and studies of MZ twins separated early in life are, anecdotally, consistent with genetic factors. These studies must be considered in light of the parallel study on alcoholism and the additional information regarding alcohol intake patterns and problems, as well as other substance patterns, before any final conclusion can be drawn.

TWIN RESEARCH ON SUBSTANCES OTHER THAN ALCOHOL

There are few studies relating to misuse of prescription drugs, the "street" abuse of multiple drugs, or heroin addiction. Most of the sparse data available relates to smoking and coffee.

Smoking is not the major focus of this paper. Historically, such studies are justified by the anecdotal report of similarity in smoking in the 44 separated MZ twins studied by Shields and the demonstration of a probable level of heritability for abstinence vs use of tobacco shown by Partanen et al [25, 36]. The use of coffee was also briefly discussed by those authors. While showing no level of heritability for abstinence vs coffee drinking, subjects did demonstrate the probability of some hereditary influence in heavy vs light use of caffeine [25]. In addition, in a study of 11 MZ twins, Abe et al were able to show probable concordance for some of the effects of caffeine [1].

FUTURE TWIN RESEARCH IN SUBSTANCE ABUSE

Of all areas of substance abuse, the twin data on drinking practices and alcoholism appear to be the strongest. Despite the methodological problems outlined earlier in this chapter, it is most impressive that twin studies have consistently demonstrated a level of heritability for abstinence vs drinking and quantity and frequency of alcohol intake. A separate investigation has demonstrated the probable heritability of alcoholism itself. These studies could be strengthened through additional data on alcoholism and prospective studies of twins attempting to outline the nature of the biological factors that are inherited.

One could also envision a series of studies of MZ vs DZ twins looking at factors such as personality, metabolism of enthanol, acute reaction to the drug, the development of tolerance, or propensity toward chronic consequences as a fruitful area for future study. Similar paradigms could be used to study propensities towards misuse of other substances including tobacco, caffeine, and drugs of abuse.

Twin research in substance abuse could also turn towards attempting to identify relevant environmental factors. Thus, for example, the cotwin control method could be more extensively applied to twin research on substances, and studies of twins reared apart could add additional information. Regarding the latter, a variety of studies are now in progress at the University of Minnesota. Of course, twin research can be very important in increasing our understanding of the genetics of all substances of abuse.

In summary, twin studies can add important information through expanding our knowledge of alcoholism. A need is most acute in dealing with twin studies involving substances other than alcohol and in expanding the present methodologies.

REFERENCES

1. Abe K: Reactions to coffee and alcohol in monozygotic twins. J Psychosomatic Res 12:199–203, 1968.
2. Allen MG, Greenspan SI, Pollin W: The effect of parental perceptions on early development in twins. Psychiatry 39:65–71, 1976.
3. Allen MG, Pollin W, Hoffer A: Parental, birth, and infancy factors in infant twin development. Am J Psychiatry 127:33–41, 1971.
4. Cadoret RJ, Cain CA, Grove WM: Development of alcoholism in adoptees raised apart from alcoholic biologic relative. Arch Gen Psychiatry 37:561–563, 1980.
5. Carter-Saltzman L, Scarr S: MZ or DZ? Only your blood grouping laboratory knows for sure. Behav Genet 7:273–280, 1977.
6. Cohen DJ, Dibble E, Grawe JM, Pollin W: Separating identical from fraternal twins. Arch Gen Psychiatry 29:465–469, 1973.
7. Cotton NS: The familial incidence of alcoholism: A review. J Stud Alc 40:89–116, 1979.
8. Fabsitz RR, Garrison RJ, Feinleib M, Hjortland M: A twin analysis of dietary intake: Evidence for a need to control for possible environmental differences in MZ and DZ twins. Behav Genet 8:15–25, 1978.
9. Gershon ES, Bunney WE, Leckman JF, Van Eerdeqegh M, DeBauche A: The inheritance of affective disorders: A review of data and of hypotheses. Behav Genet 6:227–261, 1976.
10. Gesell A, Thompson H: Learning and growth in identical infant twins. Genet Psychol Monogr 6:1–19, 1929.
11. Goodwin D: Is alcoholism hereditary? Arch Gen Psychiatry 25:545–549, 1971.
12. Goodwin D, Guze SD: "Psychiatric Diagnosis." New York: Oxford University Press, 1979.

13. Goodwin DW, Schulsinger F, Hermansen L, Guze SB, Winokur G: Alcohol problems in adoptees raised apart from alcoholic biological parents. Arch Gen Psychiatry 28:238–243, 1973.
14. Hill SY, Goodwin DW, Cadoret R, Osterland CK, Doner SM: Association and linkage between alcoholism and eleven serological markers. J Stud Alc 36:981–992, 1975.
15. Horn JM, Plomin R, Rosenman R: Heritability of personality traits in adult male twins. Behav Genet 6:17–30, 1976.
16. Jonsson E, Nilsson T: Alkoholkonsumption ho s monozygota och dizygota tvillingar. Nord Hyg Tidskr 49:21, 1968.
17. Kaij L: "Alcoholism in Twins." Stockholm: Almqvist & Wiksell, 1960.
18. Kidd KK, Matthysee S: Research designs for the study of gene–environment interactions in psychiatric disorders. Arch Gen Psychiatry 35:925–932, 1978.
19. Kopun M, Propping P: The kinetics of ethanol absorption and elimination in twins and supplementary repetitive experiments in singleton subjects. Eur J Clin Pharmacol 11:337–344, 1977.
20. Loehlin JC, Nichols RC: "Heredity, Environment, & Personality." Austin, Texas: University of Texas Press, 1976.
21. Lykken DT: The diagnosis of zygosity in twins. Behav Genet 8:437–473, 1978.
22. Lykken DT, Tellegen A, DeRubeis R: Volunteer bias in twin research: The rule of two-thirds. Soc Biol 25:1–9, 1978.
23. Lytton H, Martin NG, Eaves L: Environmental and genetical causes of variation in ethological aspects of behavior in two-year-old boys. Soc Biol 24:200–211, 1977.
24. Newman HH, Freeman FN, Holzinger KJ: "Twins: A Study of Heredity and Environment." Chicago: University of Chicago Press, 1937.
25. Partanen J, Bruun K, Markkanen T: "Inheritance of Drinking Behavior." Helsinki: Keskuskirjopaino-Centraltryckeriett, 1966.
26. Radlow R, Conway TL: Consistency of alcohol absorption in human subjects. Presented at the American Psychological Association, Toronto, Canada, 1978.
27. Robins LN: Sturdy childhood predictions of adult antisocial behaviour: Replications from longitudinal studies. Psychol Med 8:611–622, 1978.
28. Schlesser MA, Winokur G, Sherman BM: Genetic subtypes of unipolar primary depressive illness distinguished by hypothalamic-pituitary-adrenal axis activity. Lancet 7:739–741, 1979.
29. Schuckit MA: Alcoholism and sociopathy-diagnostic confusion. Quart J Stud Alc 34:157–164, 1973.
30. Schuckit MA: Alcohol and affective disorder: Diagnostic confusion. In Goodwin DW (ed): "Alcoholism and Depression." New York: Spectrum Press 1979, pp 9–19.
31. Schuckit MA: "Drug and Alcohol Abuse: A Clinical Guide to Diagnosis and Treatment." New York: Plenum Press, 1979.
32. Schuckit MA: Alcoholism and genetics: Possible biological mediators. Biol Psychiatry 15:437–447, 1981.
33. Schuckit MA: Alcohol absorption rate in men at high risk for the future development of alcoholism. Alcoholism: Clinical and Experimental Research (in press).
34. Schuckit MA, Goodwin DA, Winokur G: A study of alcoholism in half siblings. Am J Psychiatry 128:1132–1136, 1972.
35. Schuckit MA, Rayses V: Ethanol ingestion: Differences in blood acetaldehyde concentrations in relatives of alcoholics and controls. Science 203:54–55, 1979.
36. Shields J: "Monozygotic Twins." London: Oxford University Press, 1962.
37. Shields J: Heredity and environment. In Eysenck HJ, Wilson GD (eds): "A Textbook of Human Psychology." Lancaster, England: MTP Press, 1976, pp 145–160.
38. Shields J, Gottesman I: Cross-national diagnosis of schizophrenia in twins. Arch Gen Psychiatry 27:725–730, 1972.
39. Slater E, Cowie VA: "The Genetics of Mental Disorders." London: Oxford University Press, 1971.
40. Vesell ES: Pharmacogenetics: Multiple interactions between genes and environment as determinants of drug response. Am J Med 66:183–187, 1979.
41. Vesell ES, Page JG, Passancanti GT: Genetic and environmental factors affecting ethanol metabolism in man. Clin Pharmacol Ther 12:192–201, 1971.

Twin Research 3: Epidemiological
and Clinical Studies, pages 71—76
© 1981 Alan R. Liss, Inc., 150 Fifth Avenue, New York, NY 10011

Adoption Studies of Alcoholism

Donald W. Goodwin

Department of Psychiatry, University of Kansas Medical Center, Kansas City

One approach to separating "nature" from "nurture" in the etiology of alcoholism is to study individuals separated from their alcoholic biological relatives soon after birth and raised by nonalcoholic adoptive parents. Beginning in 1970, the present author and his colleagues started a series of adoption studies in Denmark, supported by the National Institute of Alcohol Abuse and Alcoholism, intended to investigate further the possibility that alcoholism in part had genetic roots [4, 5]. The studies have gone through three phases. The most recent was completed in 1977.

PHASE ONE

Because men are more likely to develop drinking problems than are women, the first phase of the study involved studying a sample of Danish males who had a biological parent with a hospital diagnosis of alcoholism and who had been adopted in the first few weeks of life to nonrelatives. The control group, consisting of age-matched men without, as far as was known, alcoholism in their biological parents, was selected from a large pool of adoptees. A psychiatrist interviewed the total sample of 133 men (average age, 30), 55 of whom had a biological parent who was alcoholic, matched with 78 controls with no known alcoholism in their parents (it was possible some did have alcoholic parents, but there was no record of this in the central registries maintained in Denmark). The interviewer did not know whether the interviewees were sons of alcoholics or sons of presumed nonalcoholics and the study was "blind" from its inception until the data were analyzed. Experimenter bias therefore could not have been a factor in the study.

The results of the study can be summarized as follows:

1) Ten of the 55 probands (sons of alcoholics) were alcoholic, using both specific criteria and a history of treatment for alcoholism. Of the 78 controls, 4 met the criteria for alcoholism but none had received treatment. The difference was significant at the 0.02 level.

2) The probands were no more likely to be heavy drinkers or drinkers with occasional problems from drinking than were the controls. About 40% of each group were heavy drinkers, defined as daily drinkers who drank six or more drinks at least several times a month. Having a biological parent who was alcoholic in-

creased the likelihood of the son being alcoholic but did not increase the chance of his being classified as a heavy drinker.

3) The interviewer, a trained psychiatrist, obtained a complete psychiatric history and performed a mental status examination. The probands were no more likely to receive a diagnosis of depression, sociopathy, drug abuse, or other diagnosable psychiatric conditions than were the controls. Both groups had sizable numbers of individuals diagnosed as having various personality disturbances, but these vaguely described traits were as common in the control group as in the probands.

From these data it could be concluded that sons of alcoholics were about four times more likely to be alcoholic than were sons of nonalcoholics, despite having no exposure to the alcoholic biological parent after the first few weeks of life. Moreover, they were likely to be alcoholic at a relatively early age (in their 20's) and have a form of alcoholism serious enough to warrant treatment. Having a biological parent who was alcoholic apparently did not increase their risk of developing psychiatric disorders other than alcoholism and did not predispose to heavy drinking in the absence of alcoholism. The familial predisposition to alcoholism in this group was *specific* for alcoholism and *not on a continuum* with heavy drinking.

PHASE TWO

Some of the probands had brothers who had been raised by their alcoholic biological parents (most of the alcoholic parents, by the way, were fathers). The sons of alcoholics raised by their alcoholic biological parents also had a high rate of alcoholism, compared to controls consisting of nonadopted men raised by nonalcoholic parents. Their rate of alcoholism, however, was no greater than was the rate observed in their brothers raised by nonalcoholic foster parents (about 18% in both groups).

The conclusion from the first two phases was that alcoholism was transmitted in families and that the increased susceptibility to alcoholism in men occurred about equally in men raised by their alcoholic biological parents and men raised by nonalcoholic foster parents. In other words, if indeed there was a genetic predisposition to alcoholism, exposure to the alcoholic parent did not appear to augment this increased susceptibility.

PHASE THREE

The final phase of the study involved studying the daughters of alcoholics, both those raised by foster parents and those raised by their alcoholic biological parents. The sample consisted of 49 proband women (adopted-out daughters of alcoholics) and 48 controls (adopted-out daughters of presumed nonalcoholics). As was the case of the former studies, the interviews were conducted blindly, with no chance of biased results. The subjects were between the age of 30 and 41, with a mean age of 35. The major findings were as follows:

1) One of the probands was clearly alcoholic and another was a serious problem drinker who failed to meet the criteria completely for alcoholism. Two of the controls were alcoholic. The three women diagnosed as being alcoholic had all received treatment for their alcoholism. Hence 4% of the women in both groups

were either alcoholic or serious problem drinkers. The sample was too small to draw definite conclusions from this, but since there is an estimated prevalence of alcoholism among Danish women of about 0.1% to 1%, the data suggest that there may indeed be an increased prevalence of alcoholism in the two groups. Since nothing is known about the parents of the control women, other than that none had a biological parent with a hospital diagnosis of alcoholism, possibly the two alcoholic controls had parents who had alcohol problems. The parents could not be located and there was no way of determining whether they were alcoholics. However, it was interesting that both of the alcoholic controls had foster parents who were described as alcoholic, suggesting that environmental exposure to alcoholism may contribute to alcoholism in women but not in men.

2) More than 90% of the women in both groups were abstainers or very light drinkers. This contrasted to the Danish male adoptees: About 40% of the latter were heavy drinkers.

3) Family history studies have suggested that alcoholics often have male relatives who are alcoholic or sociopathic and female relatives who are depressed [14]. In this study, complete psychiatric histories were obtained and mental status examinations were performed. Among the adopted women, there was a low rate of depression in both groups, with no more depression in the daughters of the alcoholics than in the controls. Among daughters of alcoholics raised by their alcoholic parents, depression was significantly more present than in controls. There was no evidence of increased susceptibility to other psychiatric disorders in the daughters of alcoholics, whether raised by foster parents or their own alcoholic biological parents.

It therefore appears that alcoholism in women may have a partial genetic basis, but that sample size in the present study precluded any definitive conclusion. Since the great majority of the women were very mild drinkers, it is possible that social factors discouraging heavy drinking may suppress a genetic tendency where one exists. There was no evidence of a genetic predisposition to depression in the daughters of alcoholics. At any rate, if such a predisposition exists, apparently environmental factors are required to make the depression clinically manifest. Regarding the daughters raised by their alcoholic parents, it is not possible to determine whether their increased rate of depression was due to environmental factors precipitating a genetic predisposition or due entirely to environmental factors.

It should be noted that some evidence indicates that women develop alcoholism at a later age than do men, and possibly these 35-year-old women had not all entered the age of risk for alcoholism. Further follow-up studies are needed to explore this possibility.

Four similar studies have been conducted. Roe [10] obtained information about 49 foster children in the 20–40-year age group, 22 of normal parentage and 27 with a biological parent described as a "heavy drinker." Among children with heavy-drinking parents, 70% were users of alcohol, compared to 64% in the control parentage group. In adolescence, two children of "alcohol parentage" got into trouble because of drinking too much as compared to one in the "normal parentage" group. The authors found that adopted children of heavy drinkers had more adjustment problems in adolescence and adulthood than did adopted children of nonalcoholics, but the differences were not significant and neither group had adult drinking problems. They concluded there was no evidence of hereditary influences on drinking.

This conclusion, however, can be questioned on several grounds. First, the sample was small. There were only 21 men of alcoholic parentage and 11 of presumed normal parentage. Since women, particularly at the time of the study, were at very low risk for alcoholism, discovering they had no problem with alcohol was not unexpected. Second, although the biological parents of the proband group were described as "heavy drinkers," it is unclear how many would justify a diagnosis of alcoholism. Most had a history of antisocial behavior, and apparently none had been treated for drinking problems. All of the biological parents of the proband group in the Danish study received a hospital diagnosis of alcoholism at a time when this diagnosis was rarely employed in the country where the study took place.

Schuckit et al [11] also studied a group of individuals reared apart from their biological parents where either a biological parent or a "surrogate" parent had a drinking problem. The subjects were significantly more likely to have a drinking problem if their biological parent was considered alcoholic than if their surrogate parent was alcoholic. Studying 32 alcoholics and 132 nonalcoholics, most of whom came from broken homes, it was found that 62% of the alcoholics had an alcoholic biological parent compared to 20% of the nonalcoholics. This association occurred irrespective of personal contact with the alcoholic biological parent. Simply living with an alcoholic parent appeared to have no relationship to the development of alcoholism.

Bohman [1] studied 2,000 adoptees born between 1930 and 1949 by inspecting official registers in Sweden for notations about alcohol abuse and criminal offenses in the adoptees and their biological and adoptive parents. There was a significant correlation between registrations for abuse of alcohol among biological parents and their adopted sons. Registered criminality in the biological parents did not predict criminality or alcoholism in the adopted sons. The higher the number of registrations for alcoholism in the biological parents, the greater was the incidence of registration for alcohol abuse in the adopted children. These results support a genetic hypothesis for the development of alcoholism and closely parallel those found in the Goodwin et al [4] study of adopted sons of alcoholics.

Cadoret and Gath [2] studied 84 adult adoptees (18 years or older) separated at birth with no further contact with their biological relatives. Alcoholism occurred more frequently in the adoptees whose biological background included an individual with alcoholism than it did in adoptees without this biological background. Alcoholism did not correlate with any other biological parental diagnosis. Childhood "conduct disorder" was significantly higher in those adoptees who later received a diagnosis of alcoholism or problem drinking.

Both of the above adoption studies produced results closely similar to those found in the Danish adoption studies [4]. In other words, alcoholism in the biological parents predicted alcoholism in their male offspring raised by unrelated adoptive parents but did not predict other psychiatric illness (such as criminality). In both the Danish studies [4] and the Cadoret and Gath study [2], alcoholics had an increased incidence of childhood "conduct disorder" but no higher incidence of other psychopathology.

Two studies have been reported bearing on possible genetic modes of transmission. Kaij and Dock [8] tested the hypothesis of a sex-linked factor influencing the occurrence of alcoholism by comparing alcohol abuse rates in 136 sons of the sons, vs 134 sons of the daughters, of 75 alcoholics. No substantial difference between the groups of grandsons was found in frequency of alcoholism, suggesting that a sex-linked factor was not involved. The total sample was also used to calculate the risk of registration for alcohol abuse among the grandsons; rate of registration by the grandsons' fifth decade of life was 43%, approximately three times that of the general male population. This result is incompatible with an assumption of a recessive gene's being involved in the occurrence of alcoholism, although it fits with the assumption of a dominant gene.

Investigating the possibility that children of alcoholics metabolize alcohol differently from children of nonalcoholics, Utne et al [13] compared the disappearance rate of blood alcohol in two groups of adoptees, ten of whom had a biological parent who was alcoholic and ten of whom came from nonalcoholic parentage. There was no significant difference in the elimination rate of ethanol.

There has been speculation that a genetic factor influencing the development of alcoholism might involve atypical liver alcohol dehydrogenase. Recent data [12] indicate a high frequency of ADH polymorphism among Japanese. Analysis of 40 autopsied liver specimens showed that 34 had atypical ADH phenotype. Since there appears to be a relatively low rate of alcoholism in Orientals, the fact that possibly 85% of Japanese carry an atypical liver ADH suggests that alcohol sensitivity may result from increased acetaldehyde formation in individuals carrying atypical ADH gene and that, conversely, non-Orientals with a low incidence of atypical ADH may be more at risk for alcoholism than are Orientals.

FAMILIAL ALCOHOLISM

Jellinek [6], 40 years ago, proposed a diagnostic category called "familial alcoholism." The Danish studies, in particular, seem to support this concept. Familial alcoholism, as described by Jellinek and supported by the Danish data, consists of the following features: 1) a family history of severe, unequivocal alcoholism, 2) early onset, 3) bender-type alcoholism requiring treatment at a relatively young age, and 4) no increased susceptibility to other types of substance abuse or diagnosable psychiatric illness.

From a research standpoint, separating "familial" from "nonfamilial" alcoholism may reveal some interesting and useful correlations. About half of alcoholic patients on many alcoholism wards give a family history of alcoholism. Separating alcoholic patients into these groups would therefore, yield similarly sized cells for comparison purposes.

One study [7] found that, if an alcoholic had one family member who was alcoholic, in 82% of cases there were two or more family members who were alcoholic, further strengthening the concept of familial alcoholism.

Another study [9] found that 69% of women alcoholics who were "spree" drinkers, as opposed to 22% of women alcoholics who were "nonspree" drinkers, had fathers who were heavy drinkers. As Cotton [3] points out, many additional variables, such as age of onset of heavy drinking, the interval between the first drink and heavy drinking, the efficacy of different treatment modalities, or the frequency of marriage to an alcoholic spouse, may differentiate alcoholics who have a family history of alcoholism from those who do not.

REFERENCES

1. Bohman M: Genetic aspects of alcoholism and criminality — through a material of adoptions. Arch Gen Psychiatry 35:269–276, 1978.
2. Cadoret R, Gath A: Inheritance of alcoholism in adoptees. Br J Psychiatry 132:252–258, 1978.
3. Cotton NS: The familial incidence of alcoholism, a review, J Stud Alc 40:89–116, 1979.
4. Goodwin DW, Schulsinger F, Hermansen L, Guze SB, Winokur G: Alcohol problems in adoptees raised apart from alcohol biological parents. Arch Gen Psychiatry 28:238–243, 1973.
5. Goodwin DW, Schulsinger F, Moller N, Hermansen L, Winokur G, Guze SB: Drinking problems in adopted and nonadopted sons of alcoholics. Arch Gen Psychiatry 31:164–169, 1974.
6. Jellinek EM, Jolliffe N: Effect of alcohol on the individual. Quart J Stud Alc 1:110–181, 1940.
7. Lucero RJ, Jensen KF, Ramsey C: Alcoholism and teetotalism in blood relatives of abstaining alcoholics. Quart J Stud Alc 32:183–185, 1971.
8. Kaij L, Dock K: Grandsons of alcoholics. Arch Gen Psychiatry 32:1379–1381, 1975.
9. Parker FB: Sex-role adjustment in women alcoholics. Quart J Stud Alc 33:647–657, 1972.
10. Roe A: The adult adjustment of children of alcoholic parents raised in foster homes. Quart J Stud Alc 5:378–393, 1944.
11. Schuckit MA, Goodwin DW, Winokur G: A half-sibling study of alcoholism. Am J Psychiatry 128:1132–1136, 1972.
12. Stamatoyannopoulas G, Chen SH, Fukui M: Liver alcohol dehydrogenase in Japanese: High population frequency of atypical form and its possible role in alcohol sensitivity. Am J Hum Genet 27:789–796, 1975.
13. Utne HE, Hansen F, Vallo R, Winkler K, Schulsinger F: Unpublished communication. Ethanol elimination rate in adoptees with and without parental disposition towards alcoholism, 1977.
14. Winokur G, Reich T, Rimmer J, Pitts F: Alcoholism: III. Diagnosis and familial psychiatric illness in 259 alcoholic probands. Arch Gen Psychiatry 23:104, 1970.

Twin Research 3: Epidemiological
and Clinical Studies, pages 77 — 87
© 1981 Alan R. Liss, Inc., 150 Fifth Avenue, New York, NY 10011

Investigations Into the Genetics of Alcohol Dependence and Into Its Effects on Brain Function

H.M.D. Gurling, R.M. Murray, and C.A. Clifford

Department of Psychiatry (H.M.D.G., R.M.M.), and Department of Psychology (C.A.C.), Institute of Psychiatry, London

INTRODUCTION

A number of investigators have used twins in an effort to determine whether there is a genetic predisposition to alcohol consumption or alcohol dependence. Other studies have employed the cotwin control method to examine environmental and psychological correlates of alcohol dependence, some of which may be causally related to, and others a product of, the alcohol dependence [5, 7, 9, 22, 23].

This chapter will review these two approaches and also present preliminary findings from a twin study being carried out using the Maudsley Hospital twin register.

Genetic and Pharmacogenetic Studies of Alcohol Use in Twins

Several groups have studied the in vivo metabolism of alcohol in human twins [12, 20]. Vessel [33] found that the heritability of ethanol degradation was 0.98, implying that environmental influences were very small. Kopun and Propping were prompted to repeat this study and found a much lower heritability, 0.41 [18]. These studies have been reviewed in greater detail elsewhere [21], but both were conducted on small numbers of twins, making the use of biometric analysis inappropriate.

Investigations into normal and heavy alcohol consumption that have been conducted on larger numbers of twins do not show such a strong genetic effect as the pharmacogenetic studies. The results, which are summarised in Table 1, show a small to moderate increase in concordance in monozygotic (MZ) over dizygotic (DZ) twins for amount or frequency of alcohol consumption [7, 8, 17, 19, 25], and also a tendency for factors that would reduce alcohol consumption to be heritable, as shown in Table 2 [8, 16, 19].

Dr. Gurling is supported by a grant from the Research Fund of the Bethlem Royal and Maudsley Hospital.

TABLE 1. Twin Studies, Normal and Excessive Use

Author	N Pairs	Sex	Characteristic Studied	Concordance[a] MZ	DZ	MZ/DZ Ratio	h²
Partanen et al [26]	729	M	Lack of control				0.14
			Amount				0.36
			Density				0.39
Loehlin [19]	850	M + F	Excessive use				0.36
Conterio and Chiarelli [8]	77	M	Quantity drunk	65	44	1.5	
Cederlöf et al [7]	5,025	M	Normal drinking	1.46	1.34	1.09	
		F	Normal drinking	1.44	1.34	1.07	
		M	Excessive drinking	4.96	3.3	1.5	
		F	Excessive drinking	13.12	6.12	2.14	
Kaij [17]	111	M	Average and above average consumers	45.2	28.8	1.57	

[a]Percentage values, except for Cederlöf's study showing coincidence rates based on whole population sample of twins.

TABLE 2. Twin Studies — Heritable Factors Favouring Nonconsumption

Author	N Pairs	Sex	Characteristic studied	Concordance MZ	DZ	MZ/DZ Ratio	h²
Loehlin [19]	850	M + F	Hangover				0.62
			Never a heavy drinker				0.52
Jonsson and Nilsson [16]	7,500	M + F	Non-consumption	22%	16%	1.4	
Conterio and Chiarelli [8]	77	M	Alcohol use or not	100%	86%	1.4	
			Wine drinking or not	94%	84%	1.1	

Twin Studies of Alcohol Dependence

Previous investigations of twin probands with an established alcohol dependence syndrome have been carried out on small numbers. Kaij [17] studied 14 MZ and 31 DZ alcoholic probands who had reached the stage of drinking to avoid withdrawal symptoms. His proband method concordance rates in this class were 71.4% and 32.3% for MZ and DZ twins, respectively. Tienari [32] who reported on 13 MZ twins included both heavy abusers and the severely dependent. He reported a pairwise concordance of 38.5%. Both studies can be criticised because of their sampling methods. Kaij's probands were selected on the basis of having been reported to the Swedish Temperance Board on account of coming to the attention of the police or because of being a nuisance to their families. Almost all of Tienari's probands had some form of personality disorder or psychosis. In both cases, therefore, alcoholism could conceivably have occurred secondary to either personality deviance or psychosis, and the genetic predisposition could have been primarily to these disorders rather than to alcoholism itself.

THE PRESENT STUDY

Since 1948 the Maudsley Hospital has maintained a psychiatric twin register that has provided the data base for several important twin studies [14, 30]. We have used this register to identify a consecutive series of same-sexed alcoholic probands. These comprise 20 male and 15 female MZ twins and 33 male and 11 female DZ twins.

Information regarding the probands and their cotwins has been gathered by a number of means. These include a standardised psychiatric screening instrument, the SADS-L [31] and a standardised alcohol interview schedule [6]. In addition, record searches were carried out and information was obtained using the National Health Service Central Patient Register and the Department of Health Mental Health computer files for all hospital admissions in England and Wales.

The study is in progress and at present the identical twin probands and their cotwins have been investigated more thoroughly than the nonidentical twins. So far, however, reliable information has been obtained on 56 pairs of twins at interview by either the senior author or by another Maudsley Hospital psychiatrist. Zygosity has been determined by a physical resemblance questionnaire and, through the kindness of the Medical Research Council and Dr. Ruth Sanger of University College, London, by study of a series of more than 12 blood groups.

We have deliberately chosen to present our findings in terms of dependence on alcohol rather than alcoholism. The reason for this is that alcoholism is notoriously difficult to define, and many definitions include social criteria (eg, arrests for drunken driving) that reflect public attitudes to excessive drinking rather than the drinking behavior itself. The definition of the alcohol dependence syndrome we have used is that outlined by Edwards and Gross [11] and later adopted by the World Health Organization [10]. It may be summarised as follows: 1) a narrowing in the repertoire of drinking behavior, 2) salience of drink-seeking behavior, 3) increased tolerance to alcohol, 4) repeated withdrawal symptoms, 5) repeated relief or avoidance of withdrawal symptoms by further drinking, 6) subjective awareness of a compulsion to drink, 7) reinstatement of the syndrome after abstinence.

Our preliminary results shown in Table 3 suggest pairwise concordance rates for the alcohol dependence syndrome of 21% for the MZ and 25% for the DZ twins.

Analysis of the age distribution of these twins shows that 38% were still below the age of 40 when last seen, and so alcohol dependence may yet develop in a proportion of cotwins. It is nevertheless clear that our preliminary findings do not show the same tendency for alcohol dependence to be heritable as Kaij found in Sweden. Indeed, the concordance for both DZ and MZ twin are similar to the prevalence of alcohol dependence in first-degree family members.

It is of course possible that our eventual findings for 78 as opposed to the present 56 pairs will show slightly higher concordance rates for the MZ than DZ twins. But, at the present time, the identical twins have been more fully investigated, so this concordance is unlikely to increase very much. There are a number of other possible reasons for the discrepancy between Kaij's findings and ours. First, he studied only men, whereas we included women. Second, the samples differed with regard to the frequency of psychiatric disturbance. Third, patterns of alcohol consumption in the general population in Sweden in the immediate postwar period

TABLE 3. Pairwise Concordance for the Alcohol-Dependence Syndrome in 56 Pairs of Maudsley Twins

	Males	Females	Both
MZ pairs	5/15 (33%)	1/13 (8%)	6/28 (21%)
DZ pairs	6/20 (30%)	1/8 (13%)	7/28 (25%)

differ from those in the United Kingdom a generation later. Fourth, different criteria for alcohol dependence were used.

We would not at this point like to exclude the possibility that heredity does contribute to liability to alcohol dependence, particularly in view of information we have on reared-apart identical twins who abuse alcohol. Five such pairs of reared-apart twins are known to us and in two pairs all four twins are severely dependent. However, the first of these pairs were raised in separate households in the same heavy cider-drinking village of South West England, and therefore were subject to similar enviromental pressures. The twins of the second pair, who are Irish, were unknown to each other until the age of 24 years but both had been in the merchant navy, an occupation conducive to the development of problem drinking. Thus, although the existence of two pairs of reared-apart MZ twins concordant for alcohol dependence might at first suggest a major genetic component, knowledge of the life histories of these twins demonstrates that environmental factors may have contributed to their concordance.

Our study also sheds some light on the question of whether twinning itself has any influence on the likelihood of becoming alcohol-dependent, a possibility raised by the relatively few chronic alcoholic MZ twins that Kaij was able to find on the Swedish National Twin Register. The prevalence of alcoholism in all the twins attending the Maudsley Hospital since 1948 is 6.2% and the proportion of alcoholics in the general hospital population is 5.9%. Therefore it does not seem likely that twinning has a strong positive or negative effect on the development of alcoholism.

COGNITIVE DEFICITS AND CEREBRAL PATHOLOGY

Alcoholism occasionally causes very gross cognitive deficit as in the memory loss of Korsakoff's syndrome, which is associated with pathological changes in the mammillary bodies. In addition, air encephalography and computerised brain tomography have shown changes in the cerebral morphology of severely dependent alcoholics, similar to the cerebral atrophy found in dementia.

It has recently been shown by a number of different workers that alcoholics perform less well on certain cognitive tests than normal drinking controls [4, 24, 27, 29]. The more recent of these studies have shown some correlation between cognitive tests and morphological change as found on brain scans, but the correlations are low. In fact, Wilkinson and Carlen [34] found no correlation between tests of the Halstead Reitan battery and degree of morphological change as found on computerised tomography. Ron et al [28] found a correlation between the digit symbol subtest of the WAIS and ventricular size. Another investigation by Bergman et al [1] did not have a control group but claimed to find correlations between learning and memory deficits and subcortical damage, and between the Halstead Reitan Impairment Index and cortical lesions. All the studies tend to show that psychological impairment is less related to lifetime alcohol consumption than to length of abstinence before testing.

In this area of research, the problem of finding adequately matched controls appears to be very great. Kaij [17] used the cotwin control method and concluded that his cognitive tests failed to distinguish between alcohol abusers and their cotwins. Other cotwin control studies have not addressed the question of cognitive deficit, but Bergman and Norlin [2] found that high alcohol consumers had a more field-dependent cognitive style and later [3] reported no difference in Rorschach responses in alcohol-discordant twins.

Cognitive Tests

In the present study a series of eight cognitive tests have been employed on 13 pairs of MZ twins. Four of these pairs were concordant for alcohol abuse and nine were discordant. Three of the nine discordant twin pairs were selected from the Institute of Psychiatry "normal" twin register, described elsewhere in this volume, on the basis that one of the twins was an extremely heavy drinker (> 10 cl pure alcohol daily). The remainder were from the series of alcoholic probands and their cotwins discussed in the first part of this chapter. The nine alcohol abusers who were tested had almost identical levels of educational attainment and developmental histories to their cotwins. All but one alcohol abuser had been abstinent for at least 2 months. The following tests were used: 1) Spatial Little Men (test of right/left orientation), 2) symbol digit test (from WAIS), 3) verbal memory (paired words, forced choice), 4) perceptual analysis, 5) visuospatial memory, 6) Mill Hill vocabulary tests, 7) tactual performance test, and 8) Wisconsin card sorting test (Nelson modification).

Tests 7 and 8 were carried out in the traditional manner but the other six were administered in a computerised format devised by our colleague Dr. William Acker on whom we were heavily reliant. The tests, which are known as the Maudsley Automated Psychological Screening Battery, were specifically designed to detect cognitive deficit across a wide range of skills and include accurate measurement of reaction times in tasks of varying difficulty. The findings for the nine discordant pairs are presented in Tables 4 and 5.

Matched-pair t-tests were calculated to determine levels of significance (single-tailed). The results of the untimed tests (Table 4) show significant deficits among the alcohol abusers for left/right orientation and tactual performance. It is of interest that the within-pair differences for the two verbal tests (Mill Hill and verbal memory) were negligible, confirming previous finding that heavy alcohol abuse has a differentially adverse effect on performance measures [13, 15].

No significant differences were found in reaction times (Table 5). However, the alcohol abusers showed a nonsignificant tendency to be slower in the tactual performance and the symbol digit tests. There was a tendency for the alcohol abusers to have reaction times that were faster in the right/left orientation test and the verbal and visuospatial memory tests. This may indicate that, when the task at hand is not one primarily of speed, the alcohol abusers are more impulsive.

TABLE 4. Cotwin Control Study — Tests Without Reaction Times

Test	N pairs	Sum of within-pair differences[a]	t	Significance[b]	Correlation with atrophy score
Right/left orientation errors	9	−43	1.97	P < 0.05	0.45
Verbal memory, correct	9	0	0	NS	0.27
Mill Hill, correct	9	+ 1	0.01	NS	−0.12
Visuospatial memory,					
Memory	9	+14	0.74	NS	−0.02
distractors	9	−52	1.44	NS	0.63
Tactual performance					
Shape	7	− 9	3.58	P < 0.01	−0.07
location	7	−14	2.54	P <0.02	0.65
Wisconsin sorting,					
Total errors	7	−21	0.49	NS	0.47
Perserverative errors	7	−31	1.13	NS	0.42

[a]Negative sign implies alcoholic twins performed worse.
[b]Single-tailed.

TABLE 5. Cotwin Control Study — Psychological Tests With Reaction Times (RT)

Test	N pair	Sum of within-pair differences (in seconds)[a]	t	Significance[b]	Correlation with atrophy score
Right/Left orientation RT	9	− 1.28	0.37	NS	0.37
Verbal memory,					
Correct RT	9	− 3.08	0.87	NS	0.05
Incorret RT		− 12.50	1.43	NS	0.70
Mill Hill, RT	9	+ 3.30	0.01	NS	0.02
Tactual performance,					
Dominant hand	7	+ 836	1.14	NS	0.13
Non-dominant hand	7	+ 175	0.32	NS	0.36
Both hands	7	+1096	1.12	NS	−0.03
Symbol digit	9	+ 0.78	1.00	NS	−0.39
Visuospatial memory RT	9	− 1.90	0.85	NS	−0.22

[a]Positive score: Alcohol abusers slower.
[b]Single-tailed.

Computerised Tomography

Brain scans were performed using an EMI CT 1010 scanner on all 18 twins and the results were interpreted with the help of Dr. M. Ron of the Institute of Psychiatry. An example of the differences found in the scans of a 45-year-old pair of identical twins who were highly discordant for alcohol consumption is shown in Figure 1.

The cerebral sulci, sylvian fissure, and interhemispheric fissure for all the twins were categorised into levels of abnormality, indicating a lessening of brain size. The cross-sectional ventricular and brain areas were measured directly on two consecutive tomograms. The measurements were combined as a ventricle/brain ratio and averaged for each individual.

Twins were allocated atrophy scores from the ventricle/brain ratios if they fell into certain ranges ascertained from a control series [28]. A combined atrophy score was determined by summing the categorical scores. A score of zero indicates normality and gross cerebral atrophy yields a score of 10. The combined atrophy score for all the alcohol abusers and normal cotwins is shown in Table 6 together with the within-pair difference.

The correlated t-test for within-pair atrophy score differences shows a highly significant difference ($P < 0.02$) between the alcohol abusers and their cotwins. It can be seen, however, that the so-called normal cotwins also have some atrophy. This can be attributed to the older age of three of the pairs, in whom a degree of atrophy could be expected.

An important question that has not been adequately answered in previous studies is whether the brain scan changes in alcoholics correlate with cognitive deficits. Inspection of Tables 4 and 5 shows that there is a correlation between the tests showing significant cognitive deficits and the total atrophy score. (The tables show within-pair correlation coefficients.) The values are 0.45 for right/left orientation and 0.65 for the location subtest of the tactual performance test. It can also be seen that, where the cognitive tests show a tendency for the alcohol abusers to perform less well, the correlations with the total atrophy score are also positive.

These findings demonstrate a correlation between abnormalities on brain scan and cognitive deficit for performance skills that are localised in the nondominant hemisphere. It appears that the cotwin control method is a particularly valuable approach in this area of investigation because it overcomes the problems of finding adequately matched control groups. When the sample size of twins is increased, it may be possible to detect psychological impairment in individuals who are heavy drinkers as opposed to those who are alcohol-dependent.

TABLE 6. Computerised Tomography

	Alcohol abusers	Normal cotwins
Total atrophy score for each group of twins	36	9
Mean atrophy score (9 pairs)	4	1
Mean within-pair difference	2.22[a]	

[a]t = 2.88, P < 0.02.

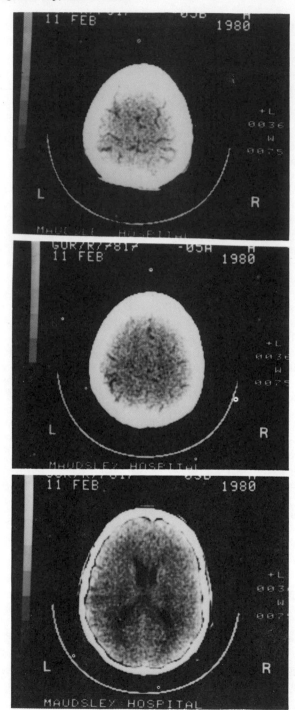

Fig. 1. Monozygotic Twins. a) Normal Cotwin

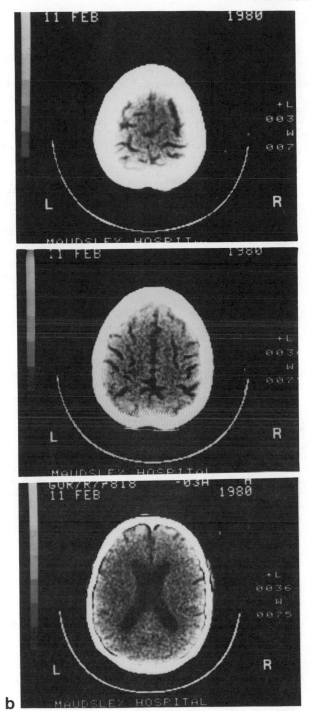

b)Alcoholic Proband

REFERENCES

1. Bergman H, Borg S, Hindmarsh T, Idestrom CM, Mutzell S: In Begleiter H, Kissen B (eds): "Biological Effects of Alcohol." Plenum Press, New York: 1980.
2. Bergman H, Norlin B, Borg S, Fyrö B: Field dependence in relation to alcohol consumption: A cotwin control study. Percep Motor Skills 41:855–859, 1975.
3. Bergman H, Norlin B, Borg S, Koppen S, Starck A, Zotterman A: Structuring and articulation of Rorschach inkblots in relation to alcohol consumption: A cotwin control study. Percep Motor Skills 46:947–952, 1978.
4. Boeke PE: Some remarks about alcohol dementia in clinically treated alcoholics. Br J Addict 65:173–180, 1970.
5. Borg S, Fyrö F, Myrhed M: Psychosocial factors in alcohol discordant twins. Br J Addict 74:189–198, 1979.
6. Caetano R, Edwards G, Oppenheim AN, Taylor C: Building a standardised alcoholism interview schedule. Drug Alcohol Depend 3:185–197, 1978.
7. Cederlöf R, Friberg L, Lundman T: The interactions of smoking, environment and heredity and their implications for disease aetiology. Acta Med Scand 202 Suppl 612:1–128, 1977.
8. Conterio F, Charelli B: Study of the inheritance of some daily life habits. Heredity 17:347–359, 1962.
9. De Faire U: Ischaemic heart disease in death discordant twins. A study of 205 male and female pairs. Acta Med Scand Suppl 568:109, 1974.
10. Edwards D, Gross MM, Keller M, Moser J, Room R: "Alcohol-Related Disabilities." WHO Offset Publication No. 32, 1977.
11. Edwards G, Gross MM: Alcohol dependence: Provisional description of a clinical syndrome. Br Med J 1:1058–1061, 1976.
12. Forsander O, Eriksson K: Forekommer Det Etnologiska Skillnader 1 Alkoholens Amnesomättninger Alkoholpolitik. 37:115, 1974.
13. Glosser G, Butters N, Kaplan E: Visuoperceptual processes in brain damaged patients on the digit-symbol substitution test. Int J Neurosci 7:59–66, 1977.
14. Gottesman II, Shields J: "Schizophrenia and Genetics: A Twin Study Vantage Point." New York: Academic Press, 1972.
15. Jones BM: Verbal and spatial intelligence in short and long term alcoholics. J Nerv Ment Dis 153:292–297, 1971.
16. Jonsson E, Nilsson T: Alkoholkonsumtion hos monozygota och dizygota tvillingpar Nord Hyg Tidskr 49:21–25, 1968.
17. Kaij L: "Alcoholism in Twins." Stockholm: Almqvist and Wiksell, 1960.
18. Kopun M, Propping P: The kinetics of ethanol absorption and elimination in twins and supplementary repetitive experiments in singleton subjects. Eur J Clin Pharmacol 11:337–344, 1977.
19. Loehlin JC: An analysis of alcohol-related questionnaire items from the National Merit Twin Study. Ann NY Acad Sci 197:117–120, 1972.
20. Lüth KF: Untersuchungen Uber Die Alkoloblutkorzenkrationach Alcoholgaben bei 10 Eineiigen Und 10 Zweieiigen Zwillingspaaren. Dtsch Z Gerichtl Med 32:145–164, 1939.
21. Murray RM, Gurling HMD: Genetic contributions to normal and abnormal drinking. In Sandler M (ed): "Psychopharmacology of Alcohol." New York: Raven Press, pp 90–105, 1980.
22. Myrhed M: Alcohol consumption in relation to factors associated with ischaemic heart disease. Acta Med Scand Suppl 567, 1974.
23. Myrhed M, Bergstrom K: Liver enzymes in alcohol discordant twins. Acta Med Scand 200:1–2, 87–91, 1976.
24. Parker ES, Noble EP: Alcoholic consumption and cognitive function in social drinkers. J Stud Alcohol 38:1224–1232, 1977.
25. Partanen J. Bruun K, Markkanen T: "Inheritance of Drinking Behaviour." Helsinki: The Finnish Foundation for Alcohol Studies, 1966.
26. Partanen J, Bruun K, Markkanen T: "Inheritance of Drinking Behaviour: A Study on

Intelligence, Personality and Use of Alcohol of Adult Twins." Helsinki: Finnish Foundation for Alcohol Studies No. 14, 1966, p 159.

27. Ron MA: Brain damage in chronic alcoholism: A neuropathological, neuroradiological and psychological review. Psychol Med 7:103–112, 1977.

28. Ron MA, Acker W, Lishman WA: Dementia in chronic alcoholism. A clinical, psychological and CAT study. In Obiols et al (eds): "Biological Psychiatry Today." Elsevier, North Holland, 1979.

29. Ryan C, Butters N, Montgomery K: Memory deficits in chronic alcoholics. Continuities between the "intact" alcoholic and the alcoholic Korsakoff patient. In Begleiter H, Kissen B (eds): "Alcohol Intoxication and Withdrawal." New York: Plenum Press, 1979.

30. Slater E, Shields J: Genetical aspects of anxiety in studies of anxiety. Lader M (ed). Br J Psychiatry. Special Publication. No. 3 Headley Bros., 1969.

31. Spitzer RL: "Critical Issues in Psychiatric Diagnosis." New York: Raven Press, 1978.

32. Tienari P: Psychiatric illnesses in identical twins. Acta Psychiatry Scand Suppl 171, 1963.

33. Vessel ES, Page JG, Passananti GT: Genetic and environmental factors affecting ethanol metabolism in man. Clin Pharmacol Ther 12:192–201, 1971.

34. Wilkinson DA, Carlen PL: Neuropsychological and neurological assessment of chronic alcoholism: Discrimination between groups of alcoholics. J Stud Alcohol 41:129–139, 1980.

Twin Research 3: Epidemiological
and Clinical Studies, pages 89—96

A Twin Study of Psychomotor Performance During Alcohol Intoxication: Early Results

N.G. Martin, J.B. Gibson, J.G. Oakeshott, A.V. Wilks, G.A. Starmer, J. Craig, and J. Perl

Department of Population Biology, Research School of Biological Sciences, Australian National University, Canberra (N.G.M, J.B.G., J.G.O., A.V.W.), and Department of Pharmacology, University of Sydney (G.A.S., J.C., J.P.)

It is a commonplace observation that some people are greatly affected by even small doses of alcohol while others seem relatively tolerant to even large doses. How much of this variation in susceptibility to intoxication is genetically determined? Are there environmental factors that influence susceptibility to alcohol?

In an attempt to answer these questions, we are measuring 18–35-year-old twins on a number of psychomotor tasks related to driving skills including motor coordination, body sway, hand steadiness, reaction time, and cognitive impairment before and after ingestion of alcohol.

Our sample includes healthy twins of both sexes resident in Sydney and aged between 18 and 35. Each twin participating attends a testing session beginning about 9:00 AM, having eaten a light, nonfatty breakfast about an hour earlier. Four sets of variables are measured during an 8-hour session: personality and drinking history, parameters of the blood ethanol profile, and physiological and behavioural responses following ethanol ingestion. Before testing begins, a 20-ml blood sample and a urine sample are collected; one aliquot of blood is used for typing to establish zygosity and another aliquot of blood and the urine sample are used for quantitative haematological and biochemical assays, including mean corpuscular volume and plasma levels of gamma-glutamyl transpeptidase, aspartate aminotransferase, alkaline phosphatase, and triglycerides, all of which are putative indicators of previous drinking experience [8].

Subjects are trained on apparatus used to test psychomotor performance and then "prealcohol" (T_0) measurements are taken of all the physiological and behavioural tests. They are then given an alcohol dose of 0.75 g ethanol/kg body weight diluted to 10% v/v in sugarless lemon squash (equivalent to about ⅔ to a full bottle of wine) and are asked to drink it in 20 minutes. After a further 20 minutes, "postalcohol" testing begins with repeated measurements of breath alcohol, blood alcohol, blood pressure, pulse, skin temperature, motor coordination, body sway, hand steadiness, simple and complex reaction times, cognitive impairment, mental alertness, and mood state. Each subject is measured for each of these five times at hourly intervals (T_1 to T_s), although additional readings of breath and blood alcohol are taken at more frequent intervals to increase information about the profile.

The sex, age and zygosity characteristics of the 79 pairs successfully tested during 1979 are given in Table 1. Twenty-nine of these pairs were tested twice to provide data on the repeatability of the traits being measured, allowing us to estimate the relative contributions of measurement error and environmental influences sensu stricto to E_1 (individual environmental variance).

The total of 79 pairs tested so far is inadequate for a full genetic analysis. Power calculations by Martin et al [6] show that the sample sizes in most twin studies to date on traits of intermediate inheritance have been too small to give any confidence in the results obtained. The information gained from a twin study increases with sample size, but investigations involving fewer that 100 pairs have a very low probability of providing a critical test of relevant hypotheses when used for traits that are incompletely inherited [see references in 3]. Our study aims to collect data on at least 200 pairs of twins, so the analysis presented below is to be regarded as illustrative but not substantive.

We illustrate one method we intend using to analyse our results with data from a task involving arithmetic computation. The apparatus is the A.K.T.G. (Arbeit und Konzentration Testgräte; Zak, Simbach am Inn, West Germany) on which the subject has to respond to as many simple arithmetic computations (eg, $3 + 5 = ?$, $9 - 3 = ?$) as possible in 2 minutes. Numbers of correct and incorrect responses are recorded but we shall consider only the former, and means for these over all subject-days are shown in Table 2.

The deterioration and recovery curves are congruent for males and females, but only in females is the deterioration from prealcohol performance significant at 50 and almost significant ($c = 1.92$) at 110 minutes. Females do better than males on all trials, significantly so on all but the two occasions when subjects are most intoxicated. Most noteworthy are the large standard deviations around each mean, which demonstrate the great variability of performance we have observed at this task.

The improvement of scores over prealcohol values in the final two trials indicate that there is a significant practice effect. This is seen again in results from those subjects who volunteered to repeat the entire testing day between 2 and 6 months

TABLE 1. Composition of Twin Sample Tested During 1979

	MZF	MZM	DZF	DZM	DZO	Total
Pairs tested on first occasion	23	18	15	10	13	79
Pairs tested on second occasion	9	11	5	2	2	29
Total	32	29	20	12	15	108 pair days

TABLE 2. Mean Number (and Standard Deviation) of Correct Arithmetic Computations
Performed on A.K.T.G. Apparatus. Significance of Sex Differences Indicated

Trial	Minutes after alcohol	Number correct	
		Females (N = 114)	Males (N = 94)
T_0	− 10	77.8 ± 16.7*	71.6 ± 21.7
T_1	+ 50	71.0 ± 14.2	67.6 ± 21.5
T_2	+ 110	73.7 ± 15.5	70.3 ± 20.2
T_3	+ 170	78.5 ± 14.8*	73.0 ± 20.5
T_4	+ 230	82.5 ± 15.4*	76.9 ± 20.8
T_5	+ 290	85.8 ± 17.6**	77.5 ± 21.6

*$0.01 < P < 0.05$.
**$0.001 < P < 0.01$.

TABLE 3. Repeatability of A.K.T.G. Scores Before (r) and After (r′) Correction for Practice
Effect. Significance of Difference Between Occasions Is Indicated

	Number correct − Females (N = 27)				Number correct − Males (N = 25)			
	r	r′	Occasion 1	Occasion 2	r	r′	Occasion 1	Occasion 2
T_0	0.63***	0.84***	76.37***	87.04	0.68***	0.82***	67.04***	80.20
T_1	0.57***	0.74***	68.04***	76.33	0.44*	0.60***	63.44***	77.72
T_2	0.73***	0.84***	72.22***	79.56	0.83***	0.94***	66.88***	76.60
T_3	0.70***	0.82***	76.96***	84.33	0.77***	0.83***	69.12**	76.76
T_4	0.70***	0.81***	80.93***	88.04	0.85***	0.91***	73.60***	81.12
T_5	0.76***	0.80***	85.56*	90.44	0.83***	0.86***	74.80*	80.44

*$0.01 < P < 0.05$.
**$0.001 < P < 0.01$.
***$P < 0.001$.

after their first attendance (Table 3). Scores have improved significantly in both
sexes at every trial. It is also noteworthy that recovery to prealcohol performance
takes longer on the second occasion, indicating that subjects are starting nearer
their plateau and consequently practice effects are less marked.

Most important, however, are the repeatabilities or test-retest reliabilities of performance. These are intraclass correlation coefficients between performance on the
two occasions. Practice effects between occasions will contribute to variance within
individuals and consequently decrease the raw intraclass correlations (r). However,
if we remove the systematic between-occasions effect from the within-individuals
mean square, the corrected correlations (r′) are considerably higher, most being
around 0.8, and of course this value forms the upper limit to any estimates of heritability. One minus this value is an estimate of the variance due to measurement
error between occasions. It can be seen that our measures have pleasingly high reliabilities but in both sexes the retest reliabilities are lowest at the time of largest de-
crement in performance.

Before we proceed to the genetic analysis of the data, it is worth restating the
central question we are trying to answer. Are there genetic differences affecting be-

havioural response to alcohol? In other words, are there genes influencing variation and covariation in performance between trials during intoxication that are not acting before or after intoxication?

One approach to this question is through the genetic analysis of covariance structures [1, 5, 7], which is adapted from the work of Jöreskog [4] and allows us simultaneously to test hypotheses about both the sources and structure of covariation. Because performance on the last two trials is clearly heavily contaminated by practice effects, we shall remain close to the question by restricting our analysis to the prealcohol and first three postalcohol trials. We have, in fact, dropped the last two trials in testing for the remainder of the project. Preliminary univariate analysis of the separate measurements suggests heterogeneity between males and females in the relative importance of genetic and environmental sources of variation. Because the numbers of males are even smaller than females, we shall restrict our illustrative analysis to data for the first four trials in 21 pairs of MZ and 15 pairs of DZ female twins. Between- and within-pairs mean product matrices for the two types of twin are shown in Table 4.

Analysis of the separate measurements has shown that there is significant genetic variation at each trial but that between-pairs environmental variance (E_2) does not improve the fit of models. This is not to say that E_2 is not important, but is is precisely in the case where both E_2 and additive genetic variation (D_R) are present (as is likely here), that Martin et al [6] have shown that large numbers of twins are necessary if both are to be estimated reliably. We may proceed to investigate the basis of covariation across trials but with the caveat that any estimates of $\hat{D}_R$ may be confounded with a certain amount of E_2 variation.

TABLE 4. Mean Products Matrices for Arithmetic Performance in Females on First Four Trials

MZ between pairs (df = 20)				
T_0	333.64			
T_1	197.08	241.55		
T_2	236.74	226.31	277.02	
T_3	216.95	207.61	227.31	248.02
MZ within pairs (df = 21)				
T_0	56.42			
T_1	29.19	75.73		
T_2	27.09	54.19	90.11	
T_3	34.30	60.45	44.54	84.47
DZ between pairs (df = 14)				
T_0	372.67			
T_1	275.44	242.34		
T_2	321.84	262.14	366.11	
T_3	319.57	272.92	326.42	362.50
DZ within pairs (df = 15)				
T_0	266.66			
T_1	214.13	238.80		
T_2	205.56	212.66	310.43	
T_3	200.13	152.40	182.03	206.96

Given this caveat, the only *sources* of covariation we shall consider in our models are individual environment (E_1) and additive genetic action (D_R). What then of the *structure* of covariation? In our first model we shall consider that two factors account for variance at each trial, one for each source of variation, so that H is the 4 × 1 matrix of E_1 factor loadings and Δ is the corresponding matrix of D_R loadings. We postulate that any specific variation at each trial not explained by the two common factors is solely environmental in origin, so that our model also contains a diagonal matrix E of E_1 specific standard deviations (for computational reasons these square roots are more convenient to estimate than the specific variance components themselves). Thus the model for the four expected mean products matrices may be written:

$$\Sigma_{BMZ} = HH' + E^2 + \Delta\Delta'$$
$$\Sigma_{WMZ} = HH' + E^2$$
$$\Sigma_{BDZ} = HH' + E^2 + \tfrac{3}{4}\Delta\Delta'$$
$$\Sigma_{WDZ} = HH' + E^2 + \tfrac{1}{4}\Delta\Delta'$$

The coefficients are the usual ones from a univariate model for mean squares [see, eg, 2]. To make it quite clear, the shape of the model is expanded out for one of the matrices, Σ_{BMZ} in Table 5, where η_i is an E_1 factor loading, δ_i is a D_R factor loading, and e_i is the square root of a specific E_1 variance term.

We are postulating that each individual has his own "genetic level" of performance before alcohol, but that alcohol has a uniform effect at subsequent trials in altering this level by a constant factor in every individual. In other words, our null hypothesis is that there are no genetic differences regulating behavioural response to alcohol.

If environmental variation at each trial is all random measurement error, then we expect to find no E_1 factor variance (η_i's) but only specific E_1 variance (e_i's). If, however, there are environmental differences affecting individuals' performance systematically at each trial then we expect to find an E_1 factor structure.

There are thus 12 parameters (four each of η_i, δ_i, and e_i) to estimate in our model. Each of the four matrices contributes ten unique statistics so after estimation we have 28 degrees of freedom left to test goodness-of-fit of the model. Fitting these large nonlinear models is a problem dealt with in Martin and Eaves [5] and Martin et al [7]. The residual X^2_{28} is 33.27 (P = 0.23), a quite satisfactory fit to the model. All 12 parameters were significant at least at the 0.01 level.

TABLE 5. Simplest Model for Σ_{BMZ} Written in Full

T_0	T_1	T_2	T_3
$\eta_1^2 + e_1^2 + \delta_1^2$	$\eta_1\eta_2 + \delta_1\delta_2$	$\eta_1\eta_3 + \delta_1\delta_3$	$\eta_1\eta_4 + \delta_1\delta_4$
	$\eta_2^2 + e_2^2 + \delta_2^2$	$\eta_2\eta_3 + \delta_2\delta_3$	$\eta_2\eta_4 + \delta_2\delta_4$
		$\eta_3^2 + e_3^2 + \delta_3^2$	$\eta_3\eta_4 + \delta_3\delta_4$
			$\eta_4^2 + e_4^2 + \delta_4^2$

The proportion of variance in performance at each trial due to the common factor and specific variance from each source is shown in Table 6. There are several noteworthy features. First, the E_1 specific variances are more or less constant for all four trials and correspond almost perfectly with the estimates of error variance from the repeatability correlations. Thus the specific variance between twins tested at the same trial on the same occasion is the same as the variance of the same individual tested at the same trial on two occasions. We may thus regard both of these as estimates of true measurement error.

Second, the E_1 factor loads only slightly on prealcohol preformance, most when twins are at their drunkest at T_1 and then starts to fall off at T_2 and T_3. The estimate of the loading of the E_1 factor on T_0 represents those environmental differences in the background of the cotwins that make them differ on the A.K.T.G. task, and these do not appear to be very important. However, there are clearly systematic E_1 influences that covary between the postalcohol trials, which are most important at T_1 and then decline. It appears likely that there may be systematic differences between cotwins of a pair in such things as diet and drinking history. We have recorded information on these and it will clearly be important to try to partition such influences out in later analyses. It is likely that some of these influences will also differ systematically between pairs so that, with a larger sample, we should also expect to detect significant E_2 variance.

Finally, the proportion of variance due to genetic factors (or heritability) is greatest before alcohol, drops to 0.51 at T_1, and then appears to increase slightly to 0.59 at T_3. However, this does not tell us whether there are genetic effects specifically involved in susceptibility to alcohol. If there are such genetic differences, they will affect variance and covariance between the performance on the three postalcohol trials, but they will not covary with performance on the prealcohol trial. We can test this hypothesis by fitting a second genetic factor independent of the first and loading on T_1, T_2, and T_3, but not on T_0, ie, acting in the presence of alcohol but not in its absence. A diagonal term of Σ_{BMZ} would then be of the form $\eta_i^2 + e_i^2 + \delta_{i1}^2 + \delta_{i2}^2$ and an off-diagonal term of the form $\eta_i\eta_j + \delta_{i1}\delta_{j1} + \delta_{i2}\delta_{j2}$ (i, $j \neq 1$), where δ_{i1} and δ_{i2} are loadings on the independent genetic factors I and II. Rows and columns involving T_0 do not contain terms in δ_{i2}.

TABLE 6. Breakdown of Variance in Each Trial for a Model Excluding Genetic Variation in Performance Deterioration

Trial	Individual environment		Genetic factor
	Specific	Factor	
T_0	0.16	0.08	0.76
T_1	0.12	0.37	0.51
T_2	0.19	0.26	0.55
T_3	0.18	0.23	0.59

$X_{28}^2 = 33.27$, P = 0.23.

TABLE 7. Breakdown of Variance for a Model Including a Genetic Factor for Performance Deterioration Under Alcohol

| Trial | Individual environment | | Genetic | |
	Specific	Factor	General factor	Alcohol factor
T_0	0.13	0.12	0.75	—
T_1	0.11	0.38	0.45	0.06
T_2	0.20	0.23	0.51	0.06
T_3	0.17	0.18	0.57	0.08

$X_{25}^2 = 30.82$, $P = 0.19$.

If we fit this model, then the residual X_{25}^2 is 30.82, so the three extra parameters have not produced a significant reduction in chi-square ($X_3^2 = 2.45$). The three loadings on the second genetic factor at T_1, T_2, and T_3 are small but of borderline significance around 0.05 and the breakdown of variance under this model is shown in Table 7. It is clear that if there are genetic differences affecting performance deterioration under alcohol on this task, then they are of small effect compared with individual environmental experiences and with the genetic differences that affect performance on all occasions, regardless of whether alcohol is present or absent.

However, as already mentioned, these are early results and small numbers, and it may be that the picture will change when all the data are collected. In particular we hope to resolve the role of family environmental differences (E_2). The A.K.T.G. is as much a cognitive as a psychomotor task and it may be that the story for the more strictly psychomotor tasks such as body sway and coordination will be different. Nevertheless, the data do provide an illustration of a method that should be a powerful way of detecting genetic influences on susceptibility to ethanol.

ACKNOWLEDGMENTS

This work is supported by a grant-in-aid from the Australian Associated Brewers. We are grateful to Dr. L.Y.C. Lai for zygosity determination and to the twins for their willing cooperation. Most of the twins were ascertained from a 1972 registry compiled by Professor R.J. Walsh at the University of New South Wales.

REFERENCES

1. Eaves LJ, Martin NG, Eysenck SBG: An application of the analysis of covariance structures to the psychogenetical study of impulsiveness. Br J Math Statist Psychol 30:185–197, 1977.
2. Eaves LJ, Last KA, Young PA, Martin NG: Model-fitting approaches to the analysis of human behaviour. Heredity 41:249–320, 1978.
3. Gibson JB, Oakeshott JG: Genetics of biochemical and behavioural aspects of alcohol metabolism. Aust NZ J Med (in press). 1981.
4. Jöreskog KG: Analysis of covariance structures. In Krishnaiah PR (ed): "Multivariate Analysis, III." New York: Academic Press, 1973.

5. Martin NG, Eaves LJ: The genetical analysis of covariance structure. Heredity 38:79–95, 1977.
6. Martin NG, Eaves LJ, Kearsey MJ, Davies P: The power of the classical twin study. Heredity 40:97–116, 1978.
7. Martin NG, Eaves LJ, Fulker DW: The genetical relationship of impulsiveness and sensation seeking to Eysenck's personality dimensions. Acta Genet Med Gemellol 28: 197–210, 1979.
8. Whitfield JB, Hensley WJ, Bryden D, Gallagher H: Some laboratory correlates of drinking habits. Ann Clin Biochem 15:297–303, 1978.

Twin Research 3: Epidemiological
and Clinical Studies, pages 97 – 103
© 1981 Alan R. Liss, Inc., 150 Fifth Avenue, New York, NY 10011

Olfactory Sensitivity in Twins

Helen B. Hubert, Richard R. Fabsitz, Kenneth S. Brown, and Manning Feinleib

Epidemiology Branch, National Heart, Lung, and Blood Institute (H.B.H., R.R.F., M.F.); and Laboratory of Developmental Biology and Anomalies, National Institute of Dental Research (K.S.B.), Bethesda Maryland

INTRODUCTION

There is a small but growing body of literature concerned with human variation in the ability to detect odors. Despite efforts to explain the olfactory process, there is still considerable controversy over the mechanism of perception and, consequently, the sources of individual difference. Current theories of odor detection suggest that sensitivity may be significantly influenced by genetic factors. Anatomical and physiological conditions, such as the shape of the nasal airway and the endocrine status of the body, are thought to affect "general" sensitivity to all odors [8]. It has been proposed that "specific" sensitivity to an odor may be determined by the functional group (eg, acid or base), molecular shape, or molecular size of the odorant, and its "fit" to a particular receptor site in the olfactory organ [2, 3]. Perception thus could be influenced by genetic variation in the structure of these olfactory receptors [4]. While observed distributions of sensitivity are compatible with genetic mechanisms [1, 4], and odor blindness (ie, complete or specific anosmia) has been reported to cluster in families [11, 16, 18], few studies have focused specifically on the role of heredity in normal odor perception.

An opportunity to investigate the genetic and environmental influences on olfactory perception arose during the first examination cycle of the National Heart, Lung, and Blood Institute (NHLBI) Twin Study. Although precursors to cardiovascular disease were the main focus of this investigation, the protocol at one of the five examination centers also included an ancillary study of olfactory sensitivity. This twin population was an ideal group for assessment of the extent to which the variation in odor perception was genetically rather then environmentally determined.

MATERIALS AND METHODS

Participants in the first examination phase of the NHLBI Twin Study were male veterans, 42–56 years of age, who were chosen by residence from the NAS-NRC Twin Registry [13] and who agreed to be examined at the invitation of the NHLBI.

The authors published a brief report of these results in Science 208:607–609, 9 May 1980.

Information concerning personal and family medical history, diet, and twin history also was collected at the time of the initial examination [9]. Tests of olfactory sensitivity were conducted only at the Framingham, Massachusetts, study center. Acceptable data were obtained for 51 monozygotic (MZ) and 46 dizygotic (DZ) twin pairs who appeared for examination after an overnight fast.

Serial dilutions of acetic acid, isobutyric acid, and 2-sec-butyl-cyclohexanone (cyclohexanone) were used in sequence to determine three thresholds of sensitivity for each individual. These chemical compounds were chosen since they were thought to represent different "primary" odors, "pungent," "sweaty," and "camphoraceous," respectively, described in Amoore's early stereochemical theories on olfaction [1, 2]. It should be emphasized, however, that the quality "pungent" may be different from the other two in that it arises, at least in part, from stimulation of the trigeminal nerve and is not strictly an olfactory response [5].

The serial dilution method of testing each odor required six tubes containing 50 ml of solution. Tube 1 was filled with distilled water, and tubes 2–6 with increasingly stronger solutions of the compound in water. The participant was instructed to take each tube in order, unstopper it, and sniff deeply while holding it about 1 inch from his nose. He stopped this procedure at the weakest detectable concentration, which was considered the twin's threshold of sensitivity for that particular odor.

The strongest chemical solutions (tube 6) were, respectively, 25 ml glacial acetic acid in 975 ml distilled water, 0.4 ml isobutyric acid in 1,000 ml distilled water, and a half-saturated solution of cyclohexanone. The weaker solutions were obtained by diluting each of these by factors of 4, 16, 64, and 256 (tubes 5–2 respectively). Uniform test concentrations were maintained by using stoppered tubes, which were emptied and refilled frequently with fresh solution. Although no provisions could be made to maintain a constant test environment, daily changes in air purity, temperature, or humidity should not have affected within-pair or between-zygosity comparisons, since cotwins were tested on the same day, and MZ and DZ pairs were examined randomly over time.

In order to observe heritability over the range of olfactory sensitivity, the twin and regression analyses included pairs only when both members could perceive the particular odor of interest. Preliminary observation of the data indicated that odor thresholds decreased as the study progressed. While an explanation for this phenomenon could not be found, it should be noted that all analyses of the data, whether adjusted for examination time or not, yielded similar results.

Twin analyses were done following the method of Christian et al [7]. This method relies on a test of the equality of total variances of MZ and DZ twins to determine the appropriate estimate of genetic variance. If the variances are equal, the method is comparable to the classical twin analysis [12]. However, if total variances are not equal, an unbiased "among-component" estimate of genetic variance is chosen, rather than the "within-pair" determination.

RESULTS

Figure 1 shows the cumulative distribution of odor thresholds by zygosity. Linearity of the plots for both isobutyric acid (MZ and DZ $r^2 = 0.98$) and cyclohexanone (MZ and DZ $r^2 = 0.99$) indicates that the responses to these odorants were

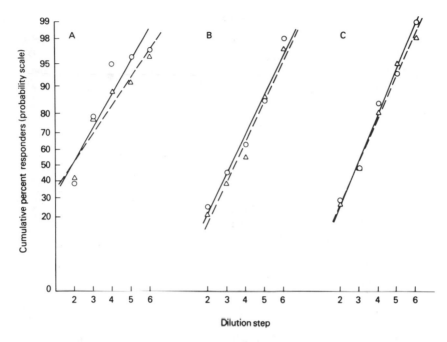

Fig. 1. The cumulative distribution of odor thresholds by zygosity for acetic acid (A), isobutyric acid (B), and cyclohexanone (C). Percents are based on 102 MZ twins (O observed data, — probit fit) and 92 DZ twins (△ observed data, --- probit fit).

approximately normally distributed. In addition, the slopes of the fitted lines were similar for MZ and DZ twins for both odorants, suggesting equal variances in all four groups.

In contrast, the plots for acetic acid were less linear (MZ r^2 = 0.84, DZ r^2 = 0.92). The distribution of responses to this compound deviated from the normal, but only at relatively high concentrations where the acid may behave more like an irritant than an odor and be sensed via the trigeminal system. Questions concerning normality indicated that nonparametric statistical techniques might be more appropriate than twin analyses in assessing heritability. In addition, the slightly lower slope for the DZ compared to the MZ population seen in the figure suggests greater heterogeneity of responses in that group (ie, unequal total variances for MZ and DZ twins).

Means and variances of the population thresholds are presented in Table 1. There were no observable differences in the MZ or DZ means for any of the three odorants, a condition which must exist before genetic analyses can be undertaken. Inequality of the MZ and DZ total variances for acetic acid indicated that the among-component estimate of genetic variance would be the appropriate unbiased measure to use to assess heritability in this case.

TABLE 1. Olfactory Threshold Means and Variances by Zygosity

	Acetic acid		Isobutyric acid		Cyclohexanone	
	MZ	DZ	MZ	DZ	MZ	DZ
No. of twin pairs	48	43	47	43	50	44
Means	2.84	2.92	3.82	3.90	3.43	3.43
Variances	0.68	1.23	1.92	1.82	1.38	1.33

TABLE 2. Summary of the Twin Analysis for Olfactory Sensitivity[a]

Odor	Intraclass correlations of sensitivity thresholds		P values of the estimate of genetic variance
	MZ	DZ	
Acetic acid	0.38	0.11	0.42[b]
Isobutyric acid	0.23	0.41	0.67
Cyclohexanone	0.10	0.04	0.53

[a]Results are adjusted for examination time.
[b]Based on the among-component estimate of genetic variance.

Results of the twin analysis on residuals (obtained after adjustment of thresholds for exam time) did not present evidence for heritability of responses to any of the odors tested (Table 2). The MZ and DZ intraclass correlation coefficients were not significantly different from one another, nor were statistical tests of the appropriate estimates of genetic variance significant. The MZ correlation for isobutyric acid was in fact smaller than the DZ correlation, contrary to what would be expected if genetic factors played a significant role in determining sensitivity. Furthermore, the DZ correlations for acetic acid and cyclohexanone were not significantly different from zero. Christian et al [6] argue that a trait cannot have significant genetic variance if twins who share on the average 50% of their genes show no correlation. The data were also analyzed using nonparametric statistical tests [17] and results were compatible with the findings discussed above.

In order to determine if any environmental or physiologic characteristics were associated with olfactory sensitivity in all twins, the data were further analyzed using multiple linear regression procedures. Variables of particular interest were age; pipe, cigar, and cigarette smoking; frequency of alcohol consumption; types of food consumed; respiratory symptoms and disease history; measures of body fatness (skinfold thicknesses and relative weight); and diabetes mellitus. Not one of these characteristics was found to be significantly associated with sensitivity to acetic acid. However, cigar or pipe smoking ($P < 0.01$), subscapular skinfold thickness ($P < 0.01$), and alcohol consumption ($P < 0.05$) were significantly and independently associated with odor thresholds for isobutyric acid (Table 3). Nonsmokers, heavier individuals, and frequent consumers of hard liquor were more sensitive to this odor than were their smoking, leaner, less indulgent counterparts. Approximately 11% of the variability in odor threshold was explained by these factors. Cigar or pipe smoking ($P < 0.01$) and skinfold thickness ($P < 0.05$) were

TABLE 3. Environmental and Physiologic Characteristics Independently Associated With Olfactory Sensitivity to Isobutyric Acid and Cyclohexanone[a]

	Significant standardized regression coefficients	
Characteristics	Isobutyric acid	Cyclohexanone
Cigar or pipe smoking	0.231	0.208
Cigarettes/day		0.189
Alcohol consumption	−0.152	
Subscapular skinfold thickness	−0.227	−0.168
Diabetes mellitus		0.201
	$R^2 = 0.11$[b]	$R^2 = 0.13$[b]

[a]Results are adjusted for examination time.
[b]Proportion of the variability in sensitivity explained by the characteristics noted (R^2).

TABLE 4. Summary of the Twin Analysis for Olfactory Sensitivity Adjusted for Significant Environmental and Physiologic Characteristics[a]

	Intraclass correlations of sensitivity thresholds		P values of the estimate of genetic variance
Odor	MZ	DZ	
Isobutyric acid	0.38	0.07	0.02
Cyclohexanone	0.19	0.003	0.25

[a]Results are also adjusted for examination time.

also similarly related to responses to cyclohexanone (Table 3). In addition, keener perception of this odor was associated with fewer cigarettes per day (P < 0.01) and a nondiabetic state (P < 0.01). (Six percent of the twins were considered borderline or definite diabetics after clinical evaluation.) The smoking variables, skinfold thickness, and diabetes accounted for 13% of the total variability in sensitivity to this odor.

Since these associated characteristics were a potential source of bias in the twin analysis (ie, equal environmental covariances for MZ and DZ twins may have been an incorrect assumption), procedures were repeated after adjustment of thresholds for all significant factors. The results of these final analyses, presented in Table 4, support the original conclusions of the study. MZ and DZ correlations were not significantly different from one another for either odor. Although the test of the estimate of genetic variance for isobutyric acid was statistically significant, the DZ twins showed essentially no correlation, and significant genetic variance could not be assumed. It is also noteworthy that the adjusted analyses for isobutyric acid yielded a larger MZ than DZ correlation, reversing the results obtained prior to adjustment in Table 2.

Analyses of the data including the anosmics, who comprised only 5% of the twin population, also did not offer an argument for heritability. Not one of the 97 twin pairs was concordant for anosmia. Of the nine anosmic individuals, three MZ and three DZ twins could not detect acetic acid; four MZ and three DZ twins could not perceive the odor of isobutyric acid; and one MZ and two DZ twins were anosmic to cyclohexanone. The medical and occupation histories of this group proved to be quite interesting. In particular, the two individuals who could not smell any of the three odors had suffered serious eye injuries. One had completely lost an eye; the other was blinded. Conceivably, traumatic injuries to this area may have affected the olfactory system as well. Two other twins had endocrine disorders, hyperthyroidism and diabetes, which have been associated with decreased olfactory sensitivity. Scrutiny of the job histories of this group revealed that firefighters were significantly more likely to be odor blind (P < 0.001) than other kinds of workers. In fact, all three anosmic firemen were incapable of smelling the same "sweaty" odor of isobutyric acid. Although the senses of smell and taste are somewhat interrelated, no discernible differences in food preferences between the anosmic men and their cotwins could be ascertained from the food frequency questionnaire.

DISCUSSION

The results of this study suggest that heredity is not a significant factor in perception of any of the three odorants. It could be argued, however, that these conclusions are influenced in part by the size of the population studied. For instance, if it could be assumed that the adjusted intraclass correlation coefficients for isobutyric acid ($r_{MZ} = 0.38$, $r_{DZ} = 0.07$) are true estimates of population parameters, and if approximately 500 DZ twin pairs could be examined, all statistical tests would suggest that sensitivity to this odor is genetically influenced. Nonetheless, the order of magnitude of the genetic component would be small, as indicated by the size of the MZ and DZ correlation coefficients. These observations point out the need to consider sample size estimates more carefully in the planning of future twin studies.

This investigation demonstrates that environmental and physiologic characteristics including tobacco smoking, alcohol consumption, occupational exposure, body fatness, diabetes, and traumatic injury are related to olfactory response. Although the data are sparse and sometimes inconsistent, a few studies and case reports have shown that smoking and diabetes are associated with decreased sensitivity [10, 14, 15]. Deterioration of the sense of smell may be explained by changes in the nasal or olfactory mucosa due to tobacco smoke exposure. Reasons for decreased activity in diabetics remain somewhat more obscure; however, cranial neuropathy, not uncommon in diabetics, may account for this finding. The associations of body fatness and alcohol consumption with odor thresholds suggest that heightened olfactory sensitivity may be part of a complex of sensory and psychological responses that includes appreciation of food and drink. This is one aspect of human olfaction that deserves more careful attention. It could be argued that what has been measured here and considered a physiologic response is not entirely that. Since the testing method requires the individual to make a judgment after each sniff, psychological processes undoubtedly play a part in the determination of odor threshold.

Although the environmental factors and physiologic traits considered here explain only a small proportion of the variability in olfactory sensitivity to isobutyric acid and cyclohexanone, the results indicate that such characteristics may be more influential than heredity in defining the distribution of responses to these odors. In contrast, perception of the odor of acetic acid appears unaffected by any of the studied attributes, an observation consistent with the hypothesis that its detection involves a different sensory mechanism.

REFERENCES

1. Amoore JE: Specific anosmia: A clue to the olfactory code. Nature (Lond) 214:1095–1098, 1967.
2. Amoore JE: "Molecular Basis of Odor." Springfield, Illinois: Thomas, 1970, pp 28–69.
3. Beets MGJ: Pharmacological aspects of olfaction. In Moulton DG, Turk A, Johnston JW (eds): "Methods in Olfactory Research." New York: Academic Press, 1975, pp 445–472.
4. Brown KS, MacLean CM, Robinette RR: The distribution of the sensitivity to chemical odors in man. Hum Biol 40:456–472, 1968.
5. Cain WS: Contribution of the trigeminal nerve to perceived odor magnitude. Ann NY Acad Sci 237:28–34, 1974.
6. Christian JC, Feinleib M, Norton JA: Statistical analysis of genetic variance in twins. Am J Hum Genet 27:807, 1975.
7. Christian JC, Kang KW, Norton JA: Choice of an estimate of genetic variance from twin data. Am J Hum Genet 26:154–161, 1974.
8. Douek E: "The Sense of Smell and its Abnormalities." Edinburgh: Churchill Livingstone, 1974, pp 118–134.
9. Feinleib M, Garrison RJ, Fabsitz R, Christian JC, Hrubec Z, Borhani NO, Kannel WB, Rosenman R, Schwartz JT, Wagner JO: The NHLBI twin study of cardiovascular disease risk factors: Methodology and summary of results. Am J Epidemiol 106:284–295, 1977.
10. Fordyce ID: Olfaction tests. Br J Ind Med 18:213–215, 1961.
11. Glaser O: Hereditary deficiencies in the sense of smell. Science 48:647–648, 1918.
12. Haseman JK, Elston RC: The estimation of genetic variance from twin data. Behav Genet 1:11–19, 1970.
13. Jablon S, Neel JV, Gershowitz H, Atkinson GR: The NAS-NRC twin panel: Methods of construction of the panel, zygosity diagnosis and proposed use. Am J Hum Genet 19:133–161, 1967.
14. Jorgensen MB, Buch NH: Studies on the sense of smell and taste in diabetics. Acta Oto-Laryngol 53:539–545, 1961.
15. Joyner RE: Olfactory acuity in an industrial population. J Occup Med 5:37–42, 1963.
16. Patterson PM, Lauder BA: The incidence and probable inheritance of "smell blindness" to normal butyl mercaptan. J Hered 39:295–297, 1948.
17. Schwartz JT, Feinleib M: Twin heritability study. In Goldberg MF (ed): "Genetic and Metabolic Eye Disease." Boston: Little, Brown, 1974, pp 37–58.
18. Whissell-Buechy D, Amoore JE: Odour-blindness to musk: Simple recessive inheritance. Nature (Lond) 242:271–273, 1973.

Twin Research 3: Epidemiological
and Clinical Studies, pages 105—116

Morphine and Experimental Pain in Identical Twins

Edward H. Liston, John H. Simpson, Lissy F. Jarvik, and Donald Guthrie

Department of Psychiatry and Biobehavioral Sciences, University of California (E.H.L., J.H.S., L.F.J., D.G.), and Veterans Administration Medical Center, Brentwood, Los Angeles (L.F.J.)

INTRODUCTION

The problem of drug abuse has thrown into sharp relief our ignorance of the contribution made by genetic factors to individual differences in response to opiates. The paucity of genetic information in humans is particularly striking in view of the fact that the small number of experiments carried out with animals has shown genetic variability to be important in reactions to diverse substances and that in humans the presence of a genetic component has been demonstrated in response to a number of chemical and pharmaceutical agents.

Among the few attempts to show genetic influences on the effects of morphine in animals are the following: Nichols and Hsiao [32] succeeded in breeding rats with a preference for morphine, and Erikson and Kiianmaa [10] found that mice bred for alchohol preference also preferred morphine. Eidelberg et al [9] reported significant differences in locomotor activity, tolerance and "dependence" following administration of morphine for four inbred strains of mice. These and other studies [eg, 14, 33, 34, 37] suggest that there are genetic mechanisms that underlie the variability in response to morphine in laboratory animals. A useful review of recent developments in this field is presented by Broadhurst [7].

Although there are no genetic studies of the effects of morphine in humans, it has been known for many years that reactions to the administration of drugs show wide individual variation, and that genetically determined disorders can produce abnormal or exaggerated drug reactions. While a scant 18 years ago the first book on pharmacogenetics listed fewer than a dozen such compounds [25], the number has increased markedly during the last few years [eg, 2, 42]. And a relatively new disease, "malignant hyperthermia," occurring in response to potent inhalation anesthetics (eg, halothane, ether, or methoxyflurane) has been identified as an autosomal dominant trait [26].

Moreover, several studies using monozygotic (MZ) and dizygotic (DZ) twins provide evidence for genetic determinants in differential drug reactions among healthy, nonmedicated individuals. Vesell and his colleagues, for example, found significantly lower intraclass correlations for DZ than for MZ twins in rates of metabolism of phenylbutazone [44], antipyrine [45], bishydroxycoumarin [46], halothane [8], and ethanol [47]. The correlations varied from 0.87 (MZ) vs 0.53 (DZ) for ethanol to 0.52 vs 0.36 for halothane. The relative contributions of genetic factors in metabolic rates were calculated to range from 0.88 to 0.99 for these compounds, with ethanol and phenylbutazone ranking the highest. Alexanderson et al [1] reported a heritability level of 0.98 for steady state blood levels of nortriptyline. These studies indicate that, for certain drugs, the differences in rates of metabolism are mediated primarily by genetic rather than environmental factors, at least in healthy twins [cf also 6, 43].

Given the data for genetic influences on response to morphine in animals and on metabolic rates of certain other substances in humans, it seemed reasonable to examine the effects of genetic components on the reactions to morphine in humans. Morphine was chosen for two reasons. First, it is similar in its effects to heroin, a commonly abused drug; second, there is a large scientific literature on its effects, especially its analgesic properties. Since morphine is one of the most powerful and useful as well as potentially dangerous medications in the modern drug armamentarium, it is particularly important to enhance our understanding of genetic contributions to its effects in humans.

As for all centrally active drugs, the effects of morphine and other opiates vary according to dose, route of administration, host factors, and environmental settings. The most consistent responses to opiate alkaloids are analgesia, drowsiness, and respiratory depression; when given to patients in pain, there is generally relief of tension and distress. Although most of these patients consider the drug effects pleasant, only a few experience euphoria. The reasons why this unrealistic sense of well-being arises in some patients and not in others are unknown. It is also beyond our present comprehension why nausea and even vomiting follow the administration of opiates in some individuals but not in others. Indeed, there are persons who never vomit after being given morphine and, conversely, there are those who vomit each time the drug is administered. And, in a group of normal volunteers free of pain, anxiety and fear may be experienced by many, euphoria by a few, and no discernible change in mood by the remainder [22, 38]. Most normal volunteers are said to dislike the experience and prefer not to repeat it [28]. To date, no means have as yet been devised to differentiate in advance those subjects who will become euphoric from those who will become dysphoric.

Although morphine has been used as an analgesic for centuries and its properties are primarily responsible for its medical use, the exact mechanism or mechanisms of action remain unclear. This lack of precision can be attributed to the extremely complex nature of pain and its measurement, since "...'pain' represents a category of experiences, signifying a multitude of different, unique events having different causes, and characterized by different qualities varying along a number of sensory and affective dimensions" [30]. The experience of pain depends not only on physiological factors (such as stimulation of specific end organ receptors, sensory coding in the spinal cord and brain), but on psychological factors as well. The response to pain can be influenced by the individual's cultural background [19, 27, 39, 50], by past experience [31], by the person's perception of the meaning of the painful stimulus or situation [3], and by the psychological state of the individual [4].

The purpose of the study described below was to investigate concurrently the physiological and psychological parameters of responses to pain and to morphine in genetically identical individuals. A detailed report of the experimental procedure and of the effects of morphine and placebo on responses to pain and psychological measures is available elsewhere [Jarvik et al, in preparation]. The following discussion is concerned specifically with the data relating to possible contributions of genetic factors.

METHODS

Subjects (Ss) were recruited by newspaper advertisements and brief announcements on radio and television stations as part of community news broadcasts calling for male identical twins in good health and over the age of 21 years. In total, 118 twins in the Southern California area responded and were screened by telephone to determine availability and probable zygosity. Those meeting initial criteria were given appointments for further interviews. Potential subjects with obvious medical problems were eliminated at this stage, as were those who were fraternal twins, those taking drugs regularly, and those opposed to taking drugs. Zygosity was confirmed by examination of fingerprints, blood group antigens, and anthropometric data. Health status was determined by medical examinations, routine laboratory testing, and psychological and psychiatric examinations.

This process yielded ten pairs of male Caucasian monozygotic (MZ) twins between 21 and 28 years of age (Table 1). Both cotwins were single in three pairs, both married in two pairs, one married and one divorced in two pairs, and one single and one married in three pairs. Eleven Ss were employed, eight were students, and one was unemployed. The cotwins of seven pairs lived separately, and those of three pairs (all single) lived together. All Ss were nondrinkers, nonsmokers, and none habitually used drugs, although several of them had tried drugs, such as marijuana and amphetamines, in the past. All spoke English, a requirement included to facilitate psychological testing. All of them agreed to refrain entirely from using alcohol and other psychoactive substances for three days prior to starting the experiment and to eliminate other pharmacologically active substances for 24 hours prior to the experiment, including nasal sprays, beverages containing caffeine, and the like. They were also asked to arrange for transportation at the end of the experimental day, so they would not have to drive. All signed informed consents.

The experimental design has been described in detail elsewhere [Jarvik et al, in preparation]. Briefly, each subject underwent a series of physiological and psychological examinations before (45 minutes) and twice after (45 minutes and 255

TABLE 1. Zygosity Data for Sample of Ten Male Twin Pairs

Twin[a]	Age	ABH	Lewis	Rh	MNSs	Duffy	Lutheran	Kell	Kp	Kidd	P
1A	22	0	a b	rhrh	− + − +	a b	a	Kk	a	a	P
1B	22	0	a b	rhrh	− + − +	a b	a	Kk	a	a	P
2A	21	0	a b	Rh_1Rh_2	− + − +	a b	a	Kk	a	a	P
2B	21	0	a b	Rh_1Rh_2	− + − +	a b	a	Kk	a	a	P
3A	22	0	a b	Rh_1Rh_1	+ + + +	a b	a	Kk	a	a	P
3B	22	0	a b	Rh_1Rh_1	+ + + +	a b	a	Kk	a	a	P
4A	27	B	a b	Rh_0rh	+ + − +	a b	a	Kk	a	a	P
4B	27	B	a b	Rh_0rh	+ + − +	a b	a	Kk	a	a	P
5A	22	0	a b	Rh_1rh	+ + + −	a b	a	Kk	a	a	P
5B	22	0	a b	Rh_1rh	+ + + −	a b	a	Kk	a	a	P
6A	28	0	a b	rhrh	− + − +	a b	a	Kk	a	a	P
6B	28	0	a b	rhrh	− + − +	a b	a	Kk	a	a	P
7A	21	B	a b	rhrh	− + − +	a b	a	Kk	a	a	P
7B	21	B	a b	rhrh	− + − +	a b	a	Kk	a	a	P
8A	22	0	a b	rh″rh	− + + +	a b	a	Kk	a	a	P
8B	22	0	a b	rh″rh	− + + +	a b	a	Kk	a	a	P
9A	26	0	a b	Rh_1Rh_2	− + − +	a b	a	Kk	a	a	P
9B	26	0	a b	Rh_1Rh_2	− + − +	a b	a	Kk	a	a	P
10A	28	0	a b	Rh_1Rh_2	− + − +	a b	a	Kk	a	a	P
10B	28	0	a b	Rh_1Rh_2	− + − +	a b	a	Kk	a	a	P

[a]The A twin is first-born, the B twin, second.

minutes, respectively) the intramuscular injection of placebo (isotonic saline, one ml per 70 kg body weight) on the first experimental day and morphine sulfate (10 mg/ml, 1 ml per 70 kg body weight) on the second experimental day, the two injections being separated by a time interval of 1–3 weeks. Even though two subjects were scheduled for each experimental day, members of a given twin pair were never scheduled together; they participated on different days. Furthermore, twins were asked to refrain from discussing the experience with each other until both had completed the experiment.

The measures used included the following: 1) the cold pressor test [20, 51], wherein the subject immersed his hand into continuously agitated ice water (temperature of 0°–2°C) and reported the perception of pain (latency in seconds to "PAIN" response = pain threshold) as well as the limit of tolerance (latency in seconds to subject's removal of hand from the ice water: "STOP" response = pain tolerance); 2) Two self-rating scales, the National Institute of Mental Health (NIMH) mood scale [35], providing factor scores for anxiety, hostility, friendliness, carefree, cognitive loss, and fatigue; and the Addiction Research Center Inventory (ARCI) [18], from which two subscales were used, namely the Morphine-Benzedrine Group Variability Scale (MBG) and the Benzedrine Group Variability Scale (BG), the former measuring primarily euphoric aspects of mood and the latter, perceptions of clarity and rapidity of thought processes. A fourth scale (LFJ) was added, consisting of the following seven items designed to assess nonspecific drug reactions: I feel sick to my stomach; My head aches; My heart is pounding; I feel I've lost my appetite; Sometimes I am sure I get a raw deal from life; Very often no one seems to understand me; Often I feel I have been punished without cause. 3) A criterion-referenced observer rating scale of information obtained in psychiatric interviews, constructed specifically for the current study, was designed to parallel the self-rating scales mentioned above (Psychiatric Interview Rating Scale—PIRS) [Liston, in preparation]. 4) The Gottschalk-Gleser Verbal Samples (GGVS) were used to assess anxiety, hostility, alienation and withdrawal [17]. And 5) two timed tasks: the Digit Symbol Substitution (DSS) test from the Wechsler Adult Intelligence Scale [48] and a test of pencil tapping speed (Tapping) were employed [13].

The basic statistical model used to analyze the data is that of a nested experiment (subjects in twin pairs) with crossed repeated measurement (sessions across days). In this model, twin pairs form the basic experimental unit and differences due to each of the effects (days, sessions, day-session interactions) are tested by comparison of the effect with its variability across twin pairs. These effects are presented in a separate paper [Jarvik et al, in preparation]. The present report concerns itself with the comparisons of variability between twin pairs with the variability within twin pairs. Univariate methods were used throughout.

RESULTS

Two sets of dependent variables were considered in this study. The first set consists of measures of pain sensitivity and pain tolerance, and the second includes the psychiatric evaluations and the self-reports of psychological functioning.

Response to Pain—Cold Pressor Test

As defined in the methods section, two dependent variables were generated for analysis (pain threshold and pain tolerance). Preliminary examination of the data indicated that three Ss tolerated the ice-water bath for the full 5 minutes allowed before the experimenter stopped the trial. These three Ss reached the ceiling of the test prior to drug administration, making it impossible to demonstrate a drug effect for pain tolerance. For this reason, their data were not included in the analyses of variance reported below. Two of these Ss were members of a single twin pair; data from the cotwin of the third S were also excluded, reducing the sample for the analysis of variance on pain measures to eight twin pairs.

Since there were no systematic effects between the measures for the right hand and for the left hand of each subject, only the data for the right hand cold pressor test are presented in the following analyses. Inasmuch as the test was always administered to the right hand first, order effects have been eliminated.

To determine the presence of a twin factor in the absence of drugs, the pain measures were analyzed using only the data from the first (predrug) testing session of each of the two days. The analyses of variance yielded no statistically significant results in terms of a twin factor for any of predrug pain measures. Additionally, to utilize all of the available data from the ten pairs, a nonparametric approach was used, comparing intraindividual response differences with intrapair differences and with differences between unrelated individuals. Accordingly, three distributions of scores (intraindividual, intrapair, cotwins, and intrapair, unrelated) were computed each for pain threshold (PAIN) and pain tolerance (STOP). For the first distribution, each subject's score on day 1 (preplacebo administration) was subtracted from his score on day 2 (premorphine administration), yielding 20 intraindividual difference scores. Subtracting the score of one twin from the score of the cotwin provided 20 absolute intrapair differences (one for each pair on each of the two days). In order to obtain data for the unrelated pairs, subjects were matched with those run as closely as possible in terms of experiment dates, except that in no case was a twin matched with his cotwin.

Median latency scores were computed for each of these three distributions for both the PAIN and the STOP measures (Table 2). Pain threshold as measured by the PAIN response failed to show any influence of genetic relatedness, the median intraindividual, intrapair (cotwins) and unrelated pair differences being 4.0, 3.5,

TABLE 2. Differences in Pain Threshold (PAIN) and Pain Tolerance (STOP) Among Ten Twin Pairs Prior to Drug Administration

| | Absolute differences in response latencies (seconds) | | | | | |
| | Intraindividual | | Intrapair (cotwins) | | Intrapair (unrelated) | |
Measure	Median	Range	Median	Range	Median	Range
PAIN	4.0	0–15	3.5	0–20	4.5	0–22
STOP	8.0	0–86	22.0	0–263	45.5	5–285

TABLE 3. Differences in Pain Threshold (PAIN) and Pain Tolerance (STOP) Among Ten Twin Pairs Following Administration of Placebo and Morphine

| | Absolute intrapair differences in response latencies (seconds) | | | |
| | Intrapair (cotwins) | | Intrapair (unrelated) | |
Measure	Median	Range	Median	Range
PAIN–Placebo	2.5	0–27	4.5	0–13
PAIN–Morphine	5.5	1–19	5.5	0–24
STOP-Placebo	34.5	0–262	25.0	13–279
STOP-Morphine	48.0	0–217	142.5	28–276

and 4.5 seconds, respectively. There was, however, a strong suggestion that pain tolerance was associated with degree of genetic relatedness, the respective medians on the STOP measure being 8.0, 22.0, and 45.5 seconds for intraindividual, intrapair (cotwins) and unrelated pair differences. In spite of these considerable differences, none was found to reach statistical significance by nonparametric tests of intraclass correlation (Kruskal-Wallis test).

The ten pairs were also examined for differences in immediate (45 minutes) responses to morphine (Talbe 3). As was the case prior to drug administration, no significant differences in threshold (PAIN) responses between cotwins and unrelated twins were noted following administration of either placebo or morphine. Similarly, there was no significant twin pair effect present for tolerance (STOP) responses following placebo. However, there was a suggestion of genetic similarity in the tolerance (STOP) response following morphine. The median absolute response latency for unrelated pairs was nearly three times that of the cotwins, although this difference was not statistically significant when examined by nonparametric tests for intraclass correlation (Kruskal-Wallis test). Correcting the response latency data by subtracting predrug values (first testing session) from postdrug values (second testing session) produced similar, though smaller and not statistically significant differences between cotwins and unrelated twins.

To summarize the cold pressor test pain results, genetic similarity was not expressed in terms of pain threshold either before or after administration of morphine, but there were trends indicating the influence of genetic factors on pain tolerance prior to and following morphine administration.

Psychological Responses

Analyses of variance across all six measurement sessions (Table 4) revealed significant twin pair effects on two measures of anxiety, the PIRS, and GGVS, with a trend in the same direction also on the NIMH Anxiety scale. That is, variability in ratings of anxiety was greater between different twin pairs than within the same twin pair. Similarly, the effects of twin pairs were significant for both the PIRS and the NIMH Hostility scales. Of the three GGVS measures of hostility, however, only the measure of Ambivalent Hostility showed a significant twin pair effect.

TABLE 4. Analysis of Variance of Within-Pair vs Between-Pair Responses on Psychological Measures Among Ten Twin Pairs

Variable[a]	F^b	P
Anxiety		
PIRS	4.71	<0.02
GGVS	5.25	<0.01
NIMH	2.51	0.05 < P < 0.10
Hostility		
PIRS	7.19	<0.005
NIMH	4.16	<0.02
GGVS		
Ambivalent	5.25	<0.01
Inward	2.11	NS
Outward	0.69	NS
Cognitive dysfunction/loss		
PIRS	3.04	<0.05
NIMH	0.64	NS
Fatigue		
PIRS	3.93	<0.05
NIMH	0.69	NS
Depression (PIRS)	2.40	0.05 < P < 0.10
Other mood scales		
Obsessive/compulsive (PIRS)	5.75	<0.01
Suspiciousness (PIRS)	10.00	<0.001
Extroversion (PIRS)	3.88	<0.05
Carefree (NIMH)	0.77	NS
Friendliness (NIMH)	1.09	NS
Timed tests		
DSS	9.91	<0.001
Tapping	7.48	<0.005

[a]See text for description of variables.
[b]There were 9 and 10 degrees of freedom for the numerator and denominator, respectively, in all comparisons.

The PIRS ratings revealed a significant effect of twin pairs on Cognitive Dysfunction and Fatigue, whereas the NIMH self-reports of Cognitive Loss and Fatigue did not. There was a trend toward a significant twin pair effect on the PIRS measure of Depression. Significant twin pair effects emerged also for the PIRS categories of Obsessive/Compulsive, Suspiciousness, and Extroversion, but not on the NIMH measures of Carefree or Friendliness. Scores on the NIMH Depression and Guilt/Shame scales did not vary sufficiently to permit statistical analysis. Both timed tests, DSS and Tapping, showed strong twin pair effects.

Neither the ARCI scales nor the LFJ scale demonstrated significant twin effects. However, eight of the 20 subjects reported becoming nauseated or were observed to vomit following the injection of morphine, and the twin pairs showed complete concordance for the presence or absence of this phenomenon. No subjects experienced these symptoms following injection of placebo.

Examination of the data for differential responses to placebo and morphine by nonparametric analysis of within-pairs vs unrelated pairs scores failed to reveal significant twin pair effects on any of the psychological measures or on the two psychomotor performance tasks.

DISCUSSION

Even though ten pairs constitute a very small sample of twins and although the study was handicapped further by the unavailability of a dizygotic comparison group and by marked intraindividual variability on many of the measures, the results suggest that genetic as well as nongenetic determinants may exert significant influences upon responses to pain and to their modification by morphine. That is, twin partners tended to be more similar in pain tolerance than were unrelated individuals. The fact that the observed differences failed to reach statistical signif-icance may be due to the small sample size, especially in light of the considerable intraindividual variability. While the failure to observe twin pair effects in pain threshold responses may be due to the absence of significant genetic similarities, it may also be related to response criteria. That is, threshold pain may be too imprecise an end point, the subjective criterion for slight pain being less reliable than criteria for pain of greater severity [5]. Moreover, morphine is known to have a lesser effect on pain threshold than on pain tolerance [5, 52].

There is an alternative explanation for the observed differences in response latencies between pain threshold and tolerance. There are strong sociocultural determinants of responses to pain associated with behavior patterns which are learned from, or influenced by, family, sex, and ethnic groups [eg, 40, 49]. It is possible that the learned component of pain perception is reflected in tolerance responses, whereas threshold responses comprise an unlearned component [29]. Thus the observed intrapair (cotwin) similarities may reflect the nongenetic common environmental influences shared by twins reared together. However, were this the reason for the observed differences, similar results should have been found for pain tolerance response latencies not only after morphine but following placebo, as well. The results, therefore, do not permit any definitive conclusions at this time.

Significant heritabilities of various personality factors have been reported in the literature [11, 15, 16, 21, 36] and the results of the psychological ratings across all testing sessions are in agreement with these earlier reports. The fact that, for the psychological ratings in general, observer ratings consistently yielded more similar values for twin partners than for unrelated individuals, while self-reports did so to a much lesser degree, might be explained in part by observer bias, since observers, even if seeing the two twin partners at different times, could not remain blind to their identities. To reduce this bias, twin partners were never seen on the same day and often more than a week elapsed between respective ratings of cotwins. More-over, two of the five verbal sample scales (GGVS) showed significantly smaller within-pair than between-pair variance and the verbal samples were scored blindly from typed protocols by persons who never saw the subjects. It is possible that the NIMH and ARCI measures are less sensitive to the effects of genetic determinants than the observer-rated instruments; but a more plausible explanation lies in the liklihood that significant differences may have gone undetected owing to the small variabilities in scores within this small sample.

The striking genetic similarity across all testing sessions in response to timed tests (DSS and Tapping), generally considered to be measures of psychomotor performance, is entirely consistent with previous reports of heritability of these skills [12, 13, 23, 24, 41].

The fact that nausea or vomiting in response to morphine administration was completely concordant for twin pairs is a finding that clearly deserves further exploration. It is interesting to note that only three of the ten pairs of twins lived together and that all three of these pairs were among the four pairs of twins who became nauseated following morphine injection. Clearly, shared environmental factors may have been of prime importance, or, genetic vulnerability to this effect of morphine might be related to other factors which, in aggregate, resulted in the cotwins' living together.

A genetic component in responses to morphine was not identified on either the psychological measures or the psychomotor performance tasks. In view of the suggested genetic similarities in pain responses, in many of the psychological measures, and in both of the psychomotor tasks across all sessions, this result is unexpected. However, the most likely explanation lies in the combination of uncontrolled state dependent variables, marked intraindividual variability and small sample size obscuring any genetic factors that may have been present.

The results of this limited study are consistent with the notion that subjective responses to narcotics are influenced by genetic components as well as environmental factors. Additional investigations with larger samples of MZ twins and comparison groups of DZ pairs are required in order to explore further these preliminary observations.

ACKNOWLEDGMENTS

This research was supported in part by grant MH-31357 from the National Institute of Drug Abuse, United States Public Health Service. Computing assistance was obtained from the Health Sciences Computing Facility, UCLA, supported by NIH Special Research Resources Grant RR-3. The assistance of Drs. Anne Spence and Robert Sparkes in carrying out examinations for determinations of zygosity and of Dr. Goldine C. Gleser in providing the scores for the written transcripts of the GGVS is hereby gratefully acknowledged.

REFERENCES

1. Alexanderson B, Evans DAP, Sjöqvist F: Steady-state plasma levels of nortriptyline in twins: Influence of genetic factors and drug therapy. Br Med J 4:764–768, 1969.
2. Asberg M, Evans DAP, Sjöqvist F: Genetic control of nortriptyline plasma levels in man: A study of the relatives of propositi with high plasma concentration. J Med Genet 8:129–135, 1971.
3. Beecher HK: "Measurement of Subjective Responses: Quantitative Effects of Drugs." New York: Oxford University Press, 1959, p 164.
4. Beecher HK: Pain: One mystery solved. Science 151:840–841, 1966.
5. Beecher HK: The measurement of pain in man: A re-inspection of the work of the Harvard group. In Soulairac A, Cahn J, Charpentier J (eds): "Pain." London: Academic Press, 1968, pp 201–213.

6. Broadhurst PL: Pharmacogenetics. In Iverson LL, Iverson SD, Snyder SH (eds): "Handbook of Psychopharmacology, Vol. 7, Principles of Behavioral Pharmacology." New York: Plenum Press, 1977, pp 265–320.
7. Broadhust PL: "Drugs and the Inheritance of Behavior." New York: Plenum Press, 1978.
8. Cascorbi HF, Vesell ES, Blake DA, Helrich M: Genetic and environmental influence on halothane metabolism in twins. Clin Pharmacol Ther 12:50–55, 1971.
9. Eidelberg E, Erspamer R, Kreinick CJ, Harris J: Differences in locomotor activity, tolerance and dependence in response to morphine among four inbred strains of mice. Eur J Pharmacol 32:329–336, 1975.
10. Eriksson K, Kiianmaa K: Genetic analysis of susceptibility to morphine addiction in inbred mice. Ann Med Exp Biol Fenn 45:389–392, 1971.
11. Eysenck HJ: The inheritance of extraversion-introversion. Acta Psychol 12:95–110, 1956.
12. Eysenck HJ, Prell DB: The inheritance of neuroticism: An experimental study. J Ment Sci 97:442–465, 1951.
13. Feingold L: A psychometric study of senescent twins. Unpublished doctoral dissertation, Columbia University, 1950.
14. Gebhart GF, Mitchell CL: Strain differences in the analgesic response to morphine as measured on the hot plate. Arch Int Pharmacodyn Ther 201:128–140, 1973.
15. Gottesman II: Heritability of personality: A demonstration. Psychol Monogr 77:1–21, 1963.
16. Gottesman II: Personality and natural selection. In Vandenberg SG (ed): "Methods and Goals in Human Behavior Genetics." New York: Academic Press, 1965, pp 63–74.
17. Gottschalk LA, Gleser GC: "The Measurement of Psychological States Through the Content Analysis of Verbal Behavior." Berkeley: University of California Press, 1969.
18. Haertzen CA, Hill HE, Bellville RE: Development of the Addiction Research Center Inventory (ARCI): Selection of items that are sensitive to the effects of various drugs. Psychopharmacologia 4:155–166, 1963.
19. Hardy JD, Wolff HG, Goodell H: "Pain Sensations and Reactions." Baltimore: Williams and Wilkins, 1952.
20. Hilgard ER: A neodissociation interpretation of pain reduction in hypnosis. Psychol Rev 80:396–411, 1973.
21. Horn JM, Plomin R, Roseman R: Heritability of personality traits in adult male twins. Behav Genet 6:17–30, 1976.
22. Jaffe JH, Martin WR: Narcotic analgesics and antagonists. In Goodman LS, Gilman A (eds): "The Pharmacological Basis of Therapeutics." New York: Macmillan, 1975, pp 245–283.
23. Jarvik LF, Kallmann FJ, Lorge I, Falek A: Longitudinal study of intellectual changes in senescent twins. In Tibbits C, Donahue W (eds): "Social and Psychological Aspects of Aging." New York: Columbia University Press, 1962, pp 839–859.
24. Kallmann FJ, Feingold L, Bondy E: Comparative adaptational, social, and psychometric data on the life histories of senescent twin pairs. Am J Hum Genet 3:65–73, 1951.
25. Kalow W: "Pharmacogenetics: Heredity and the Response to Drugs." Philadelphia: W.B. Saunders, 1962.
26. Kalow W: Topics in pharmacogenetics. Ann NY Acad Sci 179:654–659, 1971.
27. Lambert E, Libman E, Poser EG: The effect of increased salience of a membership group on pain tolerance. J Pers 28:350–354, 1960.
28. Lasagna L, von Felsinger JM, Beecher HK: Drug-induced mood changes in man. Ann Med Assoc 157:1006–1014, 1955.
29. Liebeskind JC, Paul LA: Psychological and physiological mechanisms of pain. Ann Rev Psychol 28:41–60, 1977.
30. Melzack R: "The Puzzle of Pain." New York: Basic Books, 1973, p 46.
31. Melzack R, Scott TH: The effects of early experience on the responses to pain. Comp Physiol Psychol 50:155–162, 1957.

32. Nichols JR, Hsiao S: Addiction liability of albino rats: Breeding for quantitative differences in morphine drinking. Science 157:561–563, 1967.
33. Oliverio A, Castellano C: Exploratory activity: Genetic analysis of its modification by various pharmacologic agents. In Eleftheriou BE (ed): "Psychopharmacogenetics." New York: Plenum Press, 1975, pp 99–126.
34. Page JG, Vesell ES: Hepatic drug metabolism in ten strains of Norway rat before and after pretreatment with phenobarbital. Proc Soc Exp Biol Med 131:256–261, 1969.
35. Raskin A, Schulterbrandt JG, Reatig N, McKeon JJ: Differential response to chlorpromazine, imipramine and placebo: A study of subgroups of hospitalized depressed patients. Arch Gen Psychiatry 23:164–173, 1970.
36. Scarr S: Social introversion-extraversion as a heritable response. Child Dev 40:823–832, 1969.
37. Shuster L, Webster GW, Yu G, Eleftheriou BE: A genetic analysis of the response to morphine in mice: Analgesia and running. Psychopharmacologia 42:249–254, 1975.
38. Smith GM, Beecher HK: Subjective effects of heroin and morphine in normal subjects. Pharmacol Exp Ther 136:47–52, 1962.
39. Sternbach RA, Tursky B: Ethnic differences among housewives in psychophysical and skin potential responses to electric shock. Psychophysiology 1:241–248, 1965.
40. Tursky B, Sternbach RA: Further physiological correlates of ethnic differences in response to shock. Psychophysiology 4:67–64, 1967.
41. Vandenberg SG: The hereditary abilities study: Heredity components in a pyschological test battery. Am J Hum Genet 14:220–237, 1962.
42. Vesell ES: Drug metabolism in man. Ann NY Acad Sci 179:1–773, 1971.
43. Vesell ES: Pharmacogenetics. Biochem Pharmacol 24:445–450, 1975.
44. Vesell ES, Page JG: Genetic control of drug levels in man: Phenylbutazone. Science 159:1479–1480, 1968.
45. Vesell ES, Page JG: Genetic control of drug levels in man: Antipyrine. Science 161:72–73, 1968.
46. Vesell ES, Page JG: Genetic control of dicoumarol levels in man. J Clin Invest 47:2657–2663, 1968.
47. Vesell ES, Page JG, Passananti TG: Genetic and environmental factors affecting ethanol metabolism in man. Clin Pharmacol Ther 12:192–201, 1971.
48. Wechsler D: "Manual for the Wechsler Adult Intelligence Scale." New York: Psychological Corporation, 1955.
49. Weisenberg M, Kreindler ML, Schachat R, Werboff J: Pain: Anxiety and attitudes in black, white, and Puerto Rican patients. Psychosom Med 37:123–135, 1975.
50. Wissler C: The sun dance of the Blackfoot Indians. American Museum of Natural History Anthropology Papers 16:223–270, 1921.
51. Wolf S, Hardy JD: Studies on pain: Observations on pain due to local cooling and on factors involved in the "cold pressor" effect. J Clin Invest 20:521–533, 1941.
52. Wolff BB, Kantor TG, Jarvik ME, Laska E: Response of experimental pain to analgesic drugs. Clin Pharmacol Ther 7:224–238, 1966.

Twin Research 3: Epidemiological
and Clinical Studies, pages 117—130
© 1981 Alan R. Liss, Inc., 150 Fifth Avenue, New York, NY 10011

Twin Research in Coronary Heart Disease

Kåre Berg

*Institute of Medical Genetics, University of Oslo, and Department of
Medical Genetics, City of Oslo*

INTRODUCTION

Several twin studies on atherosclerotic disease, particularly on coronary heart
disease (CHD) and on factors thought to predispose for such disease, have appeared. These studies, which are too numerous to quote on this occasion, have
mostly given results suggesting that genetic factors are of considerable importance
in this category of disease. For instance, at the Second International Congress on
Twin Studies, our group presented data, from a limited twin study, indicating a
significant genetic influence on several lipid and lipoprotein parameters. In some
instances, however, the data were inconclusive, because of the limited size of the
twin series examined.

Despite the considerable attention paid over the last few years to some specific
"risk factors," it should be kept in mind that it remains highly probable that
several factors, genetic as well as environmental, contribute to the development of
this group of disorders. Thus particular attention has been paid to the hyperlipidemias for several years, and it is clear that monogenic, polygenic, and nutri-
tionally caused hyperlipidemias exist. There is an increasing interest in the role of
one specific atherogenic lipoprotein: the Lp(a) lipoprotein. In the case of high-
density lipoprotein (HDL), it is a reduced level that constitutes a risk factor.
Hypertension is also a well-established risk factor. Less attention has been paid to
the fact that there seems to be considerable familial clustering of cases of coronary
heart disease, even independent of the factors mentioned. Among the many en-
vironmental/nutritional risk factors known or suspected, the effect of smoking has
been particularly well examined.

Data included in this report are from studies supported by grants from the Norwegian Council on
Cardiovascular Diseases and the Norwegian Research Council for Science and the Humanities and by
National Institutes of Health grant HD 10291.

Our group has for a number of years been interested in the lipoprotein/athero-sclerosis field. We have tried to approach this area from several angles. Originally, our twin study approach to this problem had a rather limited scope. This has, however, been very significantly broadened over the last 4 years because of an extensive study on Norwegian same-sexed twins that is now being conducted as a joint venture between our group in Oslo and the Department of Human Genetics, Medical College of Virginia.

The central element in this project is a very extensive questionnaire study comprising several diseases and birth defects, reproductive performance, social and behavioural characteristics, and a number of normal physical traits. Because of our particular interest in this area, we are conducting a separate questionnaire subsection study of atherosclerotic diseases. Also, the study comprises a most interesting subsection on death-discordant twins. In addition to the questionnaire part, a subset of twin families is being analysed with respect to biochemical characteristics relevant to atherosclerotic disease. When applicable, these studies will comprise clinical analyses relevant to atherosclerosis. The present report comprises information relevant to atherosclerosis, available at this stage.

MATERIALS AND METHODS

The basis for this study is a population-based twin register comprising all twin pairs born in Norway from 1915 and onwards, and formed by amalgamating two previously existing registers. The questionnaire study will, eventually, comprise all available twin pairs born in Norway between 1915 and 1960. Present addresses of living twins are traced from the records of the Central Census Bureau. At first, the twins are sent a brief questionnaire aimed at establishing their likely zygosity and family status and securing their cooperation. Those who agree to cooperate are subsequently sent the second questionnaire, which is an extensive one, dealing with a considerable number of diseases, birth defects, and normal morphological or physiological traits. The response rate runs around 72−73% following the original mailing and one single reminder.

The present status of the questionnaire study for the years 1915−1951 is summarized in Table 1. More than 16,000 first questionnaires have been mailed, and over 9,000 have been returned. Approximately half of the more than 6,000 copies of the second questionnaire have been filled in and returned to us.

In a subset of 208 same-sexed twin pairs, ten genetic marker systems were examined to establish zygosity. The study showed that the zygosity information obtained from the first questionnaire had a very high degree of reliability (data to be published in detail by Magnus et al). The purpose was to include in this subset 100 female and 100 male pairs with half of the pairs being around 35 and the other half around 60 years of age.

The genetic marker studies were done by traditional methods. Serum triglycerides and cholesterol were determined by enzymatic methods employing a fast centrifugal analyser, and quantitative determination of serum apoproteins were conducted with antiserum of our own production in radial immunodiffusion tests. Lp(a) typing was done by double immunodiffusion, employing antiserum of our own production. All laboratory analyses were conducted blindly.

TABLE 1. Questionnaire Study of Norwegian Twins Born in the Years 1915—1951: Status as of June 1980

Number of same-sexed twin pairs traced	8,296
Number of first questionnaires sent	16,577
Number of first questionnaires received	9,355
Number of second questionnaires sent	6,272
Number of second questionnaires received	3,201

The data presented in this report were evaluated by chi square tests, determination of Fisher's exact P, or variance analyses. Intraclass correlation coefficients (r) were calculated and used to estimate heritability and the effect of common environment. Heritability was calculated from the formula $h^2 = 2(r_{MZ} - r_{DZ})$ and the effect of common environment as $c^2 = 2r_{DZ} - r_{MZ}$.

RESULTS

Zygosity in Pairs Where Both Members Are Alive as Opposed to Where One Member Has Died After the Age of 20 Years

According to the design of the study, the surviving member of twin pairs in which one member has died will be sent the extensive second questionnaire at a later stage. We expect the separate study of death-discordant monozygotic (MZ) twins to be particularly interesting, but we are at this stage not able to present results. However, since the first questionnaire has been returned also for pairs where one member has died, we have been able to compare the zygosity, as judged from the questionnaire information, between pairs where both are alive and pairs where one twin has died. When only deaths after the age of 20 years were counted, 42% of the same-sexed twin pairs were MZ in the group where both twins were alive, whereas the corresponding frequency was 35% in the group where one twin had died (Table 2).

Since deaths from atherosclerotic diseases would mostly not occur until after the age of 40 years, we have also made this comparison counting, in the second group, only those pairs in which the deceased twin had died when he or she was 41 years old or more. The frequency of MZ pairs was only 33% in this restricted group of death-discordant pairs (Table 3). Presumably, in this small group, a significant number of deaths was from atherosclerotic disease. At this stage, we merely consider this information as a suggestion that death discordance in middle-aged twin pairs is not independent of zygosity. The genetic causes for death concordance in MZ twins to which we are alluding are not limited to atherosclerotic disease.

Approaches to Coronary Heart Disease in Twin Studies

Among the options available, we have at this stage used the following approaches to coronary heart disease in our twin study: From the questionnaire studies, we are analysing death discordance and zygosity as already mentioned; furthermore, we are comparing monozygotic and dizygotic (DZ) twins with respect to presence of CHD.

TABLE 2. Norwegian Same-Sexed Twin Pairs Born 1915—1948: Zygosity in Pairs Where Both Are Alive vs Pairs Where One Member Has Died After the Age of 20 Years

Category	MZ		DZ		
	N	%	N	%	Total
Both twins alive	2,167	42	3,010	58	5,177
One alive, one dead 20—65 years of age	118	35	219	65	337
Total	2,285		3,229		5,514

$\chi^2 = 5.8$; $0.01 < P < 0.02$.

TABLE 3. Norwegian Same-Sexed Twin Pairs Born 1915—1948: Zygosity in Pairs Where Both Are Alive vs Pairs Where One Member Has Died at 41—65 Years of Age

Category	MZ		DZ		
	N	%	N	%	Total
Both twins alive	2,167	42	3,010	58	5,177
One alive, one dead 41—65 years of age	56	33	114	67	170
Total	2,223		3,124		5,347

$\chi^2 = 5.0$; $0.02 < P < 0.03$.

In the biochemical area, we are studying heritability of several lipid and lipoprotein parameters, incuding total serum cholesterol, serum triglycerides, low-density lipoprotein (LDL), Lp(a) lipoprotein, and the HDL apoproteins apo-AI and apo-AII. In this report, I shall summarize the questionnaire studies and the biochemical analyses.

In addition, we have examined, by a new approach, the possible restrictive effect of several normal genetic markers on environmentally caused variation in serum lipid and lipoprotein parameters. These data will be presented by Magnus et al [6]. Furthermore, a subset of twins has been examined in an effort to reveal possible genetic control of cell membrane LDL receptor activity in healthy people. This study will be presented by Golden et al [4]. Finally, Heiberg et al [5] will present results of studies on the genetic influence on blood pressure and Møller et al [8] will introduce data showing that there is a significant genetic influence on the cardiac conductive system.

Coronary Heart Disease in Monozygotic and Dizygotic Twin Pairs

For the purpose of the present report, the available information was screened with respect to presence of CHD as judged from a "yes" response to the angina pectoris and/or myocardial infarction question in the questionnaire. Both

TABLE 4. Norwegian Same-Sexed Twin Pairs (Both Members Alive) Born 1915–1940: Zygosity in Pairs Where at Least One Member Has Coronary Heart Disease (Angina Pectoris and/or Myocardial Infarction) (Data as of June 1980)

Category	No. of twin pairs		
	MZ	DZ	Total
Both members affected	19	3	22
One member affected	10[a]	9[b]	19
Total	29	12	41

$\chi^2 = 4.1$; $0.03 < P < 0.05$.
[a]In five pairs, the unaffected member had hypertension.
[b]In one pair, the unaffected member had hypertension.

TABLE 5. Norwegian Same-Sexed Twin Pairs (Both Members Alive) 60 Years Old or Younger: Zygosity in Pairs Where at Least One Member Has Coronary Heart Disease (Angina Pectoris and/or Myocardial Infarction) (Data as of June 1980)

Category	No. of twin pairs		
	MZ	DZ	Total
Both members affected	10	2	12
One member affected	2	7	9
Total	12	9	21

Fisher's exact P = 0.008.

members were affected in 19 out of 29 MZ pairs, as compared to only three out of 12 DZ pairs (Table 4). In the pairs where only one member was affected, the unaffected member had hypertension in five out of 10 MZ pairs, as opposed to in one out of nine DZ pairs. Thus the difference in likeness with respect to coronary heart disease proneness between MZ and DZ pairs may be even greater than suggested here. Taken at face value, this result appears to point to a significant genetic component to the etiology of CHD as it occurs in the general twin population.

There are sound reasons to believe that genetic factors are particularly important in coronary heart disease occurring at a relatively young age. Therefore, the data were inspected also after exclusion of affected pairs who were more than 60 years old (Table 5). At this relatively early stage of the twin study, we have full information on only 21 twin pairs with CHD by the age of 60 years or younger. Among the 12 MZ pairs in this group, both members were affected in ten cases. In the DZ group, both members were affected in two out of nine pairs. This difference between MZ and DZ pairs was highly significant (Table 5).

Taken at face value, this preliminary result suggests a concordance rate of 0.66 and 0.25 in MZ and DZ pairs, respectively, when all pairs are considered, and of 0.83 and 0.22 when only pairs with disease manifestation by the age of 60 years or younger are considered (Table 6). Although the result from this small series must be interpreted with great caution, it appears that the concordance rate may differ considerably between MZ and DZ pairs, and strikingly when only pairs with disease manifestations at a relatively young age are considered. In this preliminary summary, we have not taken into account the time elapsed between the first occurrence of CHD, and the questionnaire study. This information on discordant pairs would be highly relevant.

Heritability Analyses of Serum Lipid Levels

Table 7 shows intraclass correlation coefficients (r) for MZ and DZ male and female pairs as well as estimates of heritability and of the effect of common environment, for total serum cholesterol. A significant contribution of genes to total serum cholesterol level is suggested in males as well as in females. Table 8 shows corresponding data for serum triglycerides. We found no evidence of a genetic influence on their level in males but a clear suggestion of such an effect in females. Thus the data concerning triglycerides must be interpreted with great caution.

Heritability Study of Apoprotein B of Low-Density Lipoprotein

Heritability analyses of apo-B gave results compatible with a strong genetic influence on the concentration of this lipoprotein component (Table 9). The difference from the results obtained with total serum cholesterol analyses suggests that apo-B determination is a more useful parameter than total serum cholesterol determination. The atherogenic LDL, in which apo-B resides, is the main carrier of cholesterol in serum. However, total serum cholesterol does measure other lipoprotein components, including antiatherogenic HDL.

Heritability of Lp(a) Lipoprotein

Table 10 shows the result of Lp(a) typing of 208 same-sexed Norwegian twin pairs. The 101 MZ pairs examined exhibited no example of one member having the Lp(a+) and the other the Lp(a−) phenotype; in all cases both twins were either Lp(a+) or Lp(a−). Of the 107 DZ pairs, almost one-fourth were discordant for Lp phenotype, as would be expected.

The results obtained with the MZ pairs as well as the difference between the MZ and DZ categories would be extremely unlikely to occur if the Lp(a) phenotypes were not genetically determined.

Heritability Analyses of High-Density Lipoprotein Apoprotein Levels

HDL, the smallest lipoprotein particle that has the highest content of protein and the lowest contents of lipids, has become the subject of considerable interest in the last several years since there is strong evidence that this lipoprotein has an antiatherogenic effect. Thus people with a high HDL level have some degree of protection against CHD. Determination of the cholesterol part of HDL is possible

TABLE 6. Norwegian Same-Sexed Twin Pairs (Both Members Alive): Concordance Rates for Coronary Heart Disease (Angina Pectoris and/or Myocardial Infarction) (Data as of June 1980)

Category	MZ pairs Rate N	DZ pairs Rate N
All affected pairs	0.66 29	0.25 12
Affected pairs, 60 years or younger	0.83 12	0.22 9

TABLE 7. Fasting Norwegian Same-Sexed Twin Pairs Analysed for Total Serum Cholesterol (1980 Study) (Number of Pairs in Parentheses)

Parameter	Male pairs	Female pairs	All pairs
r_{MZ}	0.47 (33)	0.59 (43)	0.52 (76)
r_{DZ}	0.27 (34)	0.39 (47)	0.35 (81)
h^2	0.40	0.40	0.34
c^2	0.07	0.19	0.18

TABLE 8. Fasting Norwegian Same-Sexed Twin Pairs Analysed for Serum Triglycerides (1980 Study) (Number of Pairs in Parentheses)

Parameter	Male pairs	Female pairs	All pairs
r_{MZ}	0.31 (34)	0.60 (44)	0.47 (78)
r_{DZ}	0.31 (34)	0.24 (50)	0.27 (84)
h^2	0.00	0.72	0.40
c^2	0.31	−0.12	0.07

TABLE 9. Fasting Norwegian Same-Sexed Twin Pairs Analysed for Apoprotein B (1980 Study) (Number of Pairs in Parentheses)

Parameter	Male pairs	Female pairs	All pairs
r_{MZ}	0.59 (35)	0.84 (43)	0.73 (78)
r_{DZ}	0.33 (33)	0.47 (47)	0.40 (80)
h^2	0.52	0.74	0.66
c^2	0.07	0.10	0.07

but certain methodological objections exist to the use of such determination as screening or clinical method. It appears much more satisfactory to determine the protein part also of HDL, much the way as we have done for apo-B of LDL and for Lp(a) lipoprotein.

We were able to demonstrate, shortly after Miller and Miller [7] had published their hypothesis of an antiatherogenic effect of HDL, that patients with CHD do in fact have a lower level of the main HDL apoprotein: apo-AI [2, 3]. We have also reported [1] preliminary data suggesting a genetic influence on apo-AI level and possibly also on apo-AII level. However, in a recent publication, Sistonen and Ehnholm [9] reported on a seasonal variation in apo-AI level and presented data indicating only a small contribution of genes to the level of apo-AI. Because of the limited size of our previously published series [1], results obtained in the new twin series are presented here. A total of 198 same-sexed pairs were analysed (Table 11). The within-pair variance was different between MZ and DZ pairs in the total series as well as when females alone were considered (Table 11). In the male series, the F ratio for within-pair variance was not significant between MZ and DZ pairs. However, in this case, the total variance was unequal between MZ and DZ pairs (whereas it was not for females alone or for the total series).

To eliminate any introduction of a bias caused by seasonal variation or by a storage effect on serum, we also made the analyses counting only those pairs where both members had been bled on the same day. The results were essentially the same as for the total series (Table 12). We concluded that a seasonal or storage effect, as suggested by the study of Sistonen and Ehnholm [9], did not appear to be present in our series, and that our present results were in agreement with those from our preliminary twin series [1].

Table 13 summarizes results of variance analyses for apo-AII of HDL. The difference between MZ and DZ• pairs with respect to within-pair variance was highly significant, in each sex group as well as in the total series. Total variance was in all cases sufficiently similar between MZ and DZ pairs not to create any problem.

Analyses were also repeated in this case on only those pairs where both members had been bled on the same day. The results were essentially the same as those from the total series (Table 14), with the exception that the difference between MZ and DZ pairs with respect to within-pair variance became significant at the 0.001 level. Thus we found no suggestion of a seasonal or storage effect on apo-AII level. In the case of apo-AII, we had no problem with an unequal total variance between the two categories of twins. The difference between MZ and DZ pairs with respect to within-pair variance was striking.

Since we found no confounding effect such as the one described by Sistonen and Ehnholm [9] and since in only one case did we have a problem with an unequal total variance between MZ and DZ pairs, we proceeded to calculate intrapair correlation coefficients from the variance values arrived at, for apo-AI. Table 15 shows the intraclass correlation coefficients for each twin category and sex group as well as for the total series. The resulting heritability estimates were striking (Table 15).

Figure 1 shows the distribution of apo-AI levels in male twins, counting only the first twin in each pair, and Figure 2 shows the distribution of apo-AI levels in

TABLE 10. Results of Lp(a) Typing of 208 Same-Sexed Norwegian Twin Pairs
(1980 Study)

Twin category	Number of twin pairs			
	One Lp (a+) twin and one Lp (a−)	Both twins Lp (a+)	Both twins Lp (a−)	Total
MZ	0	26	75	101
DZ	23	14	70	107

TABLE 11. Norwegian Same-Sexed Twin Pairs Analysed for apo-AI (Whole Series)

Category		N	Variance			F ratio (within)
			Total	Among	Within	
Males	MZ	44	1.18	1.87	0.50	1.46
	DZ	46	0.77	0.82	0.73	
Females	MZ	54	1.07	1.61	0.54	2.00**
	DZ	54	1.19	1.31	1.08	
All	MZ	98	1.12	1.71	0.52	1.77**
	DZ	100	1.00	1.08	0.92	

**$P < 0.01$.

TABLE 12. Norwegian Same-Sexed Twin Pairs Analysed for apo-AI (Both Members
Bled Same Day)

Category		N	Variance			F ratio (within)
			Total	Among	Within	
Males	MZ	29	1.30	2.13	0.50	1.44
	DZ	22	0.78	0.85	0.72	
Females	MZ	45	1.15	1.85	0.46	2.17**
	DZ	35	1.21	1.42	1.00	
All	MZ	74	1.22	1.96	0.48	1.85**
	DZ	57	1.04	1.18	0.89	

**$P < 0.01$.

female twins. If the suggestion of a deviation from unimodality should be confirmed, the possibility that major genes influence apo-AI level cannot be discarded. A
true deviation from unimodality would point to the possibility that the high degree
of heritability found for apo-AI level may reflect the presence of such major
genes.

TABLE 13. Norwegian Same-Sexed Twin Pairs Analysed for apo-AII (Whole Series))

Category		N	Variance			F ratio (within)
			Total	Among	Within	
Males	MZ	44	41.5	69.1	14.4	2.68**
	DZ	46	50.4	62.6	38.6	
Females	MZ	54	61.2	106.0	17.0	2.34**
	DZ	54	53.5	67.6	39.8	
All	MZ	98	52.8	90.2	15.8	2.48**
	DZ	100	51.9	64.7	39.2	

**$P < 0.01$.

TABLE 14. Norwegian Same-Sexed Twin Pairs Analysed for apo-AII (Both Members Bled Same Day)

Category		N	Variance			F ratio (within)
			Total	Among	Within	
Males	MZ	29	45.8	75.7	16.9	2.87**
	DZ	22	56.9	65.6	48.5	
Females	MZ	45	63.9	112.6	16.3	2.54**
	DZ	35	55.6	70.2	41.4	
All	MZ	74	56.5	97.0	16.5	2.67***
	DZ	57	55.7	67.4	44.1	

**$P < 0.01$.
***$P < 0.001$.

Table 16 shows intrapair correlation coefficients and heritability estimates for male and female pairs as well as for the total series, with respect to apo-AII level. In this case too, the heritability estimates were high, and this is in contrast to the only moderately high estimates obtained in our preliminary study [1].

Neither in males (Fig. 3) nor in females (Fig. 4) was there any suggestion of a deviation from unimodality in the distribution of apo-AII levels.

DISCUSSION

Several approaches to the study of CHD are employed in the collaborative study of Norwegian twins between the Institute of Medical Genetics, University of Oslo, and the Department of Human Genetics, Medical College of Virginia. At this time, we have been able to present, from the questionnaire study, preliminary data on death discordance and zygosity and on CHD in MZ and DZ twins. As the study proceeds, the questionnaire study will provide data on the offspring of MZ twins that will be analysed by the half-sib model, and a separate subsection on death-discordant twins should provide information relevant to the etiology of several diseases, including atherosclerotic disease.

TABLE 15. Norwegian Same-Sexed Twin Pairs (N = 198) Analysed for apo-AI (Values From Computations Based Only on Pairs Where Both Members Were Bled on the Same Day Are Given in Parentheses)

Parameter	Male pairs	Female pairs	All pairs
r_{MZ}	0.58 (0.62)	0.50 (0.60)	0.53 (0.61)
r_{DZ}	0.06 (0.08)	0.10 (0.17)	0.08 (0.14)
h^2	1.0 (1.0)	0.80 (0.86)	0.90 (0.94)

TABLE 16. Norwegian Same-Sexed Twin Pairs (N = 198) Analysed for apo-AII (Values From Computations Based Only on Pairs Where Both Members Were Bled on the Same Day Are Given in Parentheses)

Parameter	Male pairs	Female pairs	All pairs
r_{MZ}	0.66 (0.63)	0.72 (0.75)	0.70 (0.71)
r_{DZ}	0.24 (0.15)	0.26 (0.26)	0.25 (0.21)
h^2	0.84 (0.96)	0.92 (0.98)	0.90 (1.0)

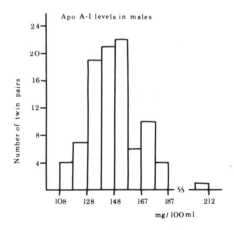

Fig. 1. Distribution of apo-AI levels in male twin pairs. Only one member of each pair has been included.

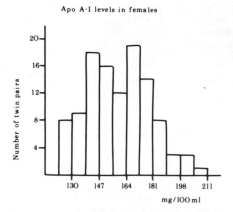

Fig. 2. Distribution of apo-AI levels in female twin pairs. Only one member of each pair has been included.

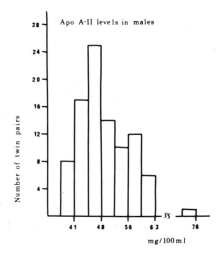

Fig. 3. Distribution of apo-AII levels in male twin pairs. Only one member of each pair has been included.

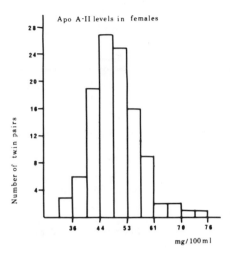

Fig. 4. Distribution of apo-AII levels in female twin pairs. Only one member of each pair has been included.

From a subset of approximately 200 same-sexed twin pairs, we have been able to present biochemical data relevant to the heritability of serum lipid and lipoprotein parameters, and to estimate a possible restrictive effect of normal genetic marker systems on continuous variables. Furthermore, cell culture studies have suggested genetic control of cell membrane LDL receptor activity in healthy people, and clinical studies have shown that there is a genetic influence on the cardiac conductive system. We believe that the combination of an extensive, population-based twin register, of new possibilities for biochemical and cellular analyses, and of new methods for data analyses will make twin studies extremely worthwhile. The new approach to the study of restrictive effects of normal markers on biochemical, continuous parameters also seems promising. Studies on death-discordant MZ twins may uncover important information with respect to etiology of common diseases.

The information on heritability of various lipoprotein parameters, which will be reported in detail elsewhere, is in agreement with previous reports from our group. There may be a considerable gene effect on the level of apo-AI as well as apo-AII, and in the case of apo-AI, an effect of major genes is not ruled out. We see no obvious explanation for the difference between our results and those reported by Sistonen and Ehnholm [9]. However, we have (Børresen and Berg, in preparation) demonstrated potential problems in quantitative determination of apo-AI by immunological methods, since this apoprotein is present in the serum in different species of molecules. Different experimental conditions for each population may be needed for adequate quantitative determination. Also, storage problems may be of importance. Finally, we and the Finnish workers have not applied the same statistical methods.

The area where a clarification may be most needed concerns the discrepancy between MZ and DZ pairs with respect to intraclass correlation coefficients, particularly for apo-AI level (Table 15). Thus, if the very low intraclass correlation coefficients in DZ pairs were to be ignored and heritability were to be estimated from MZ twins alone, the heritability estimate would be significantly reduced. This reduced level would be of the same order of magnitude as that obtained in our previously reported, smaller twin series [1]. Clearly, further studies are needed.

Since HDL has a protective effect against atherosclerotic disease, the determination of its level by hereditary as well as environmental factors should be fully analysed, with the aim to utilize the ensuing information for preventive measures.

REFERENCES

1. Berg K: Genetic influence on variation in serum high density lipoprotein. In Gotto AM Jr, Miller NE, Oliver MF (eds): "High Density Lipoproteins and Atherosclerosis." Amsterdam/New York: Elsevier/North-Holland Biomedical Press, 1978, pp 207—211.
2. Berg K, Børresen A-L, Dahlén G: Serum-high-density-lipoprotein and atherosclerotic heart-disease. Lancet 1:499, 1976.
3. Berg K, Børresen A-L, Frick MH, Dahlén G: Serum-H.D.L. in atherosclerotic heart-disease. Lancet l:1014, 1976.
4. Golden W, Magnus P, Maartmann-Moe K, Berg K, Nance WE: Genetic control of cell membrane low-density lipoprotein (LDL) receptor activity in the absence of familial hypercholesterolemia. Paper presented at the Third International Congress on Twin Studies, Jerusalem, 1980.
5. Heiberg A, Magnus P, Berg K, Nance WE: Blood pressure in Norwegian twins. In Gedda L. Parisi P, Nance WE (eds): "Twin Research 3: Epidemiological and Clinical Studies." New York: Alan R. Liss, 1981, pp163–168.
6. Magnus P, Børrensen AL, Berg K, Nance WE: Possible restrictive effect of normal genetic markers on the variation in serum cholesterol within monozygotic twin pairs. Paper presented at the Third International Congress on Twin Studies, Jerusalem, 1980.
7. Miller GJ, Miller NE: Plasma-high-density-lipoprotein concentration and development of ischaemic heart-disease. Lancet 1:16—19, 1975.
8. Møller P, Heiberg A, Berg K: The atrioventricular conduction time: A heritable trait? Paper presented at the Third International Congress on Twin Studies, Jerusalem, 1980.
9. Sistonen P, Ehnholm C: On the heritability of serum high density lipoprotein in twins. Am J Hum Genet 32:1—7, 1980.

Twin Research 3: Epidemiological
and Clinical Studies, pages 131—138
© 1981 Alan R. Liss, Inc., 150 Fifth Avenue, New York, NY 10011

Stress and Coronary Heart Disease

Einar Kringlen
Institute of Behavioral Sciences in Medicine, University of Oslo

INTRODUCTION

There is now fairly general consensus that environmental factors in general are responsible for the increased incidence of coronary heart disease (CHD) over the last generation. The rapid increase in most Western countries and the great variation in frequency in different regions of the world speak for such a hypothesis. Any alteration of the gene pool in such a short period of time is out of the question. In addition, twin studies have found an insignificant difference with regard to concordance for CHD in monozygotic (MZ) and dizygotic (DZ) twins [1,3].

No specific environmental factors have, however, been identified. Epidemiologic research has, true enough, discovered a series of "risk factors" in CHD. Several studies have shown that factors such as age, sex, blood pressure, cholesterol, cigarette smoking, body weight, and exercise are correlated with the development of CHD. However, only age, sex, systolic blood pressure, and cholesterol are universally accepted as risk factors.

In recent times, an increasing number of clinicians have felt that personality variables and psychic strain might play a role in the etiology of CHD. Most clinicians will remember patients who, after periods of hard work eventually combined with interpersonal conflicts, suddenly have been struck down with coronary infarction. However, scrutiny of the literature shows that the existence of psychosocial factors in the etiology of CHD is not convincingly documented. This might be due to several factors. First, relatively few studies have been carried out in this field; secondly, personality and stress are difficult to measure objectively; and thirdly, most epidemiological studies have relied on questionnaires or superficial interviews where personal problems may be overlooked or denied.

The twin method might throw light on these problems. By comparing MZ and DZ twins with regard to certain diseases, it is possible to get an impression of the relative significance of heredity and environment. Through a comparison of the life histories of discordant pairs, ie, pairs in whom one twin is ill and the cotwin healthy, one can arrive at an evaluation of the environmental factors.

MATERIALS AND METHODS
Sample

One of the problems facing twin research is of course related to sampling. In general, access to a population-based twin register is needed to avoid selected samples. In particular with rare diseases, it is hard to obtain a satisfactory number of twins. In this study, we identified approximately 10,000 40–69-year-old patients of both sexes with CHD (angina pectoris, infarctus cordis) admitted to relatively large medical wards in Norway during the period 1971–75. Their names were checked against our national twin registry, which covers all twin births from 1895 [2]. After exclusion of pairs where the partner had died before the age of 40, we were left with 78 MZ and DZ pairs, of whom one or both had been hospitalized for CHD.

Methods

When the index twin had been identified, a letter was mailed, through the hospital where the patient had been treated, asking the twin to participate in the study and to fill out a short questionnaire regarding zygosity and the cotwin's name and address.

By comparing twins — which one, for instance, is a smoker and which a nonsmoker — it is possible to investigate the etiologic significance of smoking. By comparing twins in whom one is hard-working and the other is not, one can examine the influence of work behavior on the development of CHD.

It is of course hard to measure personality traits objectively. How can one measure how introverted or extroverted, how ambitious or how energetic a person is? However, if one is able to compare two persons, in this case twins with the same sex and age, the chances of obtaining reliable answers are far greater.

The semistructured interview employed lasted approximately 1 hour and covered life history with particular emphasis on work habits, life style, and personality problems, as well as somatic and psychological health during recent years before the occurrence of CHD. In particularly, we were eager to compare the twin partners. With regard to the proband, detailed medical information was available, including ECG. The cotwin was therefore particularly examined with regard to ischemic heart disease. ECG, however, was not routinely taken.

Blood pressure was measured with the patient in sitting position during the end of the visit. A venous blood sample was also taken for determination of cholesterol and zygosity diagnosis. In case of death, information was sought from the family and the surviving twin. In addition, information was supplemented by medical records from physicians and hospitals.

In this report I will present some results concerning part of the sample, namely, the 33 same-sexed twin pairs where both partners were alive when the clinical investigation took place in 1976.

RESULTS
Concordance

Of the 33 same-sexed pairs, 26 are males and 7 females. The proportion of females corresponds to the distribution in the normal population (Table 1).

TABLE 1. Same-Sexed Twin Pairs With Coronary Heart Disease According to Sex and Zygosity*

Sex	MZ	DZ	Total
Male	7	19	26
Female	3	4	7
Total	10	23	33

*Except for one MZ and one DZ pair with angina pectoris only, all cases had a coronary infarction.

TABLE 2. Concordance With Regard to Coronary Heart Infarction in MZ and DZ Twin Pairs

	MZ	DZ
Total number of pairs	9	22
Number of concordant pairs	2	3
Number of discordant pairs	7	19
Proband concordance	36%	24%
Direct pairwise concordance	22%	14%

Table 2 gives the concordance rates for MZ and DZ pairs with regard to coronary infarction.

Table 2 reveals that the concordance figures for MZ are somewhat higher than for DZ twins, namely 36% vs. 24% when the proband method is employed. The direct pairwise concordance is 22% in MZ and 14% in DZ pairs. These differences support a slight genetic disposition. However, the differences in concordance are statistically insignificant.

Discordance

Which factors discriminate between twin partners in discordant pairs? In other words, which factors in the life history are different for twins in discordantly affected pairs? Do we find that the twin with CHD has been the heavier smoker, the more nervous, the most mentally troubled?

Table 3 shows that there is one outstanding discriminating factor, namely "stressful work situation." The evaluation of the work situation was based on detailed information concerning work habits, such as type of work, tempo, pressure, and deadlines, as well as availability of pauses during work hours. In fact, in all MZ pairs studied, the twin with CHD had experienced the harder mental and physical work situation. The same pattern is apparent in DZ twins: In on-

TABLE 3. Relationship Between Premorbid Factors in Male and Female MZ and DZ Twin Pairs With Regard to Coronary Infarction

Premorbid factors	MZ				DZ			
	Twin A	Twin B	Unknown	Equal	Twin A	Twin B	Unknown	Equal
More dominant	3	1	—	3	10	3	—	7
More type A	4	1	1	1	16	3	—	1
More quick-tempered	3	2	—	1	13	5	—	2
More sensitive labile	3	2	—	2	9	2	—	8
Higher occupational status	2	1	—	4	7	1	—	12
More work pressure	7	—	—	—	13	1	—	11
More overtime	7	—	—	—	14	1	—	5
More commuting	2	—	—	5	5	1	—	14
More work conflict	1	—	—	6	3	—	—	17
More marital conflict	1	2	—	4	4	2	—	14
More other family conflict	—	—	1	6	4	1	—	15
More cigarettes	3	1	—	3	11	4	—	5
More alchohol	1	1	—	5	4	1	—	15
More tranquillizers	—	—	—	7	1	2	—	16
More inactivity	1	—	—	6	6	7	1	6
More dyspeptic	2	—	—	5	6	6	—	8
More other	—	1	—	6	2	2	—	16
More clinical depression	—	—	—	7	3	2	—	15
More other psychiatric problems	—	2	—	5	2	1	—	17

ly few cases had the workload been classified as equal. These differences are statistically significant at a 5% level. The same pattern is present in the female pairs, although the numbers are small.

Table 3 also reveals that the CHD patient was more frequently classified as a type-A personality (marked by intense striving for achievement, competitiveness, easily provoked impatience, time urgency) both in DZ and MZ. We also find that the CHD patient in discordant pairs had smoked more. With regard to inactivity during leisure time and mental problems in general, there was no difference.

Interestingly enough, heavy workload is also a strong discriminating factor in women. There are few such pairs, but it is significant that all CHD women have held several jobs, and the case histories clearly demonstrate that the CHD female twins have experienced a considerably heavier work pressure than their nonaffected cotwins.

In the following, the main findings of the study will be illustrated by a few case descriptions. The CHD twin is designated A; the healthy twin, B.

Case 1: Female MZ Pair, Born 1905

Twin A has coronary symptoms, twin B is symptom-free. The twins represent births 8 and 9 of nine children. They grew up under relatively poor conditions on a small farm in western Norway. As a child twin A was the dominant and the more independent of the twins—a role relationship that has continued into adulthood. She moved in with an elder sister to help with the sister's children at the age of 10, whereas twin B stayed at home with her parents until she had finished school at age 14. Neither of the twins received any formal education after elementary school.

Twin A developed a peptic ulcer at the age of 17 or 18 after a period of hard work. At the age of 23 she married a farmer and had four children. Her husband died of cancer in 1952.

Twin A seems to have been an extroverted and independent woman with social interests and has never experienced manifest mental problems. She has always worked hard, particularly after she lost her husband when she had to take total responsibility for family and farm. Often she had to work from early morning until midnight. At the age of 62 (in 1967) she had her first attack of myocardial infarction. The next attack came in 1970. Since 1973 she has been suffering from angina pectoris. However, for the last 2 years she has been without symptoms.

Twin B married at age 21. Her husband worked both as fisherman and as a rod worker. The couple did not have any children and twin B led, in contrast to her twin sister, a rather quiet and protected life without much work.

Compared with her sister, twin B has been more reserved and more dependent, more restless and more emotionally labile. She developed moderate hypertension at the age of 62, but her blood pressure normalized rapidly after drug therapy. At times during the last 9 years, she has felt difficulty in breathing and slight chest pains, symptoms which obviously have a psychological origin, probably caused by worrying and identification with her twin sister.

Neither of the twins is a smoker. Both have slight hypertension today—twin A, 170/120; twin B, 150/100. Both have mildly elevated cholesterol levels—twin A, 8.7; twin B, 6.8 mmoles/liter.

Comment. Twin A, who developed coronary heart disease, has higher blood pressure and higher blood cholesterol than twin B. However, the difference is negligible. The most remarkable dissimilarity in this pair seems to be related to stress and to work habits. Twin A has been exposed to considerably more psychological strain and drudgery than her twin sister. She has had to work hard all her life, and at the age of 47 she lost her husband.

Case 2: Male MZ Pair, Born 1910

Twin A suffers from coronary heart disease; twin B has no coronary symptoms. The twins represent births 4 and 5 of 11 children. They grew up partly on a farm and partly in a small village where their father ran a small factory.

Twin A married at age 26 a widow ten years older than himself, whereas twin B went to sea. From the age of 15 twin A worked as a salesman and since the age of 26 he has run his own business. After some years as a seaman, twin B has worked in construction.

Both twins have been hard-working people. However, twin A experienced considerably more stress in his work than twin B. For many years A commuted long distances between two towns, which meant that during some periods he worked both day and night. Twin B has always had regular work hours.

Twin A and his wife have no children. Their relationship has been relatively satisfactory, except for a period 10 years ago when they were separated for 3 years. Twin B, however, married at the age of 42 and has obviously experienced a satisfactory marital relationship.

Both twins are by nature pleasant and extroverted and persons of orderly, regular habits. Both twins are active and somewhat restless—perhaps twin B is more so. Both are easily moved by sad events. Twin A, for instance, never attends a funeral. Twin A drinks more than twin B, but neither of them has abused alcohol.

In general the twins have not experienced extreme hardships in life, except for A, who 20 years ago suffered a financial crisis with ensuing personal problems for 2—3 years. Neither of the twins has suffered serious psychiatric problems.

Today both have moderate hypertension—A, 180/120; B, 200/110. Both have elevated cholesterol—A, 8.4; B, 9.7 mmoles/liter. Both have been smoking for 50 years—A, approximately 15 cigarettes per day; B, 6 cigarettes a day. Twin B has had more exercise in his free time than A.

Twin A developed an acute myocardial infarction for the first time in 1974 at the age of 64. Two years later he suffered two more attacks, and since then he has been troubled by angina pectoris during periods of exercise or emotional excitement.

Comment. A male MZ pair, aged 67, discordant for coronary heart disease, has been described. The most noteworthy difference in the twins' life histories is related to work. Twin A has lived a considerably more restless and stressful life than his twin brother, with irregular rhythm and long working hours. With regard to cholesterol, blood pressure, smoking, and exercise, the differences are slight.

Case 3: Female DZ Pair, Born 1924

Twin A was struck by heart thromboses in 1974 and has suffered since from angina pectoris. She married at age 31, but she has been unhappy in her marriage because her husband has abused alcohol. Besides her work as a housewife, she has worked in a cafe, and during the years before her heart infarction she worked as a paper carrier. She has thus suffered an erratic sleep pattern in recent years.

Twin B has never suffered from any heart symptoms. She is unmarried, but supports herself and her two children by part-time work and social welfare.

Comment. The most conspicuous difference in the life histories of these twins is that A has a considerably more problematic life situation with regard to both family and work.

Case 4: Male DZ Pair, Born 1924

Twin A developed heart infarction in 1974 and has since been troubled by angina pectoris. He married at age 23, but was separated from his wife after some years because he was practically never at home. He is described by his twin brother as a work addict. He has worked days as a mechanic, and for the last 20 years he has also worked as a salesman almost every night.

Twin B suffers from moderate hypertension, but has never had any direct trouble with his heart. He married at age 22. He worked first in a factory, but has in recent years worked as a caretaker of a school.

Comment. In this case also twin A has been the more active and restless with the heavier work pressure, whereas B, who admittedly is rather tense, seems to have led a quieter life.

DISCUSSION

This study has shown that concordance with regard to coronary heart infarction is insignificantly higher in MZ than DZ twins. If one allows for some higher concordance in MZ because of the more similar environment, one can safely conclude that the genetic disposition seems to play a minor role in the etiology of coronary heart disease. The findings are in accordance with the study by Harvald and Hauge [1] from Denmark, who observed higher concordance rates in MZ than DZ twins with respect to death caused by myocardial infarction. However, the difference was slight and for male pairs not statistically significant. In a Swedish twin sample, Liljefors [3] found no difference in concordance for myocardial infarction in MZ and DZ. When angina pectoris was included, concordance was found in 7 out of 29 MZ pairs (24%) and 3 out of 22 DZ pairs (14%).

The main finding of the present investigation is that heavy work pressure is correlated to myocardial infarction in both DZ and MZ discordant twins. The twin with CHD has in most cases been exposed to a more stressful work situation. Since these differences are not only observed in DZ pairs, but also in MZ pairs and in males as well as females, it is reasonable to conclude that these factors are of causative significance.

These findings are in accordance with the study by Liljefors [3], who in a sample of 91 male twin pairs with CHD (51 MZ and 40 DZ), aged 42−67, observed that the ill twin in discordant pairs had experienced more financial problems and more overtime. In fact, it was an outstanding finding that the more seriously affected twin in MZ pairs had been the more dedicated to work. Also, Liljefors and Rahe [6] observed that hard pressure in work, heavy responsibility, short breaks during work hours, and so forth discriminated within discordant MZ twins. Other clinical investigations point in the same direction. Russeck [7,8] observed, for instance, that emotional stress and heavy work pressure associated with considerable responsibility had been common for 91 of 100 young patients prior to their coronary heart disease. Furthermore, Theorell and Floderus-Myrhed [9] discovered that heavy work load was significantly correlated to development of heart infarction in 5,000 construction workers aged 41-61 years.

With regard to personality factor A, which in fact is difficult to separate from environmental stress, the data show a significant correlation between type A behavior and infarction in DZ twins. The tendency is the same in MZ twins; however, the numbers here are small. In other words, the findings of this study are in accordance with the literature. In several studies by Rosenman and Friedman and their co-workers, type-A behavior has been correlated to myocardial infarction, even in prospective studies. [cf, eg, 6]

In this investigation there is a clear tendency that smoking is related to coronary infarction. However, in several pairs one observes that the "healthy" twin has smoked more than the infarct twin. One should also add that the difference in smoking habits was rather slight in most cases. Most epidemiological studies have observed a strong relationship between smoking and myocardial infarction. However, to what degree smoking is a causative factor is still an open question because previous twin studies have not found that smoking discriminates between CHD-discordant MZ twins. Lundman [5], in a clinical study of 200 CHD-discordant twin pairs, concluded that cigarette smoking per se most likely had no etiological relationship to coronary heart disease. Likewise Liljefors [3] could observe no association between cigarette smoking and symptoms of coronary insufficiency.

Finally, I would like to add that this sample of twins with coronary heart disease contrasts with any psychiatric sample. Few of the subjects seem to experience marital problems, which is evidenced in the extremely low number of separated or divorced cases. Extremely few have alcohol problems, and the frequency of manifest psychiatric problems is low indeed.

REFERENCES

1. Harvald B, Hauge M: Hereditary factors elucidated by twin studies. In Neel JV, Shaw MW, Schull WJ (eds): "Genetics and the Epidemiology of Chronic Diseases." Washington DC: US Department of Health, Education, and Welfare, 1965.
2. Kringlen E: Norwegian Twin Registers. In Nance WE et al: "Twin Research: Biology and Epidemiology." New York: Alan R. Liss, 1978, pp 185-187.
3. Liljefors J: Coronary heart disease in male twins. Acta Med Scand Suppl 511, 1970.
4. Liljefors J, Rahe RH: An identical twin study of psychological factors in coronary heart disease in Sweden. Psychosomat Med 32:523—542, 1970.
5. Lundman T: Smoking in relation to coronary heart disease and lung function in twins. A co-twin control study. Acta Med Scand 180 (Suppl 455), 1966.
6. Rosenman RH, Friedman M, et al: A predictive study of coronary heart disease. JAMA 189:15—22, 1964.
7. Russeck HI: Stress, tobacco and coronary disease in North American professional groups. JAMA 192:189—194, 1965.
8. Russeck HI, Russeck LG: Is emotional stress an etiologic factor in coronary heart disease? Psychosomatics 17:63—67, 1976
9. Theorell T, Floderus-Myrhed B: "Workload," a risk of myocardial infarctions: A prospective psychosocial analysis. Int J Epidemiol 6:17-21.

Twin Research 3: Epidemiological
and Clinical Studies, pages 139—148

Coronary-Prone Behavior in Adult Same-Sexed Male Twins: An Epidemiological Study

Markku Koskenvuo, Jaakko Kaprio, Heimo Langinvainio, Matti Romo, and Seppo Sarna
Department of Public Health Science, University of Helsinki

INTRODUCTION

Coronary-prone behavior pattern, type A, is associated with the prevalence of coronary heart disease (CHD) [5–10, 13, 14, 19, 25, 29, 30]. The typology developed by Friedman and Rosenman was based on structured interviews and observation of subject behavior. The coronary-prone behavior pattern designated as type A is characterized by some or all of the following: intense striving for achievement, competitiveness, easily provoked impatience, time urgency, abruptness of gesture and speech, overcommitment to vocation or profession, excesses of drive and hostility [14, 15].

For epidemiological studies, self-administrable questionnaire versions of type A measuring instruments have been developed [1, 2, 4, 11, 12, 20, 27, 31, 33]. The effect of genetic factors on coronary-prone behavior has been found to be quite small in earlier studies [3, 26, 28, 34, 35].

In a previous Finnish study the psychosocial correlates of A-type behavior measured by a questionnaire-based rating scale were described [23]. The purpose of this study was to investigate Finnish male twins for identifying familial and environmental components of coronary-prone behavior patterns.

MATERIALS and METHODS

Study Material

The material has been described earlier [16]. The Finnish Twin Registry consists of all Finnish adult same-sexed twin pairs (N = 17,357 pairs) born before 1958 and with both members alive in 1967. The questionnaire was mailed to all pairs with both members alive in 1975. The overall response rate was 89%. The measurement of study variables has been presented earlier [23]: The postal questionnaire study was carried out to obtain data on zygosity [32], smoking, alcohol use, leisure-time physical activity, weight, height, and drug usage. Psychosocial factors such as marital status, occupation and occupational history, changes of residence and employment, extroversion and lability, and type A behavior were also studied as well as various symptoms and history of disease. The compilation process of the Registry and baseline characteristics of the questionnaire study have been documented in detail [17, 18, 21]. (Note: These may be obtained from the authors.)

The study population consisted of those male twin pairs in the Finnish Twin Registry who had both responded to a mailed questionnaire in 1975. Responses from 5,419 male pairs with both members respondent were used in these analyses.

Measurement of Coronary-Prone Behavior Pattern

Type A behavior pattern was measured by the rating scale developed by Bortner [2] consisting of seven items and adapted for use in a postal questionnaire. The measurement of A-type behavior in this series has been described earlier [23]. The study material was divided into deciles by the rating score, and the highest and lowest deciles consisting of most concordant A types, and most concordant B types were designated as representing type-A and type-B behavior respectively. The criteria of A-type/B-type discordant pairs used the same cut-off points.

Statistical Methods

The differences of groups of individuals were measured using Student's t-test. Correlation coefficients were compared with Fisher's z-test. Results for analyses over age have been age-adjusted. For discordant pairs, McNemar's matched pair t-test was used.

RESULTS

Intraclass Correlations of Bortner Scale Score Points

The intraclass correlations were 0.251 for MZ pairs and 0.052 for DZ pairs (Table 1). The heritability estimates (Falconer's formula : $2 \times [r_{(MZ)} - r_{(DZ)}]$) were higher in younger than in older age groups (variation between 0.66 and –0.04). In persons over 50 years old the heritability was zero. The proportions of coronary-prone behavior concordant and discordant pairs were between 14% and 15% in age groups 18–59 years (Table 2). The proportion of A-type concordant pairs showed an age trend: The highest proportion was found in age of 30–39 years. The proportion of MZ pairs among A-type concordant pairs was greater than among B-type concordant pairs, but the difference was not statistically significant (Table 3).

TABLE 1. Intraclass Correlations and Heritability Values of Bortner Scale by Age

Age group	MZ r	DZ r	h^2	z-test I r(mz)–r(dz) I P value
18–29	0.269	0.054	0.330	< 0.001
30–39	0.230	0.046	0.368	< 0.01
40–49	0.331	0.000	0.662	< 0.001
50–59	0.067	0.083	-0.032	ns
60 +	0.109	0.129	-0.040	ns
Total	0.251	0.052	0.398	< 0.001

TABLE 2. Distribution of A- and B-Type Concordant and Discordant Male Twin Pairs by Age

Age group	A-Type concordant pairs (%)	Discordant pairs (%)	B-Type concordant pairs (%)	Total number of pairs
18–29	8.8	14.0	11.6	2,501
30–39	14.2	15.0	7.5	1,237
40–49	10.5	14.5	10.2	822
50–59	8.9	13.9	8.7	483
60 +	4.8	8.8	9.6	376
Total	10.0[a]	13.9	10.0[a]	5,419

[a]By definition.

TABLE 3. Percentage of MZ Pairs in A-Type and B-Type Concordant and Discordant Male Twin Pairs by Age

Age group	A-Type concordant pairs (%)	Discordant pairs (%)	B-Type concordant pairs (%)
18–29	40	25	34
30–39	38	24	36
40–49	43	16	26
50–59	33	28	27
60 +	38	37	58
Total	38	24	35

Correlates to Study Variables

Education and occupation. A-type persons tended to be better educated than B-type persons: there was a 1.06-fold difference (P < 0.001) (Table 4). The difference in education in discordant pair analysis showed no difference among MZ pairs, but the difference among DZ pairs was nearly on the same level as in

TABLE 4. Distribution of Means and Proportions of Occupational Variables by A- and B-Type Concordant and Discordant Male Twin Pairs

	MZ pairs		DZ pairs	
	Concordant A,A-type and B,B-type pairs	Discordant pairs: A-type and B-type	Concordant A,A-type and B,B-type pairs	Discordant pairs: A-type and B-type
Years of education	8.3	8.0	7.9	7.8
	7.7[+++]	7.9	7.5[+++]	7.5
Self-employed (%)	11.5	3.3	7.6	6.2
	3.1[+++]	3.2	3.5[++]	3.4[+]
Unskilled workers (%)	4.5	9.0	6.2	9.1
	10.7[++]	9.6	10.5[++]	10.5
Persons in administrative work (%)	10.5	9.0	7.0	5.6
	4.0[+++]	6.9	4.4[+]	5.4
Mainly sedentary work (%)	34.0	30.3	29.7	25.9
	22.6[+++]	25.2	20.6[+++]	22.1
Mean income (FMK/month)	1,950	1,930	1,930	1,980
	1,590[+++]	1,930	1,690[+++]	1,740[+++]
Household head (%)	74.1	65.2	76.5	72.0
	64.2[++]	68.4	61.3[+++]	68.5

[+]P = 0.05.
[++]P = 0.01.
[+++]P = 0.001.
[a]Age-adjusted figures; P values of differences between A-type and B-type.

individual analysis. A-type was self-employed more often than the B-type in individual analysis (2.7-fold difference, P < 0.001), but in discordant pair analysis MZ pairs showed a minimal difference and DZ pairs had a 1.82-fold difference (P < 0.05). Conversely, there were more unskilled workers among B-type in individual analysis (2-fold difference) (P < 0.001), but in discordant pair analysis there was only a 1.1-fold difference. A-type was more often in administrative (2.6–1.6-fold difference) and sedentary (1.5–1.44-fold difference) work than the B-type persons (P < 0.001). These differences were most pronounced among the 30–44-years-olds. In discordant pairs these differences were much smaller but greater for MZ pairs than for DZ pairs (1.3–1.2-fold) (P > 0.05). A-type had larger mean gross monthly incomes than B-type (P < 0.001). In discordant pairs the difference was found only among DZ pairs (P < 0.001). A-type was more often the household head (P < 0.001). In discordant pairs there was only a small difference. There were no differences with respect to the proportion in shiftwork, outdoors work, or regular nightwork. A and B types did not differ in respect to the number of changes of workplace or unemployment periods.

Life changes. A-type had more changes of residence than B-type persons (P < 0.001), particularly among those aged less than 30 (Table 5). A-type persons were more often married than B-type persons (P < 0.001), the greatest differences

TABLE 5. Distribution of Means and Proportions of Psychological and Life-Change Variables by A- and B-Type Concordant and Discordant Male Twin Pairs

	MZ pairs		DZ pairs	
	Concordant A,A-type and B,B-type pairs	Discordant pairs: A-type and B-type	Concordant A,A-type and B,B-type pairs	Discordant pairs: A-type and B-type
Mean number of changes of place of residence during whole life	2.8 2.1+++	2.6 2.7	2.5 2.0+++	2.3 2.2+++
Married (%)	63.8 51.5+++	61.3 62.1	61.4 49.6+++	56.7 51.1
Mean stress of daily activities (invert scale 4–16)	12.2 13.0+++	12.3 12.4	12.1 12.8+++	12.3 12.8++
Persons who experience that their work is very varied (%)	35.3 17.3+++	24.4 27.3	31.1 23.1+++	29.1 22.2+
Mean extroversion score (scale 0–9)	5.3 3.7+++	4.6 4.2	5.1 3.8+++	5.0 3.8+++
Mean value of life dissatisfaction (scale 4–20)	8.5 9.1+++	8.9 9.0	8.7 9.0+++	8.7 9.2++

+P = 0.05.
++P = 0.01.
+++P = 0.001.
[a]Age-adjusted figures; P values of differences between A-type and B-type.

being seen in the youngest age groups. These differences were minimal in discordant pair analysis. There was no difference in proportion of divorce in individual and pairwise analysis.

Psychological factors. A-type persons were more extroverted than B-types (1.44–1.33-fold difference) ($P < 0.001$) (Table 5). In discordant pair analysis this difference was equally high among DZ pairs ($P < 0.001$), but among MZ pairs the difference was only 1.08-fold ($P > 0.05$). The life satisfaction of the A-type persons was greater than that of the B-type persons ($P < 0.001$). The greatest differences were among those under 30. In discordant pair analysis there was difference only among DZ pairs ($P < 0.01$). A-type considered their daily activities to be more stressing than the B-type persons ($P < 0.001$), but A-type persons nonetheless considered their work to be less monotonous than the B-type persons ($P < 0.001$). These differences were found in the discordant pair analysis only among DZ pairs ($P < 0.05$).

Health behavior. With respect to smoking and use of alcohol there was a difference between MZ and DZ pairs. In the individual analysis MZ A-type twins smoked more and used liquor more often ($P < 0.001$), whereas in these variables there was no difference among DZ twins. Among discordant MZ pairs, however, there was no statistical difference.

B-type spent more time on leisure-time physical activity than A-type persons, both the time spent on each session (P < 0.001) and the number of sessions being greater (P < 0.01). The intensity of leisure-time physical activity was greater for A-type persons; that is, they reported breathlessness and sweating more often. These differences in intensity, however, were not statistically significant: there was a 1.1-fold difference among MZ pairs and no difference among DZ pairs. In discordant pair analysis there was no significant difference in frequency of leisure-time physical activity sessions or in the duration of a leisure-time physical activity session. The magnitude of difference, however, was among discordant MZ pairs of the same order as in the individual analysis.

A-type men slept less on average than B-type men (P < 0.001), the greatest difference being among those under 30. In discordant pair analysis there was no statistical difference, but the magnitude of difference among MZ pairs was on the same level as in individual analysis. The subjective quality of sleep did not differ between A and B types. Mean weight, height, and relative weight did not differ either in individual or pairwise analysis.

Drug usage. There were no significant differences in the frequency of use of the following drugs: tranquilizers, sleeping pills, antihypertensive drugs, antacids, heart drugs, analgesics, fortifying preparations, and drugs for skin diseases. The consumption of coffee, tea, and lumps of sugar did not differ.

Morbidity. There was a statistically significant difference in the prevalence of angina pectoris in the Rose questionnaire (Table 7). This difference was 4.3-fold (P < 0.01) among MZ pairs and 1.94-fold among DZ pairs (P < 0.05). Differences in angina pectoris or myocardial infarction diagnosed by a physician and severe chest pain lasting over half an hour were not significant. In the discordant pair analysis, however, it was found that both members of a discordant pair had higher morbidity than concordant pairs. Particularly, discordant pairs had a higher prevalence of myocardial infarction than concordant pairs (Table 7).

DISCUSSION

The Rating Scale for Type-A Behavior

The similarities and differences of the rating scale used in this study compared to Bortner's original findings have been discussed in an earlier paper [23]. It was concluded that the rating scale used in this study measured nearly the same type of behavior as the original scale measuring characteristics of the Rosenman-Friedman typology.

Relationships to Study Variables in Analysis of Individuals

The results of individual analysis [23] fit the typology of the ambitious and competitive person. The A-type person was better educated, more often in sedentary white-collar work with a higher income, and more often the household

TABLE 6. Distribution of Means and Proportions of Health Behavior Variables by A- and B-Type Concordant and Discordant Male Twin Pairs

	MZ pairs		DZ pairs	
	Concordant A,A-type and B,B-type pairs	Discordant pairs: A-type and B-type	Concordant A,A-type and B,B-type pairs	Discordant pairs: A-type and B-type
Frequency of use of	3.3	3.2	3.1	3.0
liquor (days/month)	2.2+++	2.9	3.0	2.7
Actual mean cigarettes	11.2	9.7	10.2	10.7
per day	8.2+++	9.8	10.0	9.9
Frequency of leisure-	6.7	7.0	6.5	6.5
time physical activity (sessions/month)	7.6+	6.2	7.6+++	7.0
Average duration of a	49	45	48	46
leisure-time physical activity session (minutes)	55++	51	55++	47
Mean hours slept	7.5	7.6	7.4	7.6
	7.6++	7.7	7.7+++	7.6

+P = 0.05.
++P = 0.01.
+++P = 0.001.
aAge-adjusted figures; P values of differences between A-type and B-type.

TABLE 7. Distribution of Proportions of Variables Measuring Symptoms of Coronary Heart Disease A- and B-Type Concordant and Discordant Male Twin Pairs

	MZ pairs		DZ pairs	
	Concordant A,A-type and B,B-type pairs	Discordant pairs: A-type and B-type	Concordant A,A-type and B,B-type pairs	Discordant pairs: A-type and B-type
Angina pectoris in	5.6	6.9	6.2	6.3
Rose questionnaire (%)	1.3++	8.7	3.2+	6.1
Angina pectoris	4.0	11.4	5.1	4.6
diagnosed by a physician (%)	2.7	9.3	4.9	4.0
Severe chest pain	6.9	10.0	6.5	7.4
lasting over ½ hour (%)	3.9	11.2	6.0	7.5
Myocardial infarct	0.7	3.2	1.8	2.4
diagnosed by a physician (%)	0.9	3.1	1.8	2.0

+P = 0.05.
++P = 0.01.
+++P = 0.001.
aAge-adjusted figures; P values of differences between A-type and B-type.

head than the B-type person. Thus the A-type person exemplifies a highly productive, status-seeking personality generally admired in Western culture. The drive for job status and achievement is shown in the ambivalent attitude of the A-type personality toward work, as seen in the result that A-type considered work to be more varying and was more satisfied with life, but also experienced daily activities to be more stressful.

The physical activity at work of A-type was less and their leisure-time physical activity sessions were of a shorter duration and less frequent but of a slightly higher intensity. A-type MZ (but not DZ) twins also smoked more and consumed more alcohol more often than B-type persons. This suggests either a difference in the intrapair relationship between MZ and DZ twins or a misclassification in measured variables.

In this study an association in men between A-type behavior pattern and angina pectoris on the Rose questionnaire was found. This was found despite the fairly low age distribution of the material and the cross-sectional nature of the study. It is quite understandable that a clear cut association between A-type behavior and manifestations of coronary disease may not be found in a cross-sectional study. For instance, those with a very high A-type score may have their behavior pattern modified after suffering a coronary event or they may be selected out by mortality.

A-type behavior has been shown to be an independent risk for different manifestations of CHD [14]. Some psychosocial factors, such as marital status and social class, which were found to correlate with A-type behavior in this study, are known to be associated with CHD in Finland [22]; therefore, the relationship of A-type behavior, psychosocial factors, and CHD should be further investigated.

Relationship to Study Variables in Pairwise Analysis

The intraclass correlations were for MZ twins on the rating scale only 0.251 and for DZ twins nearly nil (0.052). They were relatively age-dependent and decreased with age. The overall heritability for the short scale was 0.40 using Falconer's formula based on intraclass correlations. These were of the same order as found in the twin study of Rahe et al [28]. These heritability estimates, which are upper theoretical estimates of the degree of genetic determination, can be considered to be fairly low. Thus at least 60% of the variation in A–B-type behavior in the Finnish population seems to be determined by environmental factors.

The cross-sectional study situation uncovered some sources of error in the discordant pair analysis. It was quite probable that part of the so-called "discordant pairs" were artificially discordant because the ischemic heart disease or some other disease had changed their behavior. Second, the differences in background variables were systematically higher in this analysis using the extreme deciles of concordant pairs compared to the analysis using individuals [23]. This difference may be due to misclassifications in the Bortner's scale itself as used in mail questionnaire.

The discordant pair analysis showed that there were some environmental factors clearly associated with coronary-prone behavior. These were partly associated to the personality and the work and partly to the health behavior. It seems, however, that there were not many variables in this study associated with the etiological factors for A-type behavior, because heritability values were quite small and yet minimal differences were found in discordant MZ pairs. Future studies should concentrate on various relevant factors in the rearing environment [24]. The intrapair relationships and the familial effects other than genetic ones, may include many factors having a meaningful influence on behavior. So the study of trait-discordant MZ twin pairs presents many aspects that may be difficult to interpret.

The association of A-type behavior and CHD will be further clarified in prospective studies on these series.

ACKNOWLEDGMENTS

This study was supported by a grant from the Council for Tobacco Research.

REFERENCES

1. Bortner RW, Rosenman RH: The measurement of pattern A behavior. J Chron Dis 20:525-533, 1967.
2. Bortner RW: A short rating scale as a pattern measure of pattern A behavior. J Chron Dis 22:87-91, 1969.
3. Bortner RW, Rosenman RH, Friedman M: Familial similarity in pattern a behavior. Fathers and sons. J Chron Dis 23:39-43, 1970.
4. Caffrey B: Reliability and validity of personality and behavioral measures in a study of coronary heart disease. J Chron Dis 21: 191-204, 1968.
5. Defourny M, Hubin P, Luminet D: Alexithymia, "pensee operatoire" and predisposition to coronopathy. Pattern "A" of Friedman and Rosenman. Psychother Psychosom 27: 106-114, 1977.
6. Friedman M, Rosenman RH: Association of specific overt behavior pattern with blood and cardiovascular findings. JAMA 169:96-106, 1959.
7. Friedman M, Manwaring JH, Rosenman RH, Donlon G, Ortega P, Grube SM: Instantaneous and sudden death. Clinical and pathological differentiation in coronary artery disease. JAMA 225:1319-1328, 1973.
8. Groupe Coopératif de la Fondation P Neumann: Approche psychologique en épidémiologie cardiovasculaire. Nouv Presse Med 22:1955-1958, 1977.
9. Haynes SG, Levine S, Scotch N, Feinleib M, Kannel WB: The relationship of psychosocial factors to coronary heart disease in the Framingham study. I. Methods and risk factors. Am J Epidemiol 107: 362-383, 1978.
10. Heller RF: Type A behaviour and coronary heart disease. Br Med J 2:368, 1979.
11. Jenkins CD, Rosenman RH, Friedman M: Development of an objective psychological test for the determination of the coronary-prone behavior pattern in employed men. J Chron Dis 20:371-379, 1967.
12. Jenkins CD, Zyzanski SJ, Rosenman RH: Progress toward validation of a computer-scored test for the Type A coronary-prone behavior pattern. Psychosom Med 33:193-202, 1971.
13. Jenkins CD, Zyzanski SJ, Rosenman RH, Cleveland GL: Association of coronary-prone behavior scores with recurrence of coronary heart disease. J Chron Dis 24:601-611, 1971.
14. Jenkins CD: Recent evidence supporting psychologic and social risk factors for coronary disease (second of two parts). N Engl J Med 294:1033-1038, 1976.
15. Jenkins CD, Zyzanski SJ, Rosenman RH: Coronary-prone behavior: One pattern or several? Psychosom Med 40:25-43, 1978.
16. Kaprio J, Sarna S, Koskenvuo M, Rantasalo I: The Finnish Twin Registry: Formation and compilation, questionnaire study, zygosity determination procedures and research program. Prog Clin Biol Res 24B:179-184, 1978.

17. Kaprio J, Sarna S, Koskenvuo M, Rantasalo I: Baseline characteristics of the Finnish Twin Registry: Section II: History of symptoms and illnesses, use of drugs, physical characteristics, smoking, alcohol and physical activity. Publications of the Department of Public Health Science M37, Helsinki, 1978.
18. Kaprio J, Koskenvuo M, Artimo M, Sarna S, Rantasalo I: Baseline characteristics of the Finnish Twin Registry: Section I: Materials, methods, representativeness and results for variables special to twin studies. Publications of the Department of Public Health Science M47, Helsinki, 1979.
19. Keith RA: Personality and coronary heart disease: A review. J Chron Dis 19:1231-1243, 1966.
20. Kittel F, Kornitzer M, Zyzanksi SJ, Jenkins CD, Rustin RM, Degre C: Two methods of assessing the type A coronary-prone behavior pattern in Belgium. J Chron Dis 31:147–155, 1978.
21. Koskenvuo M, Langinvainio H, Kaprio J, Rantasalo I, Sarna S: The Finnish Twin Registry: Baseline characteristics: Section III: Occupational and psychosocial factors. Publication of the Department of Public Health Science M49, Helsinki, 1979.
22. Koskenvuo M, Kaprio J, Kesäniemi A, Sarna S: Differences in mortality from ischemic heart disease by marital status and social class. J Chron Dis 33:95–106, 1980.
23. Koskenvuo M, Kaprio J, Langinvainio H, Romo M, Sarna S: Psychosocial and environmental correlates of coronary-prone behavior in Finland. J Chron Dis (in press).
24. Langinvainio H, Koskenvuo M, Kaprio J. Lönnqvist J, Tarkkonen L: Finnish twins reared apart: Preliminary characterization of rearing environment. Third International Congress on Twin Studies, Jerusalem, 1980.
25. Matthews KA, Glass DC, Rosenman RH, Bortner RW: Competitive drive, pattern A, and coronary heart disease: A further analysis of some data from the Western collaborative group study. J Chron Dis 30:489–498, 1977.
26. Miller JZ, Rose RJ, Grim CE: Genetic influence on coronary behavior pattern? A twin study analysis. 20th Conference on Cardiovascular Disease Epidemiology, San Diego, March 3-5, 1980.
27. Price KP: Reliability of assessment of coronary-prone behavior with special reference to the Bortner rating scale. J Psychosom Res 23:45–47, 1979.
28. Rahe R, Hervig L, Rosenman R: Heritability of type A behavior. Psychosom Med 40:478–486, 1978.
29. Rosenman RH, Friedman M: Association of specific behavior pattern in women with blood and cardiovascular findings. Circulation 24:1173–1184, 1961.
30. Rosenman RH, Brand RJ, Jenkins D, Friedman M, Straus R, Wurm M: Coronary heart disease in the Western collaborative group study. Final follow-up experience of 8.5 years. JAMA 233:872–877, 1975.
31. Rustin R-M, Dramaix M, Kittel F, Degre C, Kornitzer M, Thilly G, de Backer G: Evaluation of technics used to define type A pattern, in the Belgian Prevention Project of cardiovascular diseases. Rev Epidemiol Sante Publ 24:497–507, 1976.
32. Sarna S, Kaprio J, Sistonen P, Koskenvuo M: Diagnosis of twin zygosity by mailed questionnaire. Hum Hered 28:241–254, 1978.
33. Shekelle RB, Schoenberger JA, Stamler J: Correlates of the JAS type A behavior pattern score. J Chron Dis 29:381–394, 1976.
34. Sholtz RI, Rosenman RH, Brand RJ: The relationship of reported parental history of the incidence of coronary heart disease in the Western collaborative group study. Am J Epid 102:350–356, 1975.
35. Theorell T, deFaire U, Schalling D, Adamson U, Askevold F: Personality traits and psychophysiological reactions to a stressful interview in twins with varying degrees of coronary heart disease. J Psychosom Res 23:89–99, 1979.

Twin Research 3: Epidemiological
and Clinical Studies, pages 149—161
© 1981 Alan R. Liss, Inc., 150 Fifth Avenue, New York, NY 10011

The Hamilton Twin Study: Comparison of Serum Lipid Levels in Monozygotic and Dizygotic Twins by Chorion Type

Manning Feinleib, Joe C. Christian, Lillian Ingster-Moore, Robert J. Garrison, W. Carl Breckenridge, and Irene Uchida

Epidemiology and Biometry Program, Division of Heart and Vascular Disease, National Heart, Lung, and Blood Institute, Bethesda, Maryland (M.F., L.I.M., R.J.G.); Department of Medical Genetics, Indiana University School of Medicine, Indianapolis (J.C.C.); Department of Biochemistry, Faculty of Medicine, Dalhousie University, Halifax, Nova Scotia (W.C.B.); and Department of Pediatrics and Pathology, McMaster University, Hamilton, Ontario (I.U.)

INTRODUCTION

There is a great deal of epidemiologic, clinical, and laboratory evidence to indicate that elevated plasma cholesterol is associated with an increased risk of atherosclerosis and its complications [11]. Both elevated cholesterol and atherosclerosis have been associated with genetic factors, specifically the autosomal-dominant form of hypercholesterolemia [1, 7]. Although environmental factors such as diet are believed to influence cholesterol levels, the major part of the variation in plasma cholesterol within populations has not been explained by identifiable genes or specific environmental influences.

In addition to rare genetic traits, there is evidence that a significant proportion of the variation in cholesterol values is familial [9, 12—14]. In virtually all twin studies reported prior to 1975, significant estimates for genetic variance were found when the within-pair variances of monozygotic (MZ) and dizygotic (DZ) twins were compared. All these studies, however, assumed the total variance of plasma cholesterol to be equal for MZ and DZ twins.

In 1969 the National Heart, Lung, and Blood Institute (NHLBI) began a study of 500 twin pairs from the National Academy of Sciences—National Research Council (NAS—NRC) panel of United States veterans of World War II and the Korean conflict [6]. These 42–56-year-old male Caucasian twins were studied for a variety of coronary heart disease risk factors including plasma lipids. The total variance for plasma cholesterol among MZ twins was found to be significantly smaller than for DZ twins. This same pattern (Table 1) was revealed in all three major lipoprotein fractions (high, low, and very low density lipoproteins) but not for triglyceride levels.

Further investigation was warranted to search for the cause of the smaller total variance for MZ twins (separate analyses had shown that the variance for DZ twins was similar to that found in free-living singleton populations). Many of the competitive factors postulated by Kempthorne and Osborne [10] to cause different total variance of MZ and DZ twins were prenatal influences. When a series of 86 pairs of same-sex newborn twins was studied, the MZ twins again had a smaller total variance than the DZ twins [2], indicating that the difference was indeed prenatal. The MZ twins of the same series were then subdivided into monochorionic (MC) and dichorionic (DC) pairs using gross and microscopic placental data collected at birth [5]. The within-mean-square for MC pairs was less than one-fifth that of the DC pairs, indicating that the source of the smaller total variance of newborn MZ twins, compared to newborn DZ twins, was due to inclusion of MZ-MC twins in the sample. In the newborn twins this finding could be due to a blending of fetal circulations because most MZ-MC twins share a common placental circulation.

To determine if the smaller variance of MC twins persisted after birth, 11 pairs each of young, adult, MZ-MC and MZ-DC twins were studied and both the within-pair and among-pair mean squares were significantly larger for the DC than for the MC twins. It was hypothesized that this variation might be due to differences in the intrauterine maternal environment between the late separation of the MC twins resulting in a shared vascular circulation and the independent circulations established by the early separation of DC twins. A larger group of adult twins with known placentation was needed to see if this difference persisted into adulthood. Such a unique panel of adult twins with known placentation was available in the Hamilton Twin Study. Placental information was recorded for a random series of 1,783 multiple births in Toronto hospitals between the years 1936 and 1959. The twins ranged in age from 18 to 41 years. In a collaborative study between McMaster University, the Lipid Research Clinic at the University of Toronto, Indiana University, and the Epidemiology and Biometry Program of

TABLE 1. F' Test for Equality of Total Variance for MZ and DZ Twins in the NHLBI Twin Study (Adapted from Christian et al [3])

Variable	Total Variance		F' ratio*	P
	DZ pairs	MZ pairs		
Total cholesterol	1,717	1,234	1.4	0.001
HDL cholesterol	216	163	1.3	0.008
LDL cholesterol	1,451	1,138	1.3	0.02
VLDL cholesterol	857	446	1.9	0.0001
Triglycerides	7,990	9,129	1.1	0.17

*Approximate degrees of freedom are 450 and 350 based on 264 DZ pairs and 250 MZ pairs.

the National Heart, Lung, and Blood Institute in Bethesda, Maryland, detailed examinations of a sample of these twins have been undertaken.

METHODS

As the basis for the study of twin zygosity, the placentas of multiple births were collected from Toronto hospitals. This project, initiated in 1936 by Norma Ford-Walker, originally included only four hospitals, and the specimens were obtained in an irregular but random fashion. By 1959, a total of ten hospitals had participated. The final sample consisted of 1,783 placentas of twins and triplets.

When the placentas were collected, the following information was obtained from the maternity wards: sex, birth order, birth weights, obvious congenital malformations, mother's name, address, age, and para/gravida. If the placenta was fresh at the time of arrival in the laboratory, cord blood was obtained for ABO, Rh, and MN red cell typing. To facilitate examination of the membranes, the placentas were left overnight in cold running water, a procedure that induced the amnion to separate from the chorion. All single or fused placentas were injected with colored rubber latex, red into the artery and blue into the vein of one of the two cords. The presence of a common blood circulation was verified when the latex penetrated the vascular network to the vessels of the other cord.

Because of the long time interval between the birth of these twins and current follow-up studies (some 20–40 years), tracing their whereabouts presented the usual problems associated with a highly mobile population in a large metropolitan area. Many twins could not be studied because of death or departure to areas too distant to allow their return to be feasible. Some twins were unwilling to participate in any research project.

The McMaster University Twin Registry thus consists of an unselected series of twins born in Toronto between 1936 and 1959 inclusive for whom the type of placentation is known. From this panel, a volunteer sample of 176 same-sex twin pairs were drawn (Table 2) to examine intrapair variations in lipoproteins among MZ twins.

TABLE 2. Number of Twin Pairs in Study Population by Zygosity, Chorion Type, Age, and Sex (Hamilton Twin Study)

Sex and age	Monozygous—monochorionic	Monozygous—dichorionic	Dizygous—dichorionic
Men			
18–24	15	14	22
25+	6	5	8
Women			
18–24	25	16	28
25+	10	10	17
Total	56	45	75

Most MZ twins have their own amniotic sacs enclosed within a single chorion and anastomoses of placental blood vessels can usually be demonstrated. Same-sex twins with a dichorionic placenta, however, can be either MZ or DZ. In order to confirm monozygosity in MC twins and to determine the zygosity of same-sex DC twins, detailed genotyping was carried out. Documentation of zygosity was done by analysis of a large number of well-established genetic markers that included red cell enzymes, immunoglobulins, haptoglobins, red cell antigens, HLA antigens, and karyotyping, as well as hair and eye color. All analyses were performed without knowledge of placental type. No conflict with placental data was found. Any error in zygosity should therefore be negligible.

The variables to be discussed in this paper are total plasma cholesterol and total plasma triglycerides, measured in the fasting state. The Toronto Lipid Research Clinic determined cholesterol and triglycerides according to the standard protocol outlined in the Manual of Laboratory Operations of the Lipid Research Clinic Program [(Ref) Manual of Laboratory Operations Lipid Research Clinics Program Vol 1, Lipid and Lysoprotein Analyses, National Institutes of Health, Bethesda, Maryland, 1974]. The laboratory staff were unaware of the identity of the samples during the analysis.

RESULTS

Preliminary examination of the data by age, sex, zygosity, and chorion type indicated that some statistical properties of the data could require adjustments for skewness and possible outliers at the extremes. Figure 1 shows the mean values for serum cholesterol and triglycerides for male twins under the age of 25 by zygosity and chorion type. Similar data are shown for a control population, namely 118 white males, ages 20—24 who were examined in the Visit 2 survey of the Lipid Research Clinics Program Prevalence Study [8]. Plus and minus one standard deviation about the mean values are also illustrated. There is no statistically significant difference among the mean values for either cholesterol or triglyceride, but there is wide variability in the standard deviations. The extremely large standard deviations for both types of dichorionic twins warranted examining the effect of deleting a single outlier from each of these groups (see hatched areas). Since the inclusion or exclusion of a single data point can influence the distributions so markedly, caution was used in interpreting the data and in considering alternative methods of analysis. The total distributions for the entire twin population were examined first. Figure 2 shows the distribution of triglyceride levels for the 176 twin pairs or 352 individuals with the abscissa in terms of actual triglyceride measurements. There is marked skewness. Although the bulk of the population is concentrated between about 50 and 150 mg/dl triglyceride, three individuals have values over 400 with the extreme being 1,200 mg/dl. Figure 3 shows the distributions of the natural logarithms of the triglyceride measurements. The three previously mentioned outliers are still conspicuous but the skewness is reduced and normality nearly achieved.

The distribution of cholesterol levels is shown in Figure 4. The vast majority of the individuals fall between 100 and 250 mg/dl cholesterol but again there are one

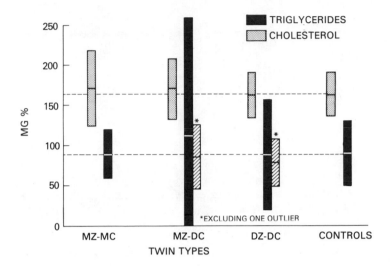

Fig. 1. Comparison of means (± ISD) for cholesterol, triglycerides for men, under 25: Hamilton Twin Study.

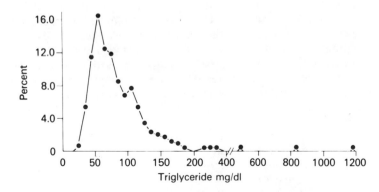

Fig. 2. Distribution of triglyceride levels: Hamilton Twin Study.

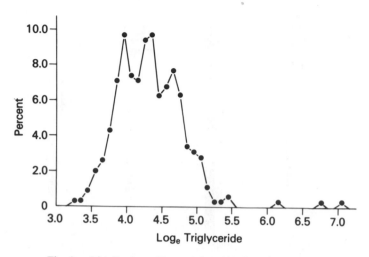

Fig. 3.   Distribution of log_e triglyceride: Hamilton Twin Study.

or two extreme values at the upper end. A logarithmic transformation as shown in Figure 5 tended to normalize the distribution in general but did not remove the outliers at the upper end of the range and highlighted a possible outlier at the lower end.

Because of the characteristics of the distributions, it was decided to analyze the data in four separate ways. First, all of the individuals were included, and no exceptions were made for any outliers. This total population and its subgroups created the statistics for both the actual lipid measurements and for the logarithmic transformations. Then the data were reanalyzed after omitting certain outliers. The criterion chosen was to exclude individuals with triglyceride values over 400 or with cholesterol levels over 350. Since the sample subjects are twin pairs, four individuals and their cotwins were thus eliminated (Table 3). All of these were males, three being under the age of 25 and one being a DZ pair over the age of 25.

Figure 6 shows the distributions of triglyceride levels for men under 25 by zygosity and chorion type and indicates the values for the excluded pairs. The two individuals excluded because of high triglyceride levels are labeled Sets 2 and 3, 2 being an MZ-DC pair and 3 being a DZ-DC pair. For the former, the cotwin also had a high triglyceride level but for the DZ pair the cotwin had a relatively low triglyceride value. MZ-MC pair labeled 1 was excluded on the basis of a high cholesterol level and their triglyceride values fall in the main part of the distribution.

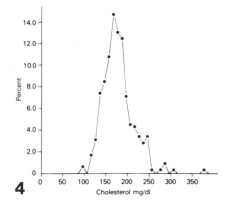

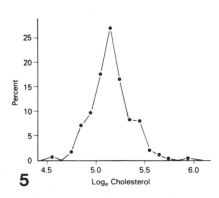

Fig. 4. Distribution of cholesterol levels: Hamilton Twin Study.

Fig. 5. Distribution of $\log_e$ cholesterol: Hamilton Twin Study.

TABLE 3. Characteristics of Excluded Twin Pairs in the Hamilton Twin Study

ID no.	Twin type	Age (yr)	Chol. (mg%)	Trig. (mg%)	Height (cm)	Weight (kg)	MRW[a]	ALC[b]
359 A	DZ	33	244	223	173.5	66.3	102	28
B		33	236	1,180	172.5	80.4	133	21
869 A	MZ	24	229	231	167.4	89.5	162	2
B	DC	24	305	830	168.4	83.1	148	18
1082 A	DZ	23	182	69	167.4	65.4	109	3
B		23	252	489	171.5	79.9	136	1
1771 A	MZ	20	143	74	183.4	77.2	109	9
B	MC	20	377	148	184.2	77.2	104	1

[a]Metropolitan Relative Weight.
[b]Total number of drinks consumed per week.

Figure 7 shows the excluded pairs of male twins under age 25 according to their cholesterol levels. The pair labeled 1 was excluded on the basis of the excessively high cholesterol of one of the twins and pairs 2 and 3 are the DC sets excluded on the basis of triglyceride values. In addition, at least one member of the latter also has high cholesterol levels. For pair 1, the MZ-MC set, there is a wide discordancy between the values of the two twins, which tends to cast some doubt, a priori, on a genetic determinant of cholesterol in this set. This assumes the reliability of the zygosity determination in which, as explained previously, there is virtually full confidence.

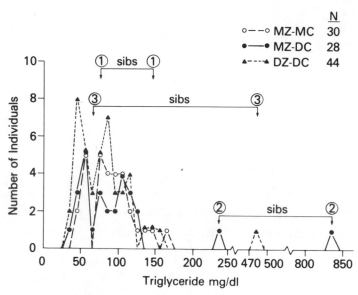

Fig. 6.   Distribution of triglyceride level by twin type, men < 25:
Hamilton Twin Study.

Comparisons of the total variances for serum cholesterol for MZ and DZ twins in the Hamilton Twin Study are shown in Table 4. The variances are shown separately for each of the four age and sex groups. The three columns on the left show the analyses for all of the twin pairs in the respective subgroups; the three columns on the right show the analyses with four pairs excluded. The row labeled "All" gives the variances for the 75 DZ pairs and the 101 MZ pairs without exclusions and for the 73 and 99 pairs, respectively, of DZ and MZ twins after the four exclusions. Contrary to the observations in the NHLBI Twin Study, the DZ pairs failed to show an increased total variance for all but one of the age and sex groups, either with or without the outliers in the distribution. The ratios of DZ total variance to MZ total variance are formally the F′ ratios, and all were expected to be greater than 1. Since there were doubts about the underlying assumptions of the normality of the distributions, no p values are indicated. In any event the directions of the ratios are contrary to the previous observations.

The comparisons of the total variances of the logarithmically transformed cholesterol values are shown in Table 5. In three of the four age and sex groups, the MZ twins have larger variances than the DZ twins whether the outliers are included or excluded, and for the older females the ratio is close to one. Again, these results are contrary to the observations in the NHLBI Twin Study.

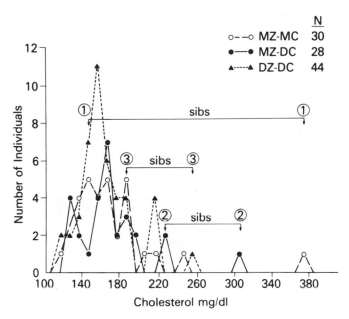

Fig. 7.   Distribution of cholesterol level by twin type, men < 25:
Hamilton Twin Study.

For triglycerides, the NHLBI Twin Study had found a relatively small, non-significantly larger variance for MZ than for DZ twins. Table 6 shows a comparison of the total variance of triglyceride levels for MZ and DZ twins in the Hamilton Twin Study. The data for the subgroups with no exclusions shows remarkable variability in the estimates of total variance. This variability is considerably reduced when the four outlier pairs are excluded. With the exception of the older women, none of the subgroups showed remarkable differences in the total variances between MZ and DZ twins. Similar results are obtained when the logarithmic transformation is applied as shown in Table 7.

Despite the fact that the comparison of total variances for cholesterol levels in the Hamilton Twin Study did not agree with the previous findings in the NHLBI Twin Study, the variances of cholesterol and log cholesterol were examined for the two types of MZ twins, the monochorionic and dichorionic. The comparisons are shown in Table 8 without any exclusions and in Table 9 with the four outliers excluded for $\log_e$ cholesterol. For three of the four subgroups, the MZ-DC twins tended to have larger variances than the MZ-MC twins. However, with the small samples involved, these do not achieve statistical significance by the formal F'

TABLE 4. Comparisons of Total Variances for MZ and DZ Twins in the Hamilton Twin Study

Cholesterol

	No exclusions			Outliers excluded		
	Total Variance			Total Variance		
Age and sex	DZ	MZ	DZ/MZ	DZ	MZ	DZ/MZ
<25, Male	785	1,820	0.43	607	683	0.89
<25, Female	927	1,089	0.85	927	1,089	0.85
25+, Male	1,398	1,381	1.01	1,278	1,381	0.93
25+, Female	938	1,041	0.90	938	1,041	0.90
All	1,049	1,368	0.77	974	1,089	0.89

TABLE 5. Comparisons of Total Variances for MZ and DZ Twins in the Hamilton Twin Study

Log_e Cholesterol

	No exclusions			Outliers excluded		
	Total Variance			Total Variance		
Age and sex	DZ	MZ	DZ/MZ	DZ	MZ	DZ/MZ
<25, Male	0.0275	0.0440	0.63	0.0230	0.0246	0.93
<25, Female	0.0327	0.0378	0.87	0.0327	0.0378	0.87
25+, Male	0.0313	0.0346	0.90	0.0280	0.0346	0.81
25+, Female	0.0283	0.0271	1.04	0.0283	0.0271	1.04
All	0.0336	0.0390	0.86	0.0318	0.0345	0.92

TABLE 6. Comparisons of Total Variances for MZ and DZ Twins in the Hamilton Twin Study

Triglycerides

	No exclusions			Outliers excluded		
	Total Variance			Total Variance		
Age and sex	DZ	MZ	DZ/MZ	DZ	MZ	DZ/MZ
<25, Male	4,673	10,785	0.43	880	822	1.07
<25, Female	790	932	0.85	790	932	0.85
25+, Male	75,052	2,182	34.4	2,104	2,182	0.96
25+, Female	1,385	707	1.96	1,385	707	1.96
All	10,383	3,979	2.61	1,120	1,076	1.04

TABLE 7. Comparisons of Total Variances for MZ and DZ Twins in the Hamilton Twin Study

Log_e Triglycerides

	No exclusions			Outliers excluded		
	Total Variance			Total Variance		
Age and sex	DZ	MZ	DZ/MZ	DZ	MZ	DZ/MZ
<25, Male	0.2179	0.2417	0.90	0.1425	0.1296	1.10
<25, Female	0.1420	0.1708	0.83	0.1420	0.1708	0.83
25+, Male	0.6160	0.2263	2.72	0.2016	0.2263	0.89
25+, Female	0.1865	0.1135	1.64	0.1865	0.1135	1.64
All	0.2414	0.1991	1.21	0.1622	0.1642	0.99

TABLE 8. Comparisons of Total Variances for Three Twin Types in the Hamilton Twin Study

Log$_e$ cholesterol (No exclusions)

Age and sex	Total Variance			Ratios		
	DZ–DC	MZ–DC	MZ–MC	DZ–DC/MZ–DC	DZ–DC/MZ–MC	MZ–DC/MZ–MC
<25, Male	0.0275	0.0421	0.0480	0.65	0.57	0.88
<25, Female	0.0327	0.0514	0.0303	0.64	1.08	1.70
25+, Male	0.0313	0.0432	0.0305	0.72	1.03	1.42
25+, Female	0.0283	0.0316	0.0235	0.90	1.20	1.34
All	0.0336	0.0452	0.0340	0.74	0.99	1.33

TABLE 9. Comparisons of Total Variances for Three Twin Types in the Hamilton Twin Study

Log$_e$ cholesterol (Outliers excluded)

Age and sex	Total Variance			Ratios		
	DZ–DC	MZ–DC	MZ–MC	DZ–DC/MZ–DC	DZ–DC/MZ–DC	MZ–DC/MZ–MC
<25, Male	0.0230	0.0246	0.0257	0.93	0.89	0.96
<25, Female	0.0327	0.0514	0.0303	0.64	1.08	1.70
25+, Male	0.0280	0.0432	0.0305	0.65	0.92	1.42
25+, Female	0.0283	0.0316	0.0235	0.90	1.20	1.34
All	0.0318	0.0420	0.0286	0.76	1.11	1.47

test. Furthermore, there are several incongruous comparisons. The DZ-DC variances are uniformly smaller than those for the MZ-DC twins and the variances for the DZ-DC twins tend to be similar to those for the MZ-MC twins.

Similar findings were observed when the outliers were excluded and, furthermore, analyses of the within-mean-squares, which should be somewhat more sensitive than analyses of the total variance, showed the same inconsistencies.

DISCUSSION

The Hamilton Twin Study represents one of the most ambitious undertakings to assemble a group of MZ twins with known chorion type. Its purpose was to assess the validity of the observation obtained in the previous NHLBI Twin Study on older men that MZ twins had smaller total variances for serum cholesterol levels than did DZ twins. In this younger population, no appreciable differences were detected in the variances of the DZ versus MZ twins for either cholesterol or log cholesterol. Whatever differences were observed appeared contrary to previous observations. Given these contrary results, it is awkward to attempt to pursue any complex rationale for minor differences among the MZ twins by chorion types. The findings are therefore inconclusive. It is tempting to recommend that further work be done to assemble larger groups of MZ twins with known chorion types but considering the large effort and high costs involved in such a study, such a recommendation seems extravagant at this time. More detailed analyses will continue on the other risk factors for heart disease gathered in the course of this study, and an attempt will be made to relate these to twin type. Perhaps these further analyses and more careful thought will shed additional understanding on the ambiguous results obtained so far.

ACKNOWLEDGMENTS

This research was supported by the National Heart, Lung, and Blood Institute contract N01-HV-72917.

REFERENCES

1. Brown MS, Goldstein JO: Familial hypercholesterolemia: A genetic defect in the low-density lipoprotein receptor. New Engl J Med 294:1386–1390, 1976.
2. Christian JC, Kang KW, Nance WE: Plasma cholesterol in newborn human twins. J Am Oil Chem 52:123a, 1975.
3. Christian JC, Feinleib M, Hulley SB, Castelli WP, Fabsitz RR, Garrison RJ, Borhani NO, Rosenman RH, Wagner J: Genetics of plasma cholesterol and triglycerides: A study of adult male twins. Acta Genet Med Gemellol 25:145–149, 1976.
4. Christian JC, Cheung SW, Kang KW, Harmath FP, Huntzinger DJ, Powell RD: Variance of plasma free and esterified cholesterol in adult twins. Am J Hum Genet 28:174–178, 1977.
5. Corey LA, Kang KW, Christian JC, Norton JA Jr, Harris RE, Nance WE: Effects of chorion type on variation in cord blood cholesterol of monozygotic twins. Am J Hum Genet 28:433–441, 1976.
6. Feinleib M, Havlik RJ, Kwiterovich PO, Tillotson J, Garrison RJ: The National Heart Institute Twin Study. Acta Genet Med Gemellol 19:243–247, 1970.

7. Frederickson DS, Levy RI: Familial hyperlipoproteinemia. In Stanbury JB, Wyngaarden JB, Frederickson DS (eds): "The Metabolic Basis of Inherited Disease." New York: McGraw-Hill, 1972, pp 545—614.
8. Heiss G, Tamir I, Davis CE, Tyroler HA, Rifkind BM, Schonfeld G, Jacobs D, Frantz ID: Lipoprotein-cholesterol distributions in selected North American populations: The Lipid Research Clinics Program Prevalence Study. Circulation 61:2:302—315, 1980.
9. Johnson BC, Epstein FH, Kjelsberg MO: Distributions and familial studies of blood pressure and serum cholesterol levels in a total community—Tecumseh, Michigan. J Chronic Dis 18:147—160, 1965.
10. Kempthorne O, Osborne RH: The interpretation of twin data. Am J Hum Genet 13:320, 1961.
11. Levy RI, Feinleib M: Risk factors for coronary artery disease and their management. In Braunwald E (ed): "Heart Disease: A Textbook of Cardiovascular Medicine." Philadelphia: WB Saunders, 1980, pp 1246—1278.
12. Martin AO, Kurczynski TW, Steinberg AG: Familial studies of medical and anthropometric variables in a human isolate. Am J Hum Genet 25:581—593, 1973.
13. Schaeffer LE, Aldersburg D, Steinberg G: Heredity, environment and serum cholesterol. Circulation 17:537—542, 1958.
14. Steinberg AG: Dependence of the phenotype on environment and heredity in the genetics of migrant and isolate populations. In Goldschmidt E (ed): "Conference on Human Population Genetics in Israel—Jerusalem 1961." Baltimore: Williams & Wilkins, 1963.

Twin Research 3: Epidemiological
and Clinical Studies, pages 163 – 168
© 1981 Alan R. Liss, Inc., 150 Fifth Avenue, New York, NY 10011

Blood Pressure in Norwegian Twins

Arvid Heiberg, Per Magnus, Kåre Berg, and Walter E. Nance

*Institute of Medical Genetics, University of Oslo (A.H., P.M., K.B), and
Department of Human Genetics, Medical College of Virginia, Richmond
(W.E.N.)*

Aggregation of increased blood pressure in families is of considerable
theoretical interest and of practical importance for preventive medicine. Twin
studies [4], family studies [5-7], and adoption studies [1] have mostly, but not
consistently, given results indicating a genetic influence on systolic as well as
diastolic pressure [for review see 6, 8]. Cultural heritability has also been implied
[7]. Many of these studies have been limited to one sex or age group. We have
therefore conducted a twin study on blood pressure in both males and females,
and in two distinctly different age groups.

MATERIALS AND METHODS

All twins were Norwegian, and generally healthy. Two series, A and B, were
examined, consisting of 200 and 36 pairs, respectively.

The twins of the A series were drawn from the Norwegian population-based
twin registry at the Institute of Medical Genetics, University of Oslo, and were in
most cases seen together. As a part of an ongoing study, they had filled in zygosity questionnaires, and blood samples had been examined for more than 15 genetic
markers. They were either 35 or 59 years of age with approximately equal
representation of the two sexes and zygosity categories within each age group.

Series B consisted of members of a twin club. Only a minority had had blood
marker tests performed. They were seen together and had answered a zygosity
questionnaire. The twins in series B were from 14 to 71 years of age, with a mean
of 37 years; 30 pairs were MZ and 6 pairs DZ.

No discrepancies were found between the results of marker studies, clinical examination, and questionnaire response. No subjects were excluded, although a
few were under antihypertensive treatment.

Blood pressure was measured with a 15-cm wide cuff on a calibrated aneroid or
mercury manometer according to the WHO methodology [9]. The lowest systolic
and diastolic (K_5) pressures were recorded and used for calculation.

In the A series the mean and standard deviation of each age and sex group
were taken as the basis for calculation of adjusted systolic and diastolic blood
pressure in terms of standard deviation units within the respective groups. In the

B series the values from the Bergen study [3] were taken as the basis for adjustment, as internal standardization was impractical owing to the small number of twins in each age group.

Analysis of variance was performed according to Christian [2]. P values lower than 0.05 were taken as statistically significant. Heritability values (h^2) were calculated from the formula $h^2 = 2(r_{DZ} - r_{MZ})$, and effect of common environment (c^2) from the formula $c^2 = 2r_{DZ} - r_{MZ}$.

RESULTS

Unadjusted Blood Pressure Values. The range, standard deviations, and mean values obtained for systolic and diastolic blood pressure in the different twins are given in Table 1. The differences between the older and the younger twins in series A are significant for both systolic and diastolic pressure in males as well as females. The mean values for series B are similar to those in the younger twins of series A. No significant skewness or kurtosis was present in any twin, sex, or age category, although some trailing toward higher values was seen. However, the number of persons with a high pressure was small.

Adjusted Values. The means, standard deviations, and total variances are given for adjusted, standard deviation unit values in Table 2. The mean of series B after adjustment is lower than that obtained for series A as a whole and this explains the differences in mean values from zero observed for the total group presented in Table 2. No significant differences between the adjusted mean values were found between different twin groups.

The F ratio between total variances approached borderline significance (0.05 < P < 0.07) for diastolic pressure in some cases, whereas no F ratio is significant for systolic pessure. The difference in total variances was mostly due to variation in females and was most pronounced in the oldest age group, but no difference between groups was found for mean values.

The values of intra-pair and inter-pair variance are given in Table 3, together with F ratios. Most F ratios were significant for MZ and some also for DZ twins.

TABLE 1. Mean Value, Standard Deviation, and Range of Lowest Recorded Systolic and Diastolic Blood Pressure in Different Groups of Norwegian Twins

Twin groups	No. of pairs	Systolic		Diastolic	
		Mean ± SD	Range	Mean ± SD	Range
Series A					
Males 35 years	38	122.4 ± 12.5	90 – 160	82.0 ± 8.5	60 – 100
59 years	51	132.2 ± 19.4	95 – 200	85.1 ± 9.4	60 – 110
Females 35 years	51	118.4 ± 11.4	85 – 150	77.3 ± 7.9	60 – 95
59 years	60	138.8 ± 20.0	100 – 200	85.9 ± 10.8	65 – 115
Males and females	200	128.8 ± 18.6		82.8 ± 9.9	
Series B	36	122.9 ± 18.7	90–178	72.5 ± 14.5	45 – 115

TABLE 2. Systolic and Diastolic Blood Pressures in Different Norwegian Twin Groups*

Twin group	Systolic Pressure				Diastolic Pressure			
	Mean ± standard deviation		Total variances		Mean ± standard deviation		Total variances	
	MZ	DZ	MZ	DZ	MZ	DZ	MZ	DZ
Series A								
Males 35 years	$0.12 \pm 1.10_{22}$	$-0.10 \pm 0.86_{16}$	1.21_{22}	0.74_{16}	$0.10 \pm 1.09_{22}$	$-0.11 \pm \mathbf{0.90}_{16}$	1.18_{22}	0.81_{16}
59 years	$-0.03 \pm 0.98_{22}$	$0.01 \pm 1.04_{29}$	0.96_{22}	1.09_{29}	$0.19 \pm 0.95_{22}$	$-0.14 \pm 1.03_{29}$	0.90_{22}	1.06_{29}
Females 35 years	$0.05 \pm 0.84_{23}$	$-0.01 \pm 1.10_{28}$	0.70_{23}	1.21_{28}	$-0.11 \pm 1.07_{23}$	$0.10 \pm 0.94_{28}$	0.70_{23}	0.88_{28}
59 years	$0.05 \pm 1.05_{32}$	$0.03 \pm 0.96_{28}$	1.11_{32}	1.12_{28}	$0.07 \pm 1.07_{32}$	$0.03 \pm 0.96_{28}$	1.11_{32}	0.83_{28}
Males and females	$0.04 \pm 1.00_{99}$	$0.02 \pm 1.00_{101}$	1.00_{99}	1.09_{101}	$0.06 \pm 1.05_{99}$	$-0.05 \pm 0.95_{101}$	1.09_{99}	0.90_{101}
Series B								
Males	$-0.29 \pm 0.87_{30}$	$-0.64 \pm 0.80_{6}$	0.76_{30}	0.64_{6}	$0.16 \pm 1.06_{30}$	$-0.26 \pm 0.77_{6}$	1.12_{30}	0.59_{6}
Females	$0.029 \pm 0.99_{51}$	$-0.073 \pm 0.99_{48}$	0.97_{51}	0.97_{48}	$0.171 \pm 1.00_{51}$	$-0.128 \pm 0.96_{48}$	0.99_{51}	0.92_{48}
Males and females	$0.074 \pm 0.97_{78}$	$-0.046 \pm 1.02_{59}$	0.94_{78}	1.03_{59}	$0.029 \pm 1.078_{78}$	$-0.001 \pm 0.92_{59}$	1.16_{78}	0.85_{59}
Both series	$-0.033 \pm 0.98_{129}$	$-0.058 \pm 1.00_{107}$	0.95_{129}	1.00_{107}	$0.085 \pm 1.05_{129}$	$-0.058 \pm 0.94_{107}$	1.094_{129}	0.884_{107}

*Adjusted mean values (± standard deviations) are given in standard deviation units, together with total variances. Number of twin pairs is indicated (subscript) behind each group.

TABLE 3. Intra- and Interpair Variances and F Ratio for Interpair/Intrapair Variance, for Systolic and Diastolic Blood Pressure in Different Groups of Norwegian Twins (Numbers Given Under F Ratio are d.f.)

Twin category	Systolic pressure						Diastolic pressure					
	MZ			DZ			MZ			DZ		
	Intra	Inter	F-ratio	Intra	Inter	F-ratio	Intra	Inter	F-ratio	Intra	Inter	F-ratio
Series A												
Males 35 years	0.41	2.05	$4.95_{21,22}$***	0.49	1.01	$2.07_{15,16}$	0.54	1.86	$3.42_{21,22}$**	0.29	1.37	$4.79_{15,16}$**
59 years	0.66	1.27	$1.94_{21,22}$	0.75	1.43	$1.90_{28,29}$*	0.77	1.04	$1.35_{21,22}$	0.85	1.27	$1.48_{28,29}$
Females 35 years	0.33	1.09	$3.35_{22,23}$**	0.85	1.57	$1.84_{27,28}$	0.53	1.79	$3.42_{22,23}$**	0.80	0.96	$1.21_{27,28}$
59 years	0.47	1.76	$3.71_{31,32}$***	0.66	1.19	$1.79_{27,28}$	0.32	1.99	$6.13_{31,32}$***	0.63	1.03	$1.63_{27,28}$
Series B	0.17	1.37	$8.09_{29,30}$***	0.15	1.24	$8.21_{5,6}$*	0.26	2.01	$7.78_{29,30}$***	0.46	0.75	$1.63_{5,6}$
All males	0.47	1.48	$3.140_{50,51}$**	0.73	1.34	$1.845_{58,59}$**	0.61	1.38	$2.26_{50,51}$**	0.61	1.31	$1.43_{58,59}$
All females	0.35	1.54	$4.423_{77,78}$***	0.73	1.34	$1.844_{7,48}$**	0.36	1.98	$5.523_{77,78}$***	0.71	1.01	$1.43_{56,59}$
Total males and females	0.40	1.51	$3.81_{128,129}$***	0.68	1.32	$1.942_{106,107}$***	0.46	1.74	$3.800_{128,129}$***	0.68	1.10	$1.623_{106,10}$*

* p<0.05
** p<0.01
*** p<0.001

TABLE 4. Intraclass Correlation Coefficients and Heritability Estimates for Systolic and Diastolic Blood Pressure in Different Groups of Norwegian Twins

Twin group	Systolic pressure			Diastolic pressure		
	r_{MZ}	r_{DZ}	h^2	r_{MZ}	r_{DZ}	h^2
Series A						
Males 35 years	0.66	0.35	0.63	0.55	0.65	−0.21
59 years	0.32	0.31	0.02	0.15	0.19	−0.08
Females 35 years	0.54	0.30	0.49	0.55	0.10	0.45
59 years	0.58	0.28	0.58	0.72	0.24	0.96
Series B	0.80	0.78	0.04	0.77	0.24	1.06
All males	0.51	0.31	0.41	0.39	0.32	0.13
All females	0.63	0.30	0.62	0.69	0.18	1.03
Total	0.60	0.32	0.56	0.59	0.24	0.71

The intraclass correlations and h^2 (heritability value) for systolic and diastolic blood pressure are given in Table 4. The estimates of effect of common environment in the combined series are 0.04 for systolic and −0.11 for diastolic pressure.

DISCUSSION

In this study, systolic and diastolic blood pressures were normally distributed, although insignificant trailing toward higher values was observed. The adjusted mean values and total variances did not show significant associations with twin type in any age or sex group, although differences from expected values were found, especially in older females. The conditions given by Christian [2] are fulfilled for all groups separately and combined.

Estimates of heritability (h^2) revealed considerable heterogeneity between age and sex groups, values from systolic pressures ranging from 0.02 to 0.63 and for diastolic pressures from −0.21 to 1.03. The h^2 value for the total series was 0.56 for systolic and 0.71 for diastolic pressure. This is in excellent agreement with estimates obtained in a larger study in males [4] and the correlation coefficients we obtained for systolic and diastolic pressure were also remarkably similar to those from that study, both for MZ and DZ twins. There was no appreciable difference in intraclass coefficients if those subjects with hypertension were excluded. Similar findings have been reported by Miall et al [6]. The heritability estimates obtained here originate from subgroups with widely different intraclass coefficients, and age and sex differences exist for both systolic and diastolic pressure. The values we have obtained should therefore be considered with caution. Nevertheless, it is of considerable interest that our results are so similar to those reported by Feinleib et al [4] from a series of twins living under conditions that are very different from those in the Scandinavian countries. When heritability estimates agree this well between different cultural settings, it is reasonable to conclude that the genetic contribution to the variation is highly significant.

ACKNOWLEDGMENTS

This work was conducted at the Institute of Medical Genetics, University of Oslo. It was supported in pat by grant No. NIH PO1 HD10291-4 from the National Institute of Child Health and Human Development to Medical College of Virginia Human Twin Panel Supplement as well as by grants from The Norwegian Council for Cardiovascular Diseases and the Norwegian Research Council on Science and The Humanities.

REFERENCES

1. Biron P, Mongeau, J-G: Familial aggregation of blood pressure and its components. Ped Clin N Am 25 (1):29–33, 1978.
1. Christian JC: Testing twin means and estimating genetic variance. Basic methodology for the analysis of quantitative twin data. Acta Genet Med Gemellol 28:35–40, 1979.
3. Eilertsen E, Humerfelt S: The blood pressure in a representative population sample. Acta Med Scand 183:293–305, 1968.
4. Feinleib M, Garrison RJ, Fabsitz R, Christian JC, Hrubec Z, Borhani NO, Kannel WB, Rosenman R, Schwartz JT, Wagner JO: The NHLBI twin study of cardiovascular disease risk factors: Methodology and summary of results. Am J Epidemiol 106:284–295, 1977.
5. Johnson BC, Epstein FH, Kjelsberg MO: Distributions and familial studies of blood pressure and serum cholesterol in a total community–Tecumseh, Michigan. J Chron Dis 18:147–160, 1965.
6. Miall WE: Genetic considerations concerning hypertension. Ann NY Acad Sci 304:18–25, 1977.
7. Morton NE, Gulbrandsen CL, Rao DC, Rhoads GG, Kagan A: Determinants of blood pressure in Japanese-American families. Hum Genet 53:261–266, 1980.
8. Tyroler HA: The Detroit project studies of blood pressure. A prologue and review of related studies and epidemiological issues. J Chron Dis 30:613–624, 1977.
9. World Health Organization: Technical Reports Series 168:9–10, 1959.

Twin Research 3: Epidemiological
and Clinical Studies, pages 169 — 178
© 1981 Alan R. Liss, Inc., 150 Fifth Avenue, New York, NY 10011

Twin Studies and Chronogenetics

L. Gedda and G. Brenci

The Gregor Mendel Institute of Medical Genetics and Twin Studies, Rome, Italy

Within the framework of a congress dedicated to gemellology, that is to the study of twins, chronogenetics is very much at home. Indeed, the research we have been doing for many years on monozygotic (MZ) twins has led us to the conclusion that there exists a basic, built-in biological timetable of hereditary origin.

It is necessary to refer to this basic, built-in genetic or hereditary timetable in order to make clear that we are not dealing here with the physicist's time, used in measuring the cosmic environment, and which living organisms derive from outside of themselves, but rather with an individual biological time, programmed by heredity and by the factors that make up heredity: chromosomes and genes (Fig. 1).

Long ago Linnaeus [8], by building his horologium florae or flower clock (Fig. 2) on the basis of the hours in which the various flower species open their petals, had shown that this phenomenon occurs in every hour of the day and night. Thus Linnaeus's flower clock demonstrates that solar time interacts with a hereditary and original time, which is characteristic of the single plant species.

Concerning twins, about 50 years ago, in 1933, Frischeisen-Köhler [7], using the metronome, showed that "personal time" measured by clapping hands or by tapping feet in the case of MZ cotwins exhibited a variability that was equal to the individual variability, whereas in the case of DZ cotwins and in the case of nontwin siblings it exhibited a different value.

At the Mendel Institute, the study of twins has given us the opportunity to observe more significant phenomena, like the "synchronisms" that are repeated in MZ twins both for normal phenomena (like weight, height, physiognomy, and so on) and for pathological phenomena (like progressive muscular dystrophy, epilepsy, retinoblastoma, and so on). These synchronisms (see, eg, Figs. 3 and 6) force us toward the conclusion that genetic information, or the lack of it, follows a kind of hereditary timing that is characteristic of the single genotype.

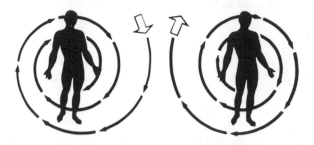

Fig. 1. Chronobiology vs chronogenetics.

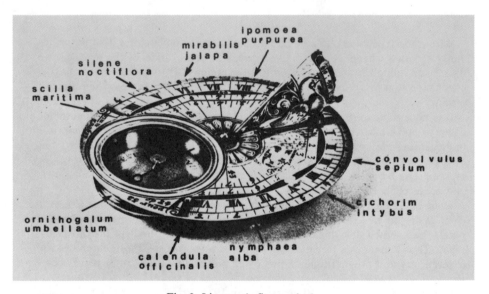

Fig. 2. Linnaeus's flower clock.

In other words, gemellology is the tree that has given us as its fruit the fourth dimension of the gene, which is the time parameter of the hereditary unit. Since the 1960s we have been talking about "ergon" as the degree of stability of the gene and about "chronon" as the length in time of its information. With these concepts we founded [4], during the 1970s the branch of "chronogenetics," which is defined as follows by the genetics glossary of Rieger et al [9]: "A branch of genetics devoted to the study of the fundamental, endogenous genetic time (hereditary biological time) with its theoretical and practical, normal and pathological implications."

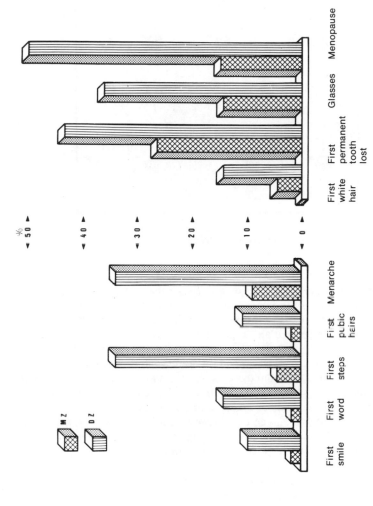

Fig. 3. Discordance values for the timing of a number of physiological phenomena in MZ vs DZ twin pairs.

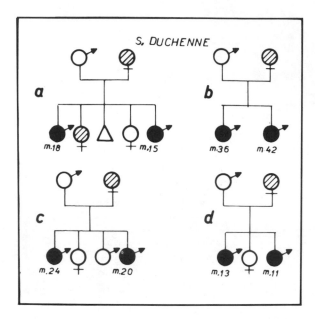

Fig. 4. Similar times of onset of muscular dystrophy in siblings of four different families.

Wherever a DNA molecule records a message that is translated into a protein structure, precisely here the DNA molecule reveals that it operates within a time frame. In order to explain the variability in the length in time of hereditary information, we have defined an "ergon-chronon system" based on three parameters of gene stability: 1) Synonymous stability, due to the different number of hydrogen bonds which, given an equal codified information, can be present in the codogenic strand; 2) redundancy stability, due to the number of repetitions of the informatic sequence; 3) repair stability, due to the interaction among the repair mechanisms of the gene and its structure.

According to this model, given equal levels of primary product, genes may have a different stability, that is to say an ergon value determined by heredity and a chronon value of corresponding information which is directly proportional to the ergon.

The extrapolation of chronogenetics from twin studies involves first of all singletons who have no ad hoc meter of comparison; that is to say, they have no twin in order to show that the mechanisms of chronogenetics must be respected here as well. Here the phenomena do not have the mathematical exactness of a comparison between twins, but nevertheless they provide evidence whose validity is not in question, and which consists in the repetition, within the family, of ontogenetic types, from the timetable for growing old to the timetable for an illness, all of which show a characteristic covariance, even in

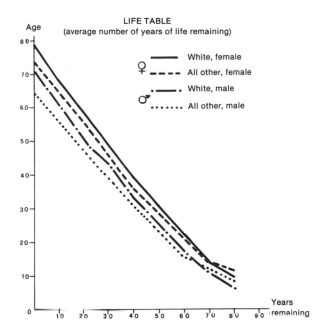

Fig. 5. Life expectancy curves for the U.S. population.

the case of individuals born in different periods, belonging to the same family. Here we are dealing not with "synchronism" but rather with "isochronism," which is the term we use to indicate the presence of a hereditary timetable far beyond the MZ twin pair, within the realm of consanguineity.

The study of synchronism in twins has led us to identify a similar sort of behavior in the actuarial curves for life expectancy in different populations. For example, in the United States these curves for men and women in the white and nonwhite population (Fig. 5) yield a chronological characterization to which we have given the name "homochronism."

Having established that the ergon-chronon system concerns every form of life, it is useful to repeat that in the case of the human species the twin test represents the preferred method for deepening the insights provided by chronogenetics. The twin pair is a living laboratory that gives us information directly regarding the hereditary biological timetable.

The study of chronogenetics introduces into the twin method the calculation of time, because it requires us to supplement the horizontal study of the twin pair with longitudinal study through observations repeated over a period of time.

The phenotypic parameters that are analyzed over time can be arranged according to a series of values, that is, according to parallel curves for the MZ

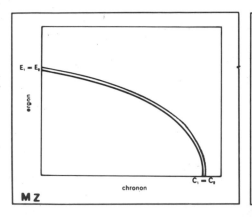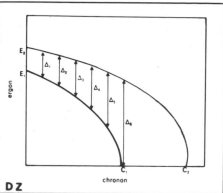

Fig. 6. The ergon-chronon system in MZ vs DZ twin pairs.

pairs and divergent curves for DZ pairs (Fig. 6). The chronogenetic parameter that can be derived from the differences that are observed at different points in time between comparable MZ and DZ pairs indicates how much of the ergon decay is due to individual mutability and how much is due to mutagenic factors in the environment.

The series of ergon decays (that is, the chronogenetic value of the decay) can be analyzed in MZ pairs in order to define the decay coefficient of the information per unit of time and thus to forecast the moment of its extinction.

In fact, if the double temporal sequence is equivalent for MZ cotwins, this shows the chronogenetic meaning of the phenomenon and the time lag between two successive moments measures the speed of variation in genetic ergon through the corresponding variation of the quantity of information in the phenotype. Thus there exist two twin tests for the study of chronogenetics: the interzygotic twin test and the monozygotic twin test.

We have used twin tests to study hereditary time at the gene level and at the chromosome level through two research projects. In the first project [5] we have used the monozygotic twin test to study the frequency of sister chromatide exchanges on lymphocitary cultures of MZ twins, and we have found a frequency of exchange that is characteristically in agreement for cotwins and divergent from one pair to the other (Table 1).

At the chromosome level, we have used the interzygotic twin test to study the blastic index, the mytotic index, and the centromeric index in chromosomes 1, 9, and 16 in a subculture of lymphocytes taken from 16 pairs of MZ and 16 pairs of DZ twins in two age groups, 8–10 and 18–20 years [3]. The results of the analysis of these data show the existence of a variation, with age, of the average values of these parameters, while the hereditary conditioning remains constant (Table 2).

TABLE 1. Frequency of Sister Chromatid Exchanges in MZ Twins. Within-Pair and Between-Pair Variability

Variability within pairs $\bar{x}_1 - \bar{x}_2 = \Delta\bar{x}$	t	df	P
$1_A \rightarrow 2_A \{14.8 - 14.7\} = 0.1$	0.239	18	≈ 0.80
$1_B \rightarrow 2_B \{16.2 - 16.4\} = -0.2$	0.424	18	≈ 0.70
$1_C \rightarrow 2_C \{17.1 - 16.9\} = 0.2$	0.373	18	≈ 0.75

Variability between pairs $\bar{x}_1 - \bar{x}_2 = \Delta\bar{x}$	t	df	P
$A \rightarrow B \{14.7 - 16.3\} = -1.6$	5.030	38	< 0.001
$A \rightarrow C \{14.7 - 17.0\} = -2.3$	6.781	38	< 0.001
$B \rightarrow C \{16.3 - 17.0\} = -0.7$	2.007	38	≈ 0.05

After Gedda et al [5].

TABLE 2. Variations With Age of Within-Pair Correlation and Heritability for the Blastic, Mitotic, and Association Indexes

Age group			Blastic index	Mitotic index	Association index
6–8 years	r	MZ	0.90	0.47	0.58
		DZ	0.53	0.33	0.63
	h		0.74	0.28	~0
16–18 years	r	MZ	0.71	0.38	0.53
		DZ	0.53	0.41	0.51
	h		0.36	~0	~0

After Gedda et al [3].

Before this, we had used the interzygotic twin test to study menarche and menopause times, and we concluded that these times are determined by hereditary factors to a degree of about 75% for menarche and about 80% for menopause [2].

A special chronogenetic research project, in which twins are at the same time the object of the research and the test with which the research is carried out, regards the moment in which the MZ twin begins his existence. In fact, in comparison to the singleton, the realization of the personal existence of the human twin is delayed, since the moment of conception does not only concern him, but also the cotwin. Thus the zygote and its cellular clone that are destined to produce a pair of identical twins do not represent, as in the case of the singleton, a single individual, but a preindividual group of cells. The twin indi-

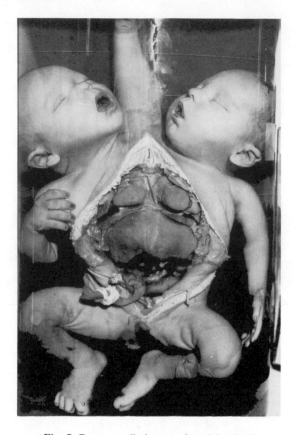

Fig. 7. Dextrocardia in one of conjoined twins.

vidual is determined when the preindividual group of cells divides into two or more totipotential parts.

The stage of the preindividual MZ clone is important not only theoretically, since this stage does not exist for the singleton, but also objectively. The phenomenon of mirror imaging goes back to the duration of the preindividual zygote. Let us pause for a moment to look at some figures derived from our research [6] on functional mirror imaging carried out on 537 twin pairs (Table 3).

Let us also think for a moment about the objective datum of siamese twins, in whom it can happen (Fig. 7) that the heart is on the left in one twin but on the right in the other [1].

From this derives our hypothesis that the division of the preindividual MZ clone that produces these twins occurred late, at a time when the preindividual

TABLE 3. Frequency of Mirror Imaging in Twins

Parameter	MZ pairs (N = 184)		DZ pairs (N = 353)	
	n	%	n	%
Hand used for writing	15	8.1	12	3.4
Hand used for throwing	30	16.3	46	13.0
Foot used for kicking	29	15.8	43	12.2
Eye used for aiming	15	8.1	19	5.4

After Gedda et al [6].

clone was already chorsclinked by the planes of segmentation that define one side in respect to the other. In this sense, mirror imaging is a chronogenetic datum on the level of the preindividual MZ clone.

The development of chronogenetic research has a definite purpose, which is to provide a scientific back-up for individualized preventive medicine.

It is commonly accepted that medicine, before it treats a disease, must attempt to prevent that disease. But the prevention we have is based on hygiene, and is thus based on average data in regard to a given population. In order to be complete, preventive medicine should be individualized; it should take into account the individual's pathologic heritage.

Along this road there are two signposts: the genealogical analysis of the family and the analysis of the decay of genotypes in question in the single individual. On this basis we can predict the onset of hereditary disease and establish the optimum individual environment to prevent the disease and the moment at which treatment will become necessary.

To extrapolate from the phenotype the "status" of genetic information and to develop on this basis a plan of individual prevention, longitudinal check-ups repeated over time can be very important, but only if the decay curve has been shown to be hereditary and if its heritability has been defined using twin research.

It is clear that the study of heritability can be based on other methods, such as the covariation among relatives, but here the notable difficulties already present in the ordinary examination of normal and pathological hereditary characteristics become enormous, especially in connection with time characteristics, because the interaction between individual time and historical time (with the latter being different even for individuals from the same families) prevents us from grasping the chronogenetic meaning of the time characteristics. Therefore, the monozygotic cotwin reference is essential to evaluate the nature and the chronogenetic meaning of the hereditary units.

There does exist in Italy as well as everywhere else the conviction that preventive medicine is the road medical science must take, and that the mere deductive applications of hygiene, of epidemiology, of environmental studies and studies of the work place are not enough. But preventive medicine must be developed in relation to the individual, because it is the genome of each individual that carries within it the timetable of his health and of his illness. Necessarily, the scientific basis of preventive medicine is genetics and more specifically chronogenetics, because this is the science that will develop the ability to draw up a calendar of the extinction of certain genes and thus set the date for the beginning of a specific preventive treatment. I think that we gemellologists have in our hands some very precious material to convince the world of medical science, to demonstrate that is is possible to carry on research for a reliable scientific basis and thus to open the door, at long last, for preventive medicine as the finest gift that twin studies can offer for the health and well-being of mankind.

REFERENCES

1. Gedda L: Il mostro di Vipiteno (Xifodimo tetrabranchio maschile). Acta Genet Med Gemellol 3:283–302, 1954.
2. Gedda L, Brenci G: Biology of the gene: The ergon/chronon system. Acta Genet Med Gemellol 18:329–379, 1969.
3. Gedda L, Del Porto G, Brenci G, D'Alessandro E, Di Fusco C, Di Tonto B, Gallina S: A twin study of cytogenetic variability. Progress report. Acta Genet Med Gemellol 26:275–276, 1977.
4. Gedda L, Brenci G: "Chronogenetics—The Inheritance of Biological Time." Springfield, Illinois: CC Thomas, 1978.
5. Gedda L, Brenci G, Di Fusco C, Noto A, Roselli E: Studies of mutability in MZ twins. In Gedda L,, Parisi P, Nance WE (eds): "Twin Research 3: Epidemiological and Clinical Studies." New York: Alan R. Liss, 1981, pp. 247–248.
6. Gedda L. Brenci G, Franceschetti A, Talone C, Ziparo R: A study of mirror imaging in Twins. In Gedda L, Parisi P, Nance WE (eds): "Twin Research 3: Twin Biology and Multiple Pregnancy." New York: Alan R. Liss, 1981, pp 167–168.
7. Frischeisen-Köhler I: "Das persönliche Tempo." Leipzig: C Thieme, 1933.
8. Linnaeus C: "Philosophia Botanica." Vienna: JT Trattner, 1763, p 278.
9. Rieger R, Michaelis A, Green MM: "Glossary of Genetics and Cytogenetics. Classical and Molecular," 4th Ed. Berlin, Heidelberg, New York: Springer-Verlag, 1976.

Twin Research 3: Epidemiological
and Clinical Studies, pages 179–185

The Age-Dependence of Disorders of Aging: Implications for Studies of Twins

Philip R.J.Burch
Department of Medical Physics, University of Leeds

INTRODUCTION

When introducing the somewhat diffuse subject of aging, many authors feel obliged to offer a definition of the phenomenon. And those of us who are unwilling to propose or endorse a definition feel obliged to explain our reluctance.

Although no general formulation has yet been adopted, one theme has dominated all others: the close connexion between aging and death. Thus, Comfort believes: "Senescence is probably best regarded as a general title for the group of effects which, in various phyla, lead to a decreasing expectation of life with increasing age" [9]. Maynard Smith's viewpoint is similar: "As an ageing process I mean any process occurring in an individual which renders that individual more likely to die in a given time interval as it grows older" [11]. Bateman's recent (1979) definition differs little from these: "...a time-dependent irreversible degeneration that accumulates until it becomes life-threatening." [2].

Although these three authors see causal links between aging and death, they avoid identifying the process directly with specific fatal diseases. They appear to regard aging as an underlying process that contributes in some nonspecific way to the shortening of life.

In my view, the notion that aging should be regarded exclusively in terms of life-shortening processes is too restrictive. It excludes some conspicuous conditions of aging, such as the loss and graying of hair, which, so far as I am aware, do not of themselves increase the risk of death.

Other gerontologists have sought to confine the label "aging" to those conditions to which all persons are susceptible. But in a survey of the age-prevalence of arcus senilis my collaborators and I deduced that only about 52% of the population are at risk [8]. This proportion is substantially less than 100%, but I see no reason why we should change the name of the condition which, again, is not obviously life-shortening. In the same survey, we found that the percentage of males at risk to "centre" baldness is somewhat higher, at about 74%, but still well under 100% [8]. The loss of hair constitutes, however, one aspect of the classical picture of the aging man.

If the description "aging" were to be confined to conditions to which every person is at more or less equal risk, then the scope for twin studies in gerontology would be drastically curtailed. The concordance for an "aging condition" in MZ twins would approximate that for comparable same-sexed DZ twins and, consequently, indications of a genetic influence on aging, which depend on differences in these concordances, would be precluded by the definition of aging. It is generally believed, however, that genetic factors play an important role not only in benign conditions such as male baldness but also in fatal disorders such as ischaemic heart disease that do much to determine the life-span. In view of the indubitable links between aging, mortality, and predisposing genes, we need to test the hypothesis that some persons are susceptible to certain aging disorders while others are not. And if there are aging disorders to which everyone is susceptible—such as the greying of hair [8]—we still need to find whether some persons are, intrinsically, more susceptible than others. In either circumstance appropriate studies of twins can be expected to provide illumination.

Efforts have also been made to distinguish between "normal" or "physiological," aging on the one hand and "pathological" aging on the other. Comfort dismisses these as "endless unfruitful discussions" [9]; I have no wish to dissent from his opinion.

These several problems of definition are, I believe, largely semantic in nature and of little scientific importance. We need, surely, to direct our efforts to understanding the causes and mechanisms of *all* age-dependent disorders regardless of nosology. For those of us participating in this symposium, it is of some importance that theories of aging with a genetic content inevitably make predictions that can be tested, to a greater or lesser degree, by the study of concordance in twins.

AUTOAGGRESSIVE THEORY OF AGING

My collaborators and I hold that many age-dependent disorders—fatal and benign—result from random "errors" in the system whose normal physiological function is the central regulation of the growth and size of target tissues throughout the body [3 — 8]. We call such disorders *autoaggressive*. A specific growth-control stem cell that has accumulated a specific set of random somatic mutations propagates a *forbidden clone* of descendant cells, the peripheral cells of which, or their secreted humoral products, attack target cells at one or more anatomical sites.

Laws of Age-Dependence

The autoaggressive mechanism appears to be subject to some surprisingly strict stochastic laws and, when certain conditions are satisfied, the age-prevalence, $P(t_e)$, of a nonlethal chronic disorder at any postnatal age t_e is given by:

$$P(t_o) = S\{1\text{-}exp\text{-}k(t_o\text{-}\lambda)^r\}^n$$

(1)

where S is the proportion of the surveyed population at genetic risk to the disorder; n is the number of sets of growth-control stem cells at somatic mutational risk; k is a kinetic constant defined by Lm^r, where L is the number of growth control stem cells at risk to somatic mutation in a single set, and m is the average rate at which each of the r genes at risk in a cell mutates, per cell at risk, per year; and λ is the average latent period between the occurrence of the last initiating somatic mutation and the first expression of the disease [3, 5].

That is to say, a specific growth-control stem cell in a genetically predisposed person that has accumulated all r specific mutations may propagate a pathogenic forbidden clone. One such forbidden clone (n = 1) often suffices to cause an autoaggressive disorder. However, in some disorders (and notably those that exhibit distinctive phases of progression), n forbidden clones may be required to produce the ultimate signs, where n is a positive integer that can range up to 10 at least. The total number of random events required to initiate the process that leads to the defined endpoint is, therefore, n r. When there are sex differences, as often happens, $P(t_o)$ needs to be specified by sex.

Between the occurrence of the last random initiating somatic mutation, and the first onset of the disorder, an interval, or *latent period*, λ, elapses. The value of λ is determined, in large part, by genetic factors and it may differ substantially from person to person within the genetically predisposed subpopulation defined by S [6].

Scope of Laws

Cited publications show numerous examples of the conformity of the age patterns of autoaggressive disorders, fatal and benign, malignant and nonneoplastic, infectious and allergic, of early and late onset, to Equation 1 and its differentiated version giving age-specific onset or death rates. (Where infectious and allergic diseases are concerned, S is calculated from onset or mortality data; it represents the proportion of the population that is a) genetically predisposed and b) successfully invaded by the specific microorganism or allergen. Although the value of S may change from year to year, the other parameters, n, r and k, remain constant.) When diagnosis is reliable and the disease process is homogeneous, conformity to the theoretical equations is usually impressive.

PROBLEMS FOR STUDIES OF TWINS

Those studies of twins that seek to explore the role of genetic factors in disease rely on demonstrating differences in concordance between MZ and DZ twin pairs. Some authors believe that the relative contributions of heredity and environment to a given disorder can be calculated and expressed quantitatively; the genetic contribution—expressed as a fraction or a percentage—is defined as *heritance*. According to our theory, such concepts are inapplicable to autoaggressive disorders. To develop a particular disorder a specific inheritance is a necessary, but not always a sufficient, condition. Given a genotype at conception that predisposes to a given disease, the organism will remain predisposed at birth, provided somatic mutation during embryogenesis does not change genes in key mesenchymal controlling cells. But given predisposition at birth, n r specific somatic mutations have to occur randomly before the disease process can be initiated. In the example of infectious and allergic diseases, the occurrence of the n r initiating somatic mutations does not suffice to cause disease; the nonimmune host must also be invaded by the appropriate precipitating agent—microorganism or allergen—before forbidden clones proliferate to attack target tissues and cause the classical symptoms and signs of disease. That is to say, inherited and environmental factors are both essential to the expression of such disorders. In many chronic autoaggressive disorders infective agents can act as exacerbators to affect the age of first onset but even in such circumstances it would be meaningless to calculate the separate contributions of environment and inheritance in terms of percentages.

PAIRWISE CONCORDANCE RATIOS AND AGE

Prevalence and Penetrance

Equation 1, defining prevalence, enables penetrance to be defined as a function of age. The penetrance, $P(t_e)$, of an autoaggressive disorder is the probability that it has been expressed, by age t_e, in a person who was genetically predisposed at birth. From Equation 1,

$$P(t_e) = \{1\text{-exp-}k(t_e\text{-}\lambda)^r\}^n$$

(2)

Because the mean value of λ is largely genetically determined and can differ quite widely from one genotype to another [6], complications will arise in the study of concordance in twins, particularly when $P(t_e)$ increases rapidly with age.

Consider the example of ischaemic heart disease (IHD) which claims more deaths than any other single disease in many medically advanced countries. The age-specific mortality, dP/dt, attributable to the main component of IHD is described [6] by:

$$dP/dt = 6kS(t_e\text{-}\lambda)^5\text{exp-}k(t_e\text{-}\lambda)^6$$

(3)

In United States whites, 1968 to 1975, the average latent period, λ (from initiation to death) was about 12 years for men and 24 years for women [6]. (IHD belongs to that general class of autoaggressive disease in which $\lambda_f = 2\lambda_M$.) From an analysis of the age-dependence of mortality ratios for various "risk factors," it is clear that sub-groups within the male population can have mean latent periods at least as short as 2 years [6].

Pairwise Concordance With Genetic Determination of Latent Period

For simplicity, let us consider a nonfatal disorder to which everyone in the population is predisposed at birth, but with kinetics and genetically determined latent periods resembling those of IHD. (The problem of concordance for simple genetic models of predisposition has been analysed [10] recently by Marshall and Knox. Problems of ascertainment have been discussed [1] by Allen and Hrubec.)

Suppose that one twin, A, of a DZ pair belongs to a specific subgroup with average latent period λ_1 and that the cotwin, B, belongs to a different subgroup with average latent period λ_2. The expected pairwise concordance, C(DZ), for the disorder in such DZ pairs at age t_e is given by:

$$C(DZ) = \{1\text{-exp-k}(t_E\text{-}\lambda_1{}^6\}\{1\text{-exp-k}(t_E\text{-}\lambda_2)^6\}$$

(4)

For MZ pairs, with both members belonging to the same genetic subgroup with average latent period λ_3, the corresponding concordance, C(MZ), is given by:

$$C(MZ) = \{1\text{-exp-k}(t_e\text{-}\lambda_3)^6\}^2$$

(5)

It follows from Equations 4 and 5 that the ratio of the concordance in MZ pairs at age, t_e, to that in DZ pairs of the same age and sex will, in general, depend on age. This gives rise to a complication that is somewhat analogous to the marked dependence of mortality ratios on age, observed for "risk factors" in connexion with IHD [6]. A simple example serves to illustrate the typical magnitude of the ratio, C(MZ)/C(DZ)—which we shall call R—and its dependence on age.

Numerical example. Suppose that the average (genetically determined) latent period between initiation and onset is 12 years. Assume that: two alleles, L1 and L2, of equal frequency (0.5), at a single autosomal locus, act as the genetic determinants of latent period; the mean latent period in the L1,L1 genotype is 4 years in L1,L2 it is 12 years; and in L2,L2 it is 20 years. (The mean value of the latent period for IHD in males is 12 years.) The weighted average pairwise concordance for MZ twins, allowing for the three possible genotypes, is readily evaluated at any age, t_e, from Equation 5. For DZ twins the calculation is more tedious because the frequencies of genotypes in all DZ pairs have to be evaluated, for all possible matings, before the weighted average concordance can be calculated.

The results obtained from this example, assuming panmictic mating, are shown by the lower curve in Figure 1; the upper curve shows the results for a similar set of assumptions, but with latent periods doubled to 8, 24, and 40 years, respectively.

It will be seen that the ratio, R, tends towards unity with advancing age as penetrance tends to unity. Given sufficiently large numbers of twins to determine concordance ratios for a disorder as a function of age, a graph of the kind shown in Figure 7 would enable the separate contributions of the two types of inheritance to be distinguished. The asymptotic value of R at high age would reflect the concordance ratio arising from those genetic factors that determine predisposition itself and would correspond to the ratios calculated by Marshall and Knox [10]; any hypothesis of the genetics of predisposition would need to be consistent with this asymptotic value of R. Similarly, hypotheses of the genetic determination of latent period would need to be consistent with the age-dependence of R.

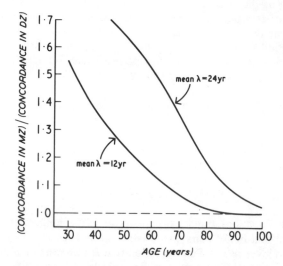

Fig. 1. Ratio of pairwise concordance in MZ twins to that in DZ twins, versus age of expression of disorder. (For details, see text and Equations 4 and 5.) Upper curve is based on a mean latent period, initiation to expression, of 24 years; lower curve is based on a mean latent period of 12 years.

CONCLUSIONS

This paper has directed attention to two distinctive types of genetic contribution to the expression of age-dependent disorders. One contribution—the orthodox [10]—simply determines whether or not a person is genetically predisposed to the disorder in question. The second, previously unrecognized contribution, influences the age at which the disorder manifests by being the main determinant of the duration of the latent period (λ) between the initiation of the active disease process and its expression in symptoms or signs.

An important parameter in twins studies is the ratio, R, of concordance (however defined) for a disorder in MZ twins to that in DZ twins. Over the age range where penetrance changes it is, of course, essential that concordances for both types of twins should be determined for a common age. For a disorder in which genetic predisposition is homogeneous, orthodox predisposing factors make a constant contribution to R, independent of age. However, the genetic influence on the latent period, λ, contributes an age-dependent factor that starts high but tends to unity as penetrance tends to 100%. Examples of this form of age-dependent contributions are shown in Figure 1.

Given sufficiently large numbers, studies of concordance for aging disorders in MZ and DZ twins should be able to shed valuable light on both types of genetic influence.

REFERENCES

1. Allen G, Hrubec Z: Twin concordance: A more general model. Acta Genet Med Gemellol 28:3–13, 1979.
2. Bateman AJ: Genetic effects on ageing. Q Rev Biol 54:330–331, 1979.
3. Burch PRJ: "An Inquiry Concerning Growth, Disease and Ageing." Edinburgh: Oliver and Boyd, 1968; Buffalo: Toronto Universty Press, 1969.
4. Burch PRJ: What limits the life span? In Benjamin B, Cox PR, Peel J (eds): "Population and the New Biology." London and New York: Academic Press, 1974, pp 31–56.
5. Burch PRJ: "The Biology of Cancer. A New Approach." Lancaster, Baltimore: Medical and Technical Publishing; University Park Press, 1976.
6. Burch PRJ: Ischaemic heart disease: Epidemiology, risk factors and cause. Cardiovascular Res 14:307–338, 1980.
7. Burch PRJ, Burwell RG: Self and not-self. A clonal induction approach to immunology. Q Rev Biol 40:252–279, 1965.
8. Burch PRJ, Murray, JJ, Jackson D: The age-prevalence of arcus senilis, greying of hair, and baldness. Etiological considerations. J Gerontol 26:364–372, 1971.
9. Comfort A: "Ageing. The Biology of Senescence." London: Routledge and Kegan Paul, 1964.
10. Marshall T, Knox EG: Disease concordance and sex similarity in twins. J Epidemiol Comm Health 34:1–8, 1980.
11. Maynard Smith J: Theories of ageing. In Krohn PL (ed): "Topics in the Biology of Aging." New York: Interscience Publishers, 1966, pp 1–27.

Twin Research 3: Epidemiological
and Clinical Studies, pages 187 — 200
© 1981 Alan R. Liss, Inc., 150 Fifth Avenue, New York, NY 10011

A Longevity Study of Twins in the Mormon Genealogy

Dorit Carmelli and Sheree Andersen

Department of Medical Biophysics and Computing, University of Utah

INTRODUCTION

Adequate data on the contribution of genetic elements to human life span for the gerontological period are scarce. The main difficulties arise in maintaining such studies over a long period of time as well as the rapid changes in environmental factors known or suspected to influence this trait and liable to ascribe considerable biases in multigenerational comparisons.

In the face of the above constraints, investigators have had recourse to twin studies. Longevity studies of twins have been done notably by Kallman and his associates [5] and by Hauge [4], who utilized the Danish twin registry during the period 1870–1910. In the former study, final life span data were collected during a 12-year follow-up period from a total of 1,603 index cases who survived age 60. They show considerable intrapair similarity in duration of life, more marked in monozygous (MZ) than in dizygous (DZ) twins, with a mean difference in life span decreasing with age. In many ways, data of this kind are the most satisfactory from a genetic standpoint. However, one must be cautious to avoid overinterpreting the contributions of genetic elements. "Results from twin studies for a wide variety of different traits and diseases show the foregoing kind of pattern with considerable regularity; one would perhaps have expected some major exceptions and, lacking them, may wonder about the power of this method [6]." If we believe however, that what genetic component there is relates not to a category "longevity" buy to the quantitative variate "length of life," information on the life experience of an adequate twin cohort may still be of considerable interest to geneticists and epidemiologists interested in this topic.

The present report summarizes the final life span of 2,242 pairs of twins born between 1800 and 1899, extracted from the Mormon Genealogy Data Base, recently computerized at the University of Utah [8]. The basic units of genealogical information are Family Group Sheets, which include for each child sex, birth order, name, date and place of birth, death and marriage events, and name(s) of marriage partner(s). A description of the data base and methods of record linking are given in Skolnick et al [8]. Twins were identified in the Mormon genealogy by systematically processing the individual file (1.2 million records), transferring to the older sib record, where it exists, and comparing respective birth dates. A threshold of less than 3 days difference in date of birth was used to denote twins. The rate of twinning in the Utah genealogy was determined by examining all live births recorded on Family Group Sheets with a demographic reference to Utah. A discussion on the interaction of twinning rates, total fertility, and average maternal age, as well as the analysis of clustering of twins in pedigrees, is presented in a separate paper [2].

The exigency of knowledge relating to total longevity of twins has prompted this dimension of our research. Our study differs from that of Kallman's [5] in that we have addressed the whole life experience of twins in the cohort of interest rather than limiting the study to those twins who survived age 60. Our data lack zygosity distinction beyond same-sexed and opposite-sexed twins and the corresponding causes of death. The latter two restrictions jointly imply confounded genetic with nongenetic effects. Informative results may nevertheless be obtained under the assumption that the correlation of same-sexed twins is significantly enhanced by the MZ component. We found this assumption substantiated by our results. The lack of information on cause of death, occupation, and other socioeconomic covariates that may influence the trait studied dictated the use of descriptive and nonparametric methods.

We proceeded in two steps. First, we evaluated a battery of correlation and concordance measures on the joint mortality distributions of the first and second born twins for same-sexed male and female twin pairs and correspondingly for the subgroup of DZ opposite-sexed twin pairs. Then we examined entire survivorship curves by standard life table and actuarial methods. The weakness of these methods lies in their relatively low statistical efficiency and their failure to throw any light on fundamental mechanisms. However, some broad conclusions seem warranted, suggesting further investigations in the nature of the familial resemblance among other types of family members, eg, sib–sib comparisons, parent–offspring, etc.

MATERIALS AND METHODS

To guard against possible bias in the death dates that were recorded, we prepared an abstract of the death data for the period of interest. Table 1 gives the distribution of recorded death dates by same-sexed male and female and opposite-sexed twin pairs for 20-year birth cohorts of the last century.

There do not appear to be identifiable patterns either in the recording or nonrecording of information. The nineteenth century of the Mormon genealogy consists of 3,631 twin pairs; 60% of these pairs have recorded death dates for both twins, 25% have one available death date, and 15% have death dates for neither twin. The distribution of available death data is uniform over time within each sex group and thus lends confidence to the assumption of representative death information of the twin cohort studied.

TABLE 1. Distribution of Death Information by Sex on Twins Born Between 1800 and 1899 in the Utah Mormon Genealogy

Year of birth	Total twins born 3,739 (100%)			Death date for both 2,242 (60%)			Death date for one 921 (25%)			Death date for neither — 576 (15%)		
	MM	FF	MF	MM	FF	MF	MM	FF	MF	MM	FF	MF
1800–39	35	34	46	22	20	26	4	5	12	9	9	11
1840–59	162	157	220	108	109	142	25	32	50	29	16	29
1860–79	420	476	506	262	293	313	91	104	130	67	79	63
1880–99	540	539	604	334	275	342	131	171	166	75	93	96
Total	1,157	1,206	1,376	726	697	823	251	312	358	180	197	199

To insure more definitive analyses, we trichotomized the data with respect to death experience of each twin pair, that is, where 1) both twins died in first year of life (infant death), 2) one of the twin pair died in infancy, and 3) both twins survived the first year of life. The motivation for this classification lies in considerations unique to infant mortality. Being prevalent in multiple births, it would unduly weight the results toward concordance were we not to make this classification. These distinctions, being made, leave us with the distribution of complete life histories as follows:

	Male–Male	Male–Female	Female–Female	Total
Both die in infancy	218	182	198	598
One survives infancy	185	255	145	585
Both survive infancy	319	386	355	1,060
Total	722	823	697	2,242

For all twin pairs with known death dates (1,060 pairs), we have employed contingency table analysis, utilizing the natural pairing. The rows, i, and columns, j, of the same-sexed tables are the age at death categories of the first and second born twin, respectively, based on the Family Group Sheet parity record. The opposite-sexed tables have rows and columns as the age at death categories of the male and female twin, respectively.

There are several measures of independence, correlation, and symmetry that lend well to categorical data of this nature. Perhaps the most common tests for independence of rows and columns are the Pearson's χ^2 statistic or the G-Likelihood Ratio. Other descriptive nonparametric association measures may be assessed which assume the value 0 when individual cell frequencies satisfy the hypothesis of independence and the maximum value of 1 when the association is "perfect." However, what perfect association means varies from one measure to another. One such measure of association, Cramer's V, is independent of sample size and may be used to compare tables with unequal sample sizes. It is derived from the χ^2 statistic using the normalizing factor $N(m-1)$, where N is the total number of pairs and m is the dimension of the table. We also recorded the Spearman's Rank Correlation Coefficient which employs the ordered age at death categories and uses the cell entries as frequencies. These measures are accompanied by Kendall's τ, which measures the correlation of the monotone relationship between two variables. It is evaluated by comparing the number of agreements in the orderings of the indices between pairs of observations with the number of disagreements.

Goodman and Kruskal [3] proposed another type of statistic, the Optimal Prediction Statistic, $\lambda_{i/j}$, which measures the gain in predicting the row variable, i, when the value of the column variable, j, is known, relative to when it is unknown. The statistic $\lambda_{j/i}$ has the complementary definition. In the case of statistical independence $\lambda_{i/j}$ will be zero, but the converse need not hold; ie, $\lambda_{i/j}$ may be zero without statistical independence present.

Intratable symmetry is another aspect of relationship that we investigated. McNemar's χ^2 statistic tests the equality of frequencies in all pairs of cells that are symmetric about the diagonal. A significant result, in the present context, implies nonsymmetry in the marginal distribution of age at death for each twin separately. The foregoing statistics, viewed in conjunction, present a diagnostic interpretation of the intrinsic relationships in the mortality distributions of the above twin cohort.

RESULTS

Twin Infant Mortality

Infant mortality is considered to be death that occurs before the first anniversary of birth and is attributed to either endogenous or exogenous causes. Endogenous deaths are those that are a direct consequence of the birth experience. They may be a result of high-risk pregnancies, which include abnormal presentations as well as congenital malformations. Exogenous infant deaths, however, are induced by some external insult, primarily infectious disease and accidents. Virtually all endogenous deaths are considered to occur in the first month of life; cumulative exogenous deaths occur proportional to $\log^3 (t + 1)$, where t is the age in days within the first year of life [1].

To avoid the complexities encountered by tables with empty cells, we have chosen to collapse the infant mortality data into four 3-month categories. The first quarter, then, is composed of endogenous and exogenous infant deaths. Same-sexed male and female twin infant mortality are represented in Table 2a and b; opposite-sexed twin infant mortality, in Table 2c. Generally it appears that the concordance of infant mortality by quarter is higher for the same-sexed female twins than for their male counterparts. Explanation for this phenomenon is evasive, but is statistically verified by our analysis. A summary of the concordance statistics, described previously, evaluated for the data in Tables 2a–c is given in Table 3. The measures of association uniformly indicate a higher concordance for the same-sexed female twins. The opposite-sexed twins experience concordance in death by quarter in the first year of life similar to the female same-sexed twins. The interpretation of the Optimal Prediction Statistic $\lambda_{j/i}$ for male same-sexed twins is such that if the quarter of death for the firstborn male twin is known, the corresponding quarter of death for his pair twin may be correctly specified approximately

TABLE 2a. Joint Distribution of Infant Mortality by Quarter for Same-Sexed Male Twins

Second born \ First born	1st	2nd	3rd	4th	Total
1st	153	10	9	5	177
2nd	4	11	2	0	17
3rd	2	3	8	1	14
4th	3	1	1	5	10
Total	162	25	20	11	218

TABLE 2b. Joint Distribution of Infant Mortality by Quarter for Same-Sexed Female Twins

Second born \ First born	1st	2nd	3rd	4th	Total
1st	150	3	1	2	156
2nd	4	13	1	0	18
3rd	2	3	8	0	13
4th	2	0	0	9	11
Total	158	19	10	11	198

TABLE 2c. Joint Distribution of Infant Mortality by Quarter for Opposite-Sexed Twins

Male twin \ Female twin	1st	2nd	3rd	4th	Total
1st	147	3	0	1	151
2nd	6	4	2	0	12
3rd	1	1	8	1	11
4th	2	0	0	6	8
Total	156	8	10	8	182

TABLE 3. Correlations and Concordances of Infant Twin Mortality by Sex of the Twin Pair

	Male twins	Female twins	Opposite-sexed
Number of pairs	218	198	182
X^2	148.54**	322.07**	239.45**
Spearman (r)	0.5677	0.7868	0.7552
Kendall (τ)	0.5466	0.7733	0.7404
Cramer (v)	0.4766	0.7363	0.6622
$\lambda_{j/i}$	0.2679	0.5500	0.4231
$\lambda_{i/j}$	0.0244	0.5714	0.4516
λ	0.1649	0.5610	0.4386
McNemar X^2 for symmetry	8.726–	1.476–	3.667–

** = Significant at .001
– = Not significant

27% of the time. The interpretation of $\lambda_{i/j}$ follows as it does for the female same-sexed and opposite-sexed counterparts. By comparison, the conditional statistic $\lambda_{i/j}$ for the male same-sexed twins, with value 2.4% shows almost no gain in prediction of the firstborn twin's quarter of death given the secondborn twin's quarter of death. None of the McNemar χ^2 statistics of symmetry was significant; however, the largest departure from symmetry is apparent for the male same-sexed twin pairs.

Table 4a-c describes the twin mortality distribution of the second group, i.e., those pairs of whom one died in infancy. The age of death of the surviving twin is shown horizontally. There does not appear to be a mortality differential in the order of birth for the same-sexed pairs, nor does sex seem to be a determinant for the opposite-sexed pairs. In an Indian sample of twins analyzed by Namboodiri et al [7], a higher mortality for the firstborn twin was observed. This result was not substantiated by our data.

The Mortality at Ages Beyond the First Year of Life

Using intervals of approximately 5 years' duration, we constructed contingency tables for the data where each twin of a pair survived the first year of life and repeated the correlation analysis as before. In addition, we performed life table analysis to compare and illustrate the overall life experience of the twins in this cohort. The joint distribution of age at death for male and female same-sexed and opposite-sexed twins is presented in Tables 5-7, respectively. Table 8 is a summary of the association measures and statistics calculated from these tables.

TABLE 4. Distribution of Age at Death of Cotwin Surviving Infant Death by Birth Order and Sex

Age at death	1-9	10-24	25-34	35-44	45-54	55-64	65-69	70-74	75-79	80-84	85+	Total
Male twin pairs												
Firstborn	22	4	21	14	9	3	3	2	3	3	11	95
Secondborn	13	4	13	17	7	8	6	3	9	6	4	90
Total	35	8	34	31	16	11	9	5	12	9	15	185
Female twin pairs												
Firstborn	15	4	8	12	12	2	2	2	1	2	10	70
Secondborn	13	5	4	16	9	8	3	0	8	4	5	75
Total	28	9	12	28	21	10	5	2	9	6	15	145
Opposite-sexed twins												
Male	27	13	4	4	10	10	8	10	20	17	9	132
Female	19	5	4	4	12	16	12	13	14	18	6	123
Total	46	18	8	8	22	26	20	23	34	35	15	255

TABLE 5. Joint Mortality Distribution of Same-Sexed Male Twins Excluding Infant Mortality

Age at death of firstborn \ Age at death of second born	1-9	10-24	25-34	35-44	45-54	55-64	65-69	70-74	75-79	80-84	85+	Total
1-9	16	2	4	3	2	5	2	3	4	5	2	48
10-24	1	2	1	0	4	4	1	1	1	2	0	17
25-34	2	1	3	0	1	0	1	1	2	1	0	12
35-44	2	0	0	2	2	3	0	3	0	0	2	14
45-54	3	0	1	2	3	6	1	2	2	0	2	22
55-64	2	1	2	3	6	11	3	3	3	4	2	40
65-69	1	2	1	2	2	5	5	1	3	3	0	25
70-74	0	1	2	0	2	4	6	11	9	3	1	39
75-79	6	1	2	3	3	1	2	4	8	5	1	36
80-84	4	0	3	1	2	3	10	7	3	6	1	40
85+	4	1	2	1	1	0	0	2	8	2	5	26
Total	41	11	21	17	28	42	31	38	43	31	16	319

TABLE 6. Joint Mortality Distribution of Same-Sexed Female Twins Excluding Infant Mortality

Age at death of firstborn \ Age at death of second born	1-9	10-24	25-34	35-44	45-54	55-64	65-69	70-74	75-79	80-84	85+	Total
1-9	26	3	4	0	6	4	0	7	3	3	4	60
10-24	5	5	2	1	0	5	2	1	4	2	0	27
25-34	1	1	2	0	0	2	0	1	1	1	0	9
35-44	2	0	1	1	2	1	1	4	2	0	2	16
45-54	3	2	1	3	5	4	1	3	3	3	0	28
55-64	7	1	1	1	5	11	4	5	4	1	2	42
65-69	4	2	3	1	6	5	5	3	4	4	1	38
70-74	4	3	0	1	2	2	3	2	5	3	1	26
75-79	2	3	3	2	3	4	2	7	8	3	4	41
80-84	4	2	0	1	2	4	4	5	4	4	5	35
85+	3	2	3	2	2	3	4	3	2	0	9	33
Total	61	24	20	13	33	45	26	41	40	24	28	355

TABLE 7. Joint Mortality Distribution of Opposite-Sexed Twins Excluding Infant Mortality

Age at death of male twin \ Age at death of female twin	1–9	10–24	25–34	35–44	45–54	55–64	65–69	70–74	75–79	80–84	85+	Total
1–9	17	1	4	6	8	3	4	5	7	4	4	63
10–24	4	3	2	3	0	4	1	3	2	0	1	23
25–34	0	2	2	3	0	1	0	1	1	0	2	12
35–44	3	3	1	1	0	0	0	2	1	3	1	15
45–54	3	3	4	3	2	2	6	5	4	3	1	36
55–64	1	6	2	2	2	6	6	4	6	3	6	44
65–69	5	2	4	0	4	5	2	2	3	7	4	38
70–74	5	6	7	2	1	6	4	5	2	2	4	44
75–79	7	2	1	3	2	1	6	8	2	4	5	41
80–84	3	3	4	0	3	3	0	6	5	9	7	43
85+	6	1	0	1	0	3	2	6	1	3	4	27
Total	54	32	31	24	22	34	31	47	34	38	39	386

TABLE 8. Correlation Measures of Age at Death in Twin Pairs by Sex Where Both Twins Survived Infant Death

	Male twins	Female twins	Opposite-sexed
Number of pairs	320	355	368
X^2 for association	137.002**	159.365**	128.021**
Spearman (r)	0.2544	0.2283	0.1566
Kendall (τ)	0.1943	0.1821	0.1166
Cramer (v)	0.1964	0.2235	0.1821
$\lambda_{j/i}$	0.0850	0.1522	0.0663
$\lambda_{i/j}$	0.0949	0.1292	0.0743
λ	0.0900	0.1408	0.0702
X^2 test for symmetry (McNemar)	54.487	55.324	76.800*

** = Significant at .001
* = Significant at .05

A pattern different from that observed for twin infant mortality emerges. Same-sexed twins have a higher concordance that the opposite-sexed pairs. The differences in association measures between male and female same-sexed twins are slight and mostly pronounced in the average prediction value, which is 14% in female pairs and 9% in male pairs. Thus, for a pair of female twins, the average reduction in error of predicting the age at death of one twin knowing the age at death of the other is about 14%. The opposite-sexed twins have an average prediction value of 7%.

Intrinsic symmetry is indicated for the joint distribution of same-sexed twins by the nonsignificant McNemar χ^2 statistics. Departure from symmetry (P $\approx$ 0.05) for the opposite-sexed twins was observed.

Actuarial Survivorship Analysis

The cohort life table is appropriate in this study for interpair twin comparisons and for a description of the corresponding survival probabilities. The life table is a statistical quantitative model restricted to the following assumptions: 1) a homogeneous population with a constant force of mortality, and 2) independence of the death events. The probability of dying in each interval, q_i, is estimated by the number of deaths experienced in the interval divided by the number alive at the beginning of the interval. The radix, or beginning population, diminishes as individuals experience mortality until none are left in the last interval. The probability of survival from one interval to another is the product of survival probabilities of the intervening intervals based on the second assumption of independence. Thus, the cumulative chance of surviving from, say, the first to the nth interval is given by $(1-q_1)$ $(1-q_2)$ . . . $(1-q_n)$.

The corresponding cumulative survivorship curves for same-sexed and opposite-sexed twins are plotted in Figures 1 and 2. The mean survival is easily estimated by finding the area under the survivorship curve. Standard errors can be derived that may be used to construct confidence intervals. Statistical comparison of two life tables, one that yields a cumulative chance of surviving P_x to age x and the other with corresponding P'_x, can be made by evaluating the statistic:

$$ Z = \frac{P_x - P'_x}{\sqrt{[se\ (P_x)]^2 + [se\ (P'_x)]^2}} $$

which is approximately, under large sample theory, normally distributed.

No significant differences were observed in survivorship curves of female same-sexed twins. We observed a significant difference in male same-sexed twins between ages 75 and 85. For the opposite-sexed twins we noted a surprisingly significant lower probability of survival, between ages 40 and 50, for the female twins than for the male cotwins. The estimated life expectancies at age one, e_1, and standard deviations are 74.45 $\pm$ 15.98 and 71.93 $\pm$ 15.34 in firstborn and secondborn male same-sexed twins, respectively. The corresponding values for female same-sexed twins are 73.68 $\pm$ 16.09 and 73.04 $\pm$ 15.84. The opposite-sexed twins have estimated life expectancies of 73.99 $\pm$ 16.18 and 73.99 $\pm$ 15.75 for the male and female cotwins. The latter strong similarity in life expectancy is somewhat remarkable.

If we believe that Mendelian variation is present and whatever genetic component there is relates to the whole quantitative variate "length of life" and not to the category "longevity" exclusively, then bimodality should show up as double sigmoid survivorship curves. No definite pattern of this type was observed. An indirect method that possibly manifests the intrinsic genetic component was under-

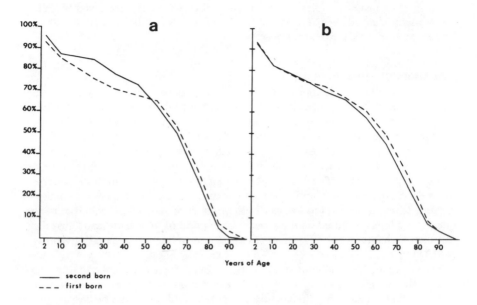

Fig. 1a) Actuarial survivorship curves for same-sexed male twins (N = 319). b) Actuarial survivorship curves for same-sexed female twins (N = 355).

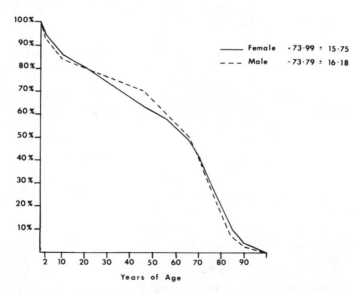

Fig. 2. Actuarial survivorship curves in opposite-sexed twins (N = 386).

taken by constructing the conditional survivorship curves of one of the twin pair, given the life experience of the other twin. We expect significant divergence between these curves and anticipate more pronounced differences for the same-sexed twins than for the opposite-sexed twins, because of the contribution of the MZ pairs. Accordingly, we partitioned the mortality experience of the same- and opposite-sexed twins by age at death of the cotwin summed over the following four categories: 1) One of the twin pair died in infancy; 2) one of the twin pair died young, 1–44 years of age; 3) one of the twin pair died in middle age, 45–69 years of age; and 4) one of the twin pair died in old age, 70+ years of age. The grouping by survival of the cotwin is coarse, comprising some very broad subdivisions, but finer classification creates the familiar problem of small sample size. Figures 3 and 4 and Table 9 summarize the expected mean and standard deviation (at age 1) by sex and age at death category of the cotwin. The results are striking. For the same-sexed twins we observed a pronounced difference in the conditional young and middle survivorship curves between ages 1 and 55 for females and 1 and 65 for males, but no difference above these ages, and complementarily we found significant differences in the conditional middle and old survivorship curves between ages greater than 55 in females and greater than 65 in males.

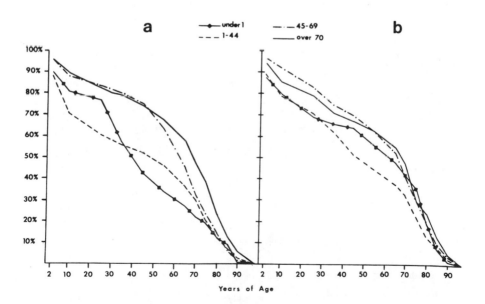

Fig. 3a) Survivorship curves in male twins conditioned on age at death of male cotwin. b) Survivorship curves in male twins conditioned on age at death of female cotwin.

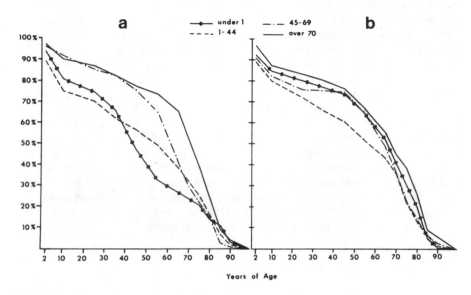

Fig. 4a) Survivorship curves of female twins conditioned on age at death of female cotwin. b) Survivorship curves in female twins conditioned on age at death of male cotwin.

TABLE 9. Estimated Mean and Standard Deviation of Life Span by Sex of Twin Pair and Age at Death of Cotwin

Sex of twin pair	Age at death of cotwin	Number of pairs	Estimated mean	Estimated SD
Female–female	Infant	145	71.15	16.13
	Young	181	69.84	15.01
	Middle	188	71.50	15.63
	Old	269	76.08	16.14
Female–male	Infant	123	72.32	15.54
	Young	141	71.33	15.41
	Middle	87	73.84	15.52
	Old	158	76.01	16.14
Male–male	Infant	185	69.66	15.76
	Young	230	70.99	15.72
	Middle	212	71.37	15.43
	Old	268	75.97	16.46
Male–female	Infant	132	72.81	15.84
	Young	113	71.10	15.62
	Middle	118	73.36	16.07
	Old	155	75.66	16.62

However, the conditional survivorship curves of females or males as dependent on the age at death of the opposite-sexed cotwin are much closer and share greater similarity to each other. No differences were observed in probability of survival of the conditional middle and old age male group. Female conditional young and middle survival curves are different between ages 45 and 55, whereas the conditional middle and old survival curves show some differences between ages 70 and 80. The male (female) survivorship curves of twins conditioned on the cotwin death in infancy show a greater similarity to the younger subgrouping in same-sexed twins than in opposite-sexed twins. The foregoing analysis manifests and confirms higher concordance in the variate "length of life" with same-sexed cotwin pairs and suggests that intrinsic genetic and/or environmental determinants might be considerably involved.

SUMMARY AND CONCLUSIONS

To summarize in a manner intended to avoid prematurely specific conclusions, we feel safe in saying that a considerable similarity in length of life was demonstrated. It was more pronounced in same-sexed twins than in opposite-sexed twins. Among the specific findings presented in this paper, some of the more salient ones follow: 1) The measures of association uniformly indicate a higher concordance for same-sexed infant female mortality than for their male counterpart. The average prediction value of the quarter of death in the first year of life female twin pairs is 44% compared to 16% in male twins. Also, some asymmetry in the distribution of infant death was indicated in males and absent for female twins. 2) Contrary to results observed by other investigators, we did not find a higher incidence of infant mortality for the firstborn twin in either sex. 3) In those twin pairs who have survived infant death, there is a clear and almost uniform resemblance in the length of life, with same-sexed twins showing a higher concordance than the opposite-sexed pairs. Again, the average prediction value was higher in female pairs, 14%, compared to 9% in male pairs. Intrinsic symmetry is indicated for the joint distribution of same-sexed twins in both sexes. 4) The conditional survivorship curves of females or males as dependent on the age at death of the same-sexed cotwin are more divergent than those conditioned on the age at death of the opposite-sexed cotwin, reaffirming the higher concordance in the variate "length of life" with same-sexed cotwin

ACKNOWLEDGMENTS

This research was supported by grants AG-02481, CA-16573, and GM-27192 from the National Institutes of Health.

REFERENCES

1. Bourgeois-Pichat J: La mesure de la mortalité infantile. Population 6:233–248, 1951.
2. Carmelli D, Hasstedt S, Andersen S: Demography and genetics of human twinning in the Utah Mormon genealogy. In Gedda L, Parisi P and Nance WE (eds): "Twin Research 3: Twin Biology and Multiple Pregnancy." New York: Alan R. Liss, 1981, pp 81–93.
3. Goodman L, Kruskal W: Measures of association for cross classifications. Am Stat Assoc J 733–763, 1954.

4. Hauge M: Hereditary factors in longevity, In Geerts SJ (ed): "Proceedings of the 11th International Congress of Genetics." New York: Terganon, 1963.
5. Kallman F: "Twin Data on the Genetics of Aging." New York: Columbia University, 1956.
6. Murphy EA: Genetics of longevity in man. In Schneider EL (ed): "The Genetics of Aging." New York: Plenum Press, 1978, pp 261-299.
7. Namboodiri N, Balakrishnan V: "A Contribution to the Study of Birth Weight and Survival of Twins Based on an Indian Sample." India: University of Kerala, 1960.
8. Skolnick M, Bean LL, Dintelman SM, Mineau GP: A computerized family history data base system. Sociol Soc Res 63:506-523, 1979.

Twin Research 3: Epidemiological
and Clinical Studies, pages 201—209
© 1981 Alan R. Liss, Inc., 150 Fifth Avenue, New York, NY 10011

Results of the 40-Year, Longitudinal Study of a Series of Twins of Berlin (450 Monozygotic and Dizygotic Twin Pairs)

Gerhard Koch

Institute of Human Genetics and Anthropology, Erlangen, Federal Republic of Germany

The first follow-up investigation of the Berlin twin series was carried out in 1954–55 [1]. It covered 265 monozygotic (MZ) (135 female and 130 male) and 230 dizygotic (DZ) (117 female and 113 male) twin pairs. The present prospective and retrospective follow-up investigation will eventually include 500 twin pairs (265 MZ and 235 DZ, both male and female). Of these, 450 are covered by the present study (235 MZ, 114 female and 121 male; 215 DZ, 107 female and 108 male), including three sets of identical triplets, three sets of dizygotic triplets, and one of tetrazygotic quadruplets.

For 41 of the 265 MZ pairs, both twins have died; for 61, one has died. In four of these cases both male twins were killed in World War II; in six cases one twin was killed and the other died. Of the 61 pairs where one twin is dead, 19 were killed in the war.

For 25 of the 235 DZ twin pairs both twins have died; in 55 cases one twin has died, whereas in four cases both twins (three male and one female) and in 18 cases one twin was killed in World War II. In five cases one twin was killed, the other died.

The ages of those twins still living range from 42 to 87 years, most having been born in the years 1920–1930, and now 50–60 years of age. Figures 1 and 2 show the oldest female MZ twin pair, both of whom are still alive. They are 86 years old, the ninth and tenth children of a ten-child family. They have always lived together, and for the past 15 years have both suffered from colon diverticulosis, as verified by x-ray.

The environment and living conditions of the twins and the effects of increasing age determine the differences in type and frequency of diseases diagnosed in the first and second follow-up investigations, particularly for tuberculosis and diabetes mellitus (Table 1). Under the unfavorable conditions during World War II and the

Fig. 1.   MZ twins No. 579.

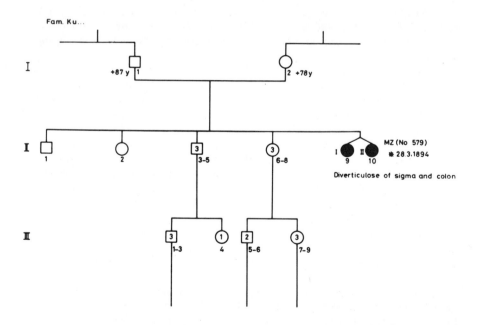

Fig. 2.   Pedigree of MZ twins No. 579.

Table 1:   Results of the first longitudinal study in 1955 and the second in 1980

	MZ □ • ○						DZ □ • ○					
	1955			1980			1955			1980		
	n	c	d	n	c	d	n	c	d	n	c	d
Tuberculosis	22	10	12	23	10	13	17	6	11	18	6	12
epidemic hepatitis	19	4	15	22	4	18	20	2	18	20	2	18
Diabetes mellitus	5	3	2	24	11	13 (5)	-	-	-	7	1	6 (1)
Slipped disk	-	-	-	6	2	4	-	-	-	11	1	10

( ): cotwin died during the war

first few years after the war, one or both of 39 twin pairs (22 MZ and 17 DZ) became ill with tuberculosis. By comparison, only one MZ twin and one DZ twin have recently contracted a fresh tubercular infection. The situation is similar for the viral infection hepatitis epidemica. It was very frequent during the war, as were other contagious diseases (dysentery, typhoid, and malaria). With diabetes mellitus, however, due to the good living and nutritional standards of the past 25 years, and dependently of age and genetic factors, a definite increase from five (all MZ twins) to 31 (24 MZ and 7 DZ twins) could be shown.

Those diseases dependent on increasing age include benign and malignant tumors, cardiovascular diseases, and the degenerative diseases of the skeletal system (spondylosis, arthrosis and slipped disc). This longitudinal study illustrates the advances in medical science of the last decades. Three of the twins have undergone a heart operation and two have lived for years with a pacemaker. The large number of slipped disc operations also indicates a medical advance; developments in neurosurgical operation techniques have without doubt contributed to the increase in such operations.

All the findings given so far are preliminary and are bound to change, as are the counts for benign and malignant tumors, which will now be discussed in detail.

Table 2 is a summary of all the malignant tumors identified in the present study: There are 38 twin pairs (13 MZ and 25 DZ) with various carcinomas, four pairs (three MZ and one DZ) with sarcomas (lymphoma, fibrosarcoma, and two melanosarcomas), three MZ twin pairs with brain tumors, and one myelocytic leukemia. This last patient was a male DZ twin who died at the age of 46. He had been treated for 15 years with psychopharmaka for a paranoid type of schizophrenia.

It was found that of the carcinoma cases, four of the 13 MZ twin pairs, 30.8%, are concordant and nine discordant. Of the 25 DZ twin pairs, four (16%) are concordant and 21 discordant.

In accordance with earlier studies of cancer in twins [8], the data obtained from this study support the theory that genetic factors are not generally of major importance as a cause of common cancers. Of the carcinomas observed, breast

Table 2: Malign tumours in twins (Results of the second study in 1980)

	MZ □ + O			DZ □ + O		
	n	c	d	n	c	d
Cancer	13	4(1)	9	25	4(2)	21
myeloid leukemia	-	-	-	1	-	1
Sarkomas	3	-	3	1	-	1
Brain tumours	3	1(1)	2	-	-	-

( ): different tumours

cancer in women and stomach cancer in men were the most frequent forms. As far as it is possible to make a comparison with such small numbers, this agrees with the cancer statistics of the general population for men and women.

Of the 12 breast cancers found among MZ and DZ twins, 11 were in only one breast and in only one case were both breasts affected.

With the MZ triplets no. 276 (Fig. 3), sister 1 had a cancer of the left breast, sister 2 of the right breast, and sister 3, who suffers from a cirrhosis of the liver is, at 58 years of age, free of cancer.

The DZ concordant twins no. 400 (Fig. 4) have a younger sister who also had breast cancer on the same side and with the same histological structure. It should be mentioned that twin 2 became ill at the age of 76.8 years, 23 years after twin 1.

Although twin studies alone have shown that genetic factors are not of major importance as a cause of common cancers, the question of a genetic precondition is not yet clear. Cancers are different in their etiology and are genetically heterogeneous. Their cause may be due not only to different genetic factors but also to various chemical and physical environmental noxious agents and viruses. These may supplement and intensify each other and become cocarcinogenic.

Morton [7] indicated that it is not possible to investigate two parameters using a single statistical method. Tattersall and Pyke [9] demonstrated in 1972 in the paper "Diabetes in Identical Twins" that the twin-family method can give further important indications as to the roles played by genetic and/or environmental factors in the origin of disease. In 1977, Nance [8] also referred to the twin-family method for cancer research. Therefore, as far as was possible, extensive familial investigations were carried out for this study also. Unfortunately it was sometimes difficult to be objective about the data on other cancer cases within the twin families. This was particularly so for those persons living in Berlin, since many hospital archives and registrar records, also registers of deaths, were destroyed during World War II.

The family Kr... in Figure 5 shows a "cancer family syndrome." It supplements — one could say — the almost identical observations of Lynch [4]. Twin 1 of the MZ twin pair no. 201, who lives in West Germany, was operated on at the age of

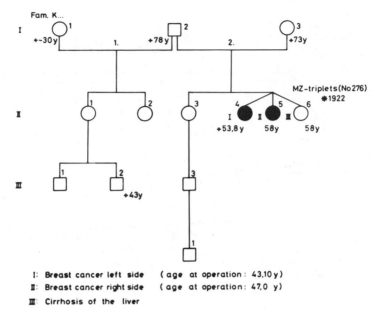

I: Breast cancer left side   (age at operation: 43,10 y)
II: Breast cancer right side (age at operation: 47,0 y)
III: Cirrhosis of the liver

Fig. 3.   Pedigree of MZ triplets No. 276.

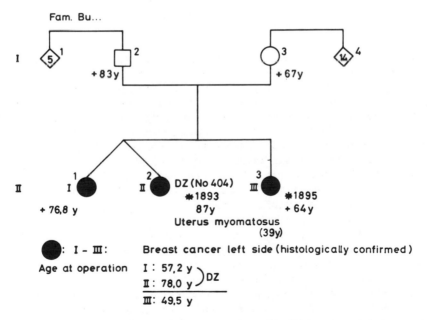

◉ : I – III: Breast cancer left side (histologically confirmed)

Age at operation   I : 57,2 y ⎞ DZ
                    II : 78,0 y ⎠
                    ───────────
                    III: 49,5 y

Fig. 4.   Pedigree of DZ twins No. 404.

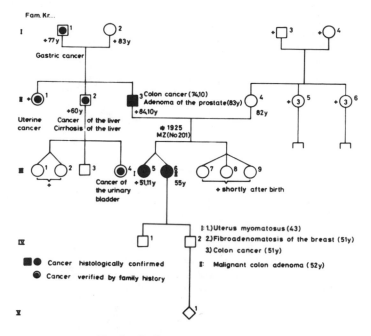

Fig. 5. Pedigree of MZ twins No. 201.

51.0 years for a cancer of the colon with liver metastases. An examination was then made of the twin sister, who had always lived in West Berlin. It was found that she had a malignant colon adenoma which was immediately operated on. The twins' father was operated on at the age of 74.1 years for a histologically confirmed colon cancer. Four other members of the family suffered from other cancers. In this case as in many other published cases, there is an autosomal-dominant hereditary cancer in the family. This family has been described here in great detail. A concentration of cancer cases was also determined for four other families. Approximately 13% of the 38 twins with cancer had two or more first-degree relatives with cancer of any anatomic site. In these families one should try to determine whether a genetic, perhaps chromosomal, or molecular defect is responsible.

These cancer families are high-risk families. They require careful genetic counseling and a life-long medical supervision of those members at risk.

The same applies for those twins and their families whose preneoplastic states were found. Figure 6 shows such a family. I am indebted for the history of this family to the proband, twin 1, himself a medical doctor.

Uterine myoma are the most common type within the large group of benign tumors (Table 3). This is also the case for women in the general population. These tumors develop at sexual maturity and, from the age of 30 onward, the curve

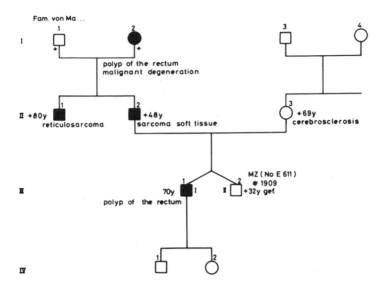

Fig. 6. Pedigree of MZ twins No. 611.

showing their occurrence becomes even steeper, reaching a peak between the 40th and 50th year. Myomas occur most frequently therefore in the years just before the menopause. According to statistics, the frequency of myomas is about 15%, but nowhere near all of them cause so much trouble — owing to their size and localization — that they need to be surgically removed. It is surprising that, despite the frequency of myomas in the general population, no larger twin study program has yet been carried out.

The present twin series includes 20 MZ and 21 DZ twin pairs, there being a decidedly higher concordance of 50% in the MZ twins than of 9.5% in the DZ twins. This suggests a major role for genetic factors in the etiology of uterine leiomyomas. All these myomas have been confirmed both by operation and by histological examination as leiomyomas. Among the patients is a concordant DZ group of triplets, where all three were operated for a leiomyoma, twins 1 and 2 at ages 28 and 33, and triplet 3 at age 37.11 years (Fig. 7).

As with the malignant tumors, other first-degree relatives in the twins' families were reported as having uterine myomas. In analogy to the "cancer family syndrome," one could speak here of a "uterine leiomyoma family syndrome" (Fig. 8).

There are also clinically and genetically different types of uterine myomas. Lynch [4] and McKusick [6] mention twin and family observations of "multiple familial cutaneous leiomyomas associated with (malignant) uterine leiomyomas." A

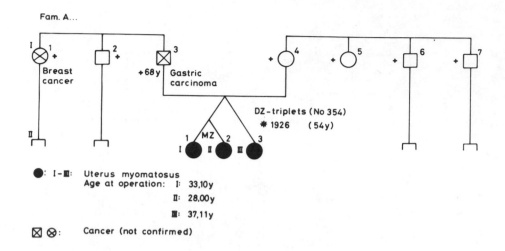

Fig. 7. Pedigree of DZ triplets No. 354.

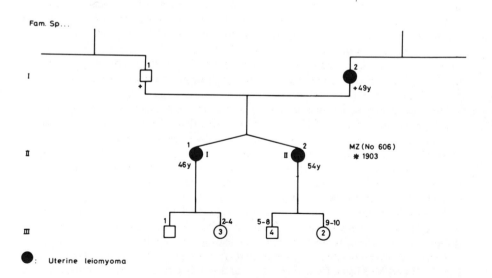

Fig. 8. Pedigree of MZ twins No. 606.

Table 3: Benign tumours in twins (Results of the second study in 1980)

	MZ □			MZ O			DZ □			DZ O		
	n	c	d	n	c	d	n	c	d	n	c	d
leiomyoma of the uterus	-	-	-	20	10	10	-	-	-	21	2	19
fibro-adenoma of the breast	-	-	-	4	1	3	-	-	-	1	-	1
fibrocystoma of the breast	-	-	-	2	-	2	-	-	-	3	-	3
adenoma of the prostate	3	1	2	-	-	-	2	-	2	-	-	-

similar association could not be established in this twin collective. However, for some of the twins, leiomyomas of the uterus and fibroadenomas of the breast were reported; that is, for a concordant MZ twin pair, for three discordant MZ twin pairs, and for one DZ twin pair.

Some of the twin and family observations also suggest a genetic origin for adenomas of the prostate. I could demonstrate this in my own family: I myself was operated on for a prostate adenoma several years ago.

I have selected benign and malignant tumors from the numerous data collected in this study since cancer research is, at the moment, of very great importance (Schwerpunktprogramm) at the Medical Faculty of the University of Erlangen-Nürnberg.

What I have reported here is only a fraction of the results to date. These data will be stored and processed by computer in conjunction with the Institute of Medical Statistics and Documentation of the University of Erlangen-Nürnberg.

REFERENCES

1. Koch G: Ergebnisse aus der Nachuntersuchung der Berliner Zwillingsserie nach 20–25 Jahren (vorläüfige Ergebnisse). Acta Genet 7:47–52, 1957.
2. Koch G: Humangenetisch-klinische Befunde bei Zwillingen. Ergebnisse aus der Nachuntersuchung der Zwillingsserie des ehemaligen Kaiser-Wilhelm Institutes für Anthropologie, menschliche Erblehre und Eugenik (Eugen-Fischer Institut) in Berlin-Dahlem nach 20–25 Jahren. J Hogl Erlangen, 1972.
3. Leutner R: Todesursachenstatistik 1973 und 1974. Bundesgesetzblatt 20:66–72; 81–91, 1977.
4. Lynch HT: "Dynamic Genetic Counseling for Clinicians." Springfield, Illinois: Charles C. Thomas, 1969.
5. Lynch HT: Skin, heredity, and cancer. In Lynch, HT: "Cancer Genetics." Springfield, Illinois: Charles C. Thomas, 1976, pp 424–470.
6. McKusick VA: Leiomyomata, heredity multiple of skin. In "Mendelian Inheritance in Man. Catalogs of Autosomal Dominant, Autosomal Recessive, and X-Linked Phenotypes." Ed. 5. Baltimore and London: The Johns Hopkins University Press, 1978, p 239.
7. Morton NE: Segregation and linkage. In Burdette WJ: "Methodology in Human Genetics." San Francisco: Holdon-Day, 1962, pp 17–52.
8. Nance WE: Relevance in twin studies in cancer research. In Mulvihill J, Müller RW, Fraumeni F Jr: "Genetics of Human Cancer." New York: Raven Press, 1977, pp 27–41.
9. Tattersall RB, Pyke DA: Diabetes in identical twins. Lancet 2:1120–1125, 1972.

Twin Research 3: Epidemiological
and Clinical Studies, pages 211—216
© 1981 Alan R. Liss, Inc., 150 Fifth Avenue, New York, NY 10011

Studies of Cancer Etiology in the Danish Twin Population. I. Breast Cancer

Niels V. Holm

Institute of Clinical Genetics and the Danish Twin Register, Odense University, Denmark

In this paper some results of a study of breast cancer (BC) based on the Danish Twin Register will be presented; the study has already been described in detail [11]. This material has been used to evaluate the validity of selection in relation to twin ascertainment procedures. Besides, the actual status of ongoing cancer studies in the Danish Twin Register will be briefly outlined.

MATERIALS AND METHODS

This twin study was based on the Danish Twin Register [8, 9]. The register contains data on all twin births that have taken place in Denmark in the period 1870—1930. Its goal is to follow all individuals from birth to a given deadline or death without paying any attention to the presence or absence of disease or to zygosity. The basic data have been obtained from the birth registries kept locally by the parishes. A search is made through local and national registries and registers of death. More than 90% of the twins have been traced so far. A questionnaire is sent to the twins as soon as they are traced. If the twins are not alive at the time of registration, their closest relative then receives the questionnaire. We try to obtain a full medical history by asking the informants to list all referrals to hospitals and to indicate the presence or absence of a number of specified diseases. Specific questions about similarity between the partners of same-sexed twin pairs are included to permit an evaluation of the zygosity diagnosis.

It is impossible to get reliable information about medical events and especially about zygosity in twins dying at an early age; therefore, when one or both twins had died before attaining the age of 6 years, they are both excluded. Also excluded are twin pairs where one or both partners had emigrated.

The total sample is followed at intervals through new questionnaires sent to all twins still alive. Once a year copies of death certificates of all registered twins who have died in the preceding year are received from the Central Register of Deaths, irrespective of whether the pair has already been traced.

In Denmark medical care including hospital service is free. All information from medical service is filed, and medical records may be perused when needed for medical research purposes without limitations by the doctors working in the twin register.

For the twin sample of this study, all replies to questionnaires and death certificates filed in the twin register for female twin pairs were screened for breast diseases whether benign or malignant. The medical and/or autopsy records have then been perused.

Included as probands were twins born in Denmark in the period 1870–1920 who were known to have developed breast cancer before 1974. In 98% the diagnosis was verified through a hospital record. All probands and cotwins were followed up to 1974.

The validity of the zygosity classification, based initially on answers to the questionnaires, has been evaluated by a comparison with the results of later blood group determination in 549 same-sexed pairs. This analysis indicated that the general reliability of the questionnaire method was high, with a frequency of misclassification below 5%.

In Denmark a cancer register [3–6] has been established from which tables of cancer morbidity during 1943–1972 have been published. The *expected* number of BC and cancer of other sites in the cotwins of BC probands was based on the tables from 1953 to 1957, because the median date of diagnosis of the present material was in that period.

In comparisons of different groups, the chi-square test or Fisher's exact test was used. When observed and expected numbers of cancers in cotwins were compared, significance tests based on a Poisson distribution were used.

In this material the BC probands have been included irrespective of death of the probands or the cotwins prior to compilation of the twin register. In some twin registers—eg, the Swedish and the Finnish—only twin pairs where both twins are alive at the time of compilation of the twin register are included. The pairwise concordance rates have been compared in the present material under these two different ascertainment procedures to see if any selection bias could be demonstrated. The birth cohorts 1870–1910 were compiled in 1954 and the birth cohorts 1911–1920 were compiled in 1964.

RESULTS

A total of 160 BC cases in 151 pairs fulfilled the proband criteria. All were probands. The detailed examination of the cotwins did not reveal any additional cases. In Table 1 the twin pairs have been classified in zygosity groups. Of 52 MZ pairs 5 were concordant; of 94 DZ pairs 4 were concordant. In 5 pairs no reliable zygosity diagnosis could be established; all these were discordant. The mean age at diagnosis of breast cancer was in accordance with that of the general population. Only small and insignificant differences could be demonstrated between concordant and discordant pairs in this respect. The time of diagnosis was also similar in concordant and discordant pairs.

The numbers of BC and cancers of other sites that developed in MZ and DZ cotwins after the diagnosis of the first BC in the pairs are presented in Table 2. In MZ cotwins, the observed to expected ratio equaled 5.7 for BC (P < 0.01) and 1.5 for cancer of other sites (P > 0.20). In DZ cotwins, the corresponding ratios equaled 2.3 (P > 0.10) and 0.9 (P > 0.30), respectively.

The pairwise concordance rates have been shown in Table 3 under two different ascertainment procedures. For both ascertainments, pairs in which one twin died prior to the appearance of BC in the pair have been excluded. In ascertainment 1 the twin pairs have been included whether or not both partners had died prior to compilation of the twin register. In ascertainment 2 only those pairs are included in whom both partners were alive at compilation of the register. Whether genetic factors are of any significant importance of a trait can be evaluated through comparison of the pairwise concordance rates in MZ and DZ twin pairs. As can be seen from Table 3, a significant difference could be demonstrated in ascertainment 2 but not in ascertainment 1.

TABLE 1. Number of Twin Pairs With Verified Breast Cancer Classified in Zygosity Groups

	MZ	DZ	UZ
Concordant pairs	5	4	0
Discordant pairs	47	90	5
Total	52	94	5

TABLE 2. Observed and Expected Number of Breast Cancer and Cancer of Other Sites in MZ and DZ Cotwins After Diagnosis of the First Breast Cancer in the Pair

	MZ cotwins		DZ cotwins	
	Observed	Expected	Observed	Expected
Breast cancer	5	0.874	4	1.716
Cancer of other sites	6	3.916	7	7.848

TABLE 3. Pairwise Concordance Rates of Breast Cancer in MZ and DZ Twin Pairs[a] in Two Different Ascertainment Procedures

	Ascertainment 1[b]	Ascertainment 2[c]
MZ twin pairs	5/45 = 0.11	5/36 = 0.14
DZ twin pairs	4/77 = 0.05	1/48 = 0.02
Significance test	P > 0.20	P = 0.049

[a]Only twin pairs in which both partners were alive at the first breast cancer in the pair are included.
[b]All twin pairs fulfilling criterion "a" are included.
[c]Only twin pairs where both partners were alive at compilation of the twin register are included.

Actual Status of Ongoing Cancer Studies in the Danish Twin Register

In collaboration with the Danish Cancer Register, all same-sexed twin pairs born in Denmark in the period 1881 – 1920 will be checked in the cancer register through a record linkage of the two registers. The Danish Cancer Register contains data on almost all malignancies diagnosed in Denmark since 1943 [3 – 6].

The intention is to apply the classical twin method in the first place to cancer of the breast, uterus, stomach, bowel, and leukemia and malignant lymphoma. To elucidate the importance of environmental factors, the case-control method will be applied. Besides, the selection problems will be examined.

DISCUSSION

Whether the higher risk in families [1, 2, 10, 12, 15, 17, 19] of developing BC is caused by genetic and/or common environmental factors has not been clarified from family studies [14, 16, 18]. The relative importance of genetic versus common environmental factors for development of BC has then to be evaluated through studies of unselected twin series. The present series provides a sample of unselected twins, because the pairs enter the register irrespective of disease. Besides, age at diagnosis and clinical characteristics in this twin sample are in accordance with the general Danish BC population.

A higher risk of BC could be demonstrated in both MZ and DZ cotwins compared to the general population. The concordance rate was highest in the MZ twin pairs but not significantly different from the DZ twin pairs, so it might be concluded that genes do not determine the development of BC to any great extent. However, the concordance rates are virtually the same as in a previous study [7], so there might really be a difference and with it some genetic determination of BC. With regard to cancer of other sites, no increased risk could be demonstrated in either MZ or DZ cotwins.

To give a valid estimate of the importance of genetic factors, the twin sample should be representative of the twin population at large. If twin pairs where one or both partners had died prior to compilation of the register are excluded, this might introduce a selection for the more healthy twin pairs.

The effect would be identical to the healthy worker effect operating in occupational health studies. In fact, this phenomenen has been demonstrated in a study from the Finnish Twin Register [13] where the observed number of cancers was lower than expected. With regard to the present sample, we would expect more concordant pairs to be excluded relative to discordant pairs, as the BC patients have an increased mortality rate. The effect on the pairwise concordance rates of exclusion has been shown in Table 3. No clear trend emerged. In the MZ group, only discordant pairs were excluded. In the DZ group, relatively more concordant than discordant pairs were excluded. The different ascertainment procedures gave two different results concerning the importance of genetic factors. This difference might of course be due to chance variation. However, the planned record linkage between the cancer register and the twin register should be able to produce a twin sample of cancer probands, which will enable us to subject this essential selection problem to a valid critical examination.

The present study of BC in an unselected twin series has indicated that genetic factors might be of some importance for the development of BC but these factors are of no importance for development of cancer of other sites.

The effect on selection in different ascertainment procedures has not come to any final conclusion. However, after a planned record linkage between the Danish Cancer Register and the Danish Twin Register, it should be possible to subject the selection problems to a valid critical examination.

This research was supported in part by Public Health Service grant CA00948 from the National Cancer Institute; by PHS grant RG09418 from the Division of Research Grants, National Institutes of Health; and by PHS grant HD00563 from the National Institute of Child Health and Human Development. Additional grants were from the Order of Odd-Fellows, Denmark, and from Hafniafonden, Den lokale Forskningsfond, Odense Sygehus, and Ingemann Bucks Fond.

REFERENCES

1. Anderson DE: Breast cancer in families. Cancer 40:1855–1860, 1977.
2. Anderson VE, Goodman HO, Reed SC: "Variables Related to Human Breast Cancer." Minneapolis: University of Minnesota Press, 1958.
3. Clemmesen J: Statistical studies in the aetiology of malignant neoplasms. I. Review and results. II. Basic tables, Denmark 1943–57. Acta Pathol Microbiol Scand (suppl 174): I:35–56; II:231, 243, 316–319, 1965.
4. Clemmesen J: Statistical studies in the aetiology of malignant neoplasms. III. Basic tables, Denmark 1958–62. Acta Pathol MicrobiolScand (suppl 209), 1969.
5. Clemmesen J: Statistical studies in the aetiology of malignant neoplasms. IV. Basic tables, Denmark 1963–67. Acta Pathol Microbiol Scand (suppl 247), 1974.
6. Clemmesen J: Statistical studies in the aetiology of malignant neoplasms. V. Basic tables, Denmark 1968–72. Acta Pathol Microbiol Scand (suppl 261), 1977.
7. Harvald B, Hauge M: Heredity of cancer elucidated by a study of unselected twins. JAMA 186:749–753, 1963.
8. Hauge M, Harvald B, Fischer M, Gotlieb-Jensen K, Juel-Nielsen N, Raebild I, Shapiro R, Videbech T: The Danish Twin Register. Acta Genet Med Gemellol 17:315–331, 1968.
9. Hauge M: The Danish Twin Register. In Mednick SA, Baert AE (eds): "An Empirical Basis for Primary Prevention: Prospective Longitudinal Research in Europe." Oxford: Oxford University Press, 1981.
10. Henderson BE, Powell D, Rosario I, Keys C, Hanisch R, Young M, Casagrande J, Gerkins V, Pike MC: An epidemiologic study of breast cancer. J Natl Cancer Inst 53:609–614, 1974.
11. Holm NV, Hauge M, Harvald B: Etiologic factors of breast cancer elucidated by a study of unselected twins. J Natl Cancer Inst 65:285–298, 1980.
12. Jacobsen O: "Heredity in Breast Cancer." Copenhagen: Nyt Nordisk Forlag, 1946.
13. Kaprio J, Teppo L, Koskenvuo M, Pukkala E: In Program and Abstracts. Third International Congress on Twin Studies, Jerusalem 16–20 June 1980, pp 93–94.
14. Lilienfeld AM: The epidemiology of breast cancer. Cancer Res 23:1503–1513, 1963.

15. Macklin MT: Comparison of the number of breast cancer deaths observed in relatives of breast cancer patients, and the number expected on the basis of mortality rates. J Natl Cancer Inst 22:927−951, 1959.
16. MacMahon B, Cole P, Brown J: Etiology of human breast cancer: A review. J Natl Cancer Inst 50:21−42, 1973.
17. Penrose LS, Mackenzie HJ, Karn MN: A genetical study of human mammary breast cancer. Br J Cancer 2:168−176, 1948.
18. Verschuer von OV: Maligne Tumoren. In Becker PE (ed): "Human Genetik. Ein kurzes Handbuch in fünf Bänden. Band III/I." Stuttgart: Thieme Verlag, 1964, pp 671−692.
19. Woolf CM: Investigation on genetic aspects of carcinoma of the stomach and breast. Univ Calif Publ Public Health 2:265−350, 1955.

Twin Research 3: Epidemiological
and Clinical Studies, pages 217 — 223
©1981 Alan R. Liss, Inc., 150 Fifth Avenue, New York, NY 10011

Cancer in Adult Same-Sexed Twins: A Historical Cohort Study

Jaakko Kaprio, Lyly Teppo, Markku Koskenvuo, and Eero Pukkala
Department of Public Health Science, University of Helsinki, and Finnish Cancer Registry, Helsinki

INTRODUCTION

It is generally accepted that most cancers are caused by environmental agents. The interplay of genetic and environmental factors is often relevant [9, 13]. Some types of cancer have been shown to follow Mendelian laws of inheritance [7], and familial aggregation has been demonstrated in a number of other specific cancers [2, 5]. Familiarity can be due both to heredity and to familial transmission of environmental carcinogenic factors [10].

Twin studies on cancer can be used for two purposes. First, they can be used to assess the role of genetic factors in the etiology of cancer in general and in that of specific cancers [1, 3, 4, 12]. As in all studies using the classical twin method, a specific estimate of genetic variance cannot be made, but rather an upper limit for the amount of genetic variance is obtained [8].

The twin method can also be applied as a case-control type of study. By studying the differences in the environmental exposures between identical twins discordant for cancer, one can attempt to identify carcinogenic factors as the twins are matched for genetic and many environmental factors. Factors that occur in both twins cannot be analyzed in such studies. To investigate the feasibility of such studies in Finland, we carried out a historical record-linkage cohort study between the Finnish Twin Registry and the Finnish Cancer Registry.

MATERIALS AND METHODS

The Finnish Twin Registry was created in 1974 from the computerized Central Population Registry by selecting all those sets of persons who satisfied the following criteria: same date of birth before 1958; same sex; same surname at birth; same community of birth; alive on January 1, 1967. The compilation process yielded 21,023 pairs, noninclusive of triplets and errors of the Central Population Registry.

A questionnaire was mailed to those alive in 1975 and with adequate address data. The questionnaire was used to establish twinship and zygosity [11] and to provide baseline data on the twin series. From the questionnaire responses and inquiries to parish records, the pairs were divided into twins and nontwins. There were 17,357 twin pairs and 3,666 singleton pairs. Zygosity could not be determined if both members of a twin pair had died before the 1975 questionnaire study, and therefore information on zygosity was not used in this study.

The Finnish Cancer Registry is a population-based, national registry in operation since 1953 [14]. It is considered to be rather complete with respect to incident cases of cancer in Finland.

Persons included in both registries were identified by comparing by computer the personal identification numbers (a 10-digit unique code assigned to each resident in Finland) of the two registries. The comparison covered the years 1967–1976: The Twin Registry dated from January 1, 1967 and the Finnish Cancer Registry's records on incident cases were complete up to 1976. The time span thus covered 10 years. The twin record linkage yielded the observed numbers of cancers of different types.

The whole series was followed up for death in 1967–1976. Age- and sex-specific person-years at risk were calculated separately for the twin population and the singleton group, all considered as individuals. The expected numbers of cancers were calculated using the national annual age- and sex-specific incidence rates for 1967–1976. Cases with the following diagnoses were excluded from the analyses: carcinoma in situ of the cervix uteri, papilloma of the urinary bladder, basal cell carcinoma of the skin, polycythaemia vera, and myelofibrosis.

Person-years at risk were also calculated for cotwins of cancer probands. If cancer had been diagnosed in both members of a twin pair after January 1, 1967, the earlier case was considered as the index case. Person-years for the cotwin were calculated from the date of diagnosis of cancer of the index case to the death of the cotwin or December 31, 1976. Expected values of cancer cases among cotwins were calculated using the national annual age-and sex-specific incidence rates.

Technical completeness of the record linkage was checked in several ways. Death certificates of twins who died of cancer after 1966 were checked. All cancers mentioned in those death certificates were found in the records of the Cancer Registry. All those persons who had reported in the 1975 questionnaire study of the Twin Registry having had cancer were either found in the record linkage or their cancer had been diagnosed before 1967.

RESULTS

The total cancer morbidity in the twin population was lower than expected for both men and women (Table 1). The relative risk for all cancers was 0.77 for men and 0.72 for women. Relative risks were below unity for all specific cancers studied as well. The relative risk was lower than unity in most age groups (Table 2). In the singleton population, the relative risk for men was slightly over unity,

TABLE 1. Observed and Expected Numbers of Cancer Cases in Finnish Series of Twins in 1967–1976

Primary site	Observed	Expected	RR
Males			
All sites	237	306.1	0.77
Lung	66	92.6	0.71
Stomach	34	36.2	0.94
Prostate	20	25.0	0.80
Other sites	117	152.3	0.77
Females			
All sites	190	264.5	0.72
Breast	45	61.1	0.74
Cervix uteri	13	17.2	0.76
Stomach	15	22.7	0.66
Ovaries	16	18.1	0.88
Corpus uteri	14	16.4	0.85
Other sites	87	129.0	0.67

TABLE 2. Observed and Expected Numbers of Cancer Cases in Finnish Twins Series in 1967–1976, by Age and Sex

Age group	Males			Females		
	Obs	Exp	RR	Obs	Exp	RR
5–9	0	0.0	0.0	0	0.0	0.0
10–14	1	1.1	0.9	0	1.0	0.0
15–19	1	3.6	0.3	5	3.4	1.5
20–24	6	4.8	1.3	8	5.3	1.5
25–29	5	5.1	1.0	6	6.6	0.9
30–34	6	6.4	0.9	3	8.4	0.4
35–39	3	9.0	0.3	12	12.7	0.9
40–44	16	13.4	1.2	10	19.1	0.5
45–49	14	20.9	0.7	22	26.6	0.8
50–54	31	26.3	1.2	23	29.2	0.8
55–59	29	36.7	0.8	21	30.2	0.7
60–64	43	55.3	0.8	15	32.8	0.5
65–69	35	52.1	0.7	26	32.5	0.8
70–74	26	34.1	0.8	19	24.7	0.8
75–79	17	19.9	0.9	12	16.2	0.7
80–84	3	10.4	0.3	6	10.0	0.6
85–	1	7.0	0.1	2	5.8	0.3
Total	237	306.1	0.77	190	264.5	0.72

whereas that for women was 0.82 (Table 3). Relative risks for specific cancers varied, owing to small sample sizes.

Because the low relative risk of cancer for twins was unexpected, and not due to technical causes, two further analyses were carried out. The relative risk of cancer increased with time (Table 4), but remained below unity for all but one year in men. In women, it increased with time and was unity or more in 1974 and later.

Total mortality of the twin series was compared to the expected mortality based on national annual age- and sex- specific mortality rates in 1967–1976. The ratio of these figures (SMR) for men remained rather unchanged (about 0.8), whereas the SMR for women increased with time (Table 5).

Within the twin series, eight cases of multiple primary cancer were found: in men two cases with cancers of the skin and prostate, two cases with cancers of the

TABLE 3. Observed and Expected Numbers of Cancer Cases in the Singleton Series in 1967–1976

Primary site	Observed	Expected	RR
Males			
All sites	88	81.2	1.08
Lung	32	25.0	1.28
Stomach	8	9.9	0.81
Prostate	8	7.5	1.07
Other sites	40	38.8	1.03
Females			
All sites	60	72.9	0.82
Breast	13	15.8	0.82
Stomach	10	7.1	1.41
Other sites	37	50.0	0.74

TABLE 4. Relative Risk of Cancer in Finnish Twin Population, by Calendar Year in 1967–1976

Year	Males			Females		
	Obs	Exp	RR	Obs	Exp	RR
1967	16	24.5	0.65	12	20.0	0.60
1968	13	25.5	0.51	7	21.3	0.33
1969	18	27.7	0.65	10	22.9	0.44
1970	26	29.1	0.89	15	23.5	0.64
1971	19	30.6	0.62	16	26.0	0.62
1972	33	31.5	1.05	19	27.2	0.70
1973	25	32.5	0.77	13	28.9	0.45
1974	28	32.5	0.86	29	29.7	0.98
1975	32	35.0	0.91	31	31.1	1.00
1976	27	37.2	0.73	38	33.9	1.12
Total	237			190		

TABLE 5. Observed and Expected Deaths in Finnish Twin Series Calendar Year (Standardized Mortality Ratios × 100), 1967-1976

	Males			Females		
Year	Obs	Exp	SMR	Obs	Exp	SMR
1967	78	99.7	78	23	53.8	43
1968	82	105.7	78	16	59.8	27
1969	84	114.3	73	20	66.4	30
1970	86	116.5	74	33	66.8	49
1971	99	127.4	78	28	73.5	38
1972	101	126.6	80	29	73.6	39
1973	112	129.4	87	54	75.1	72
1974	126	135.7	93	73	81.6	89
1975	115	136.3	84	72	83.7	86
1976	112	142.1	79	72	86.6	83

TABLE 6. Observed and Expected Numbers of Cancer Cases in Cotwins of Cancer Probands in the Finnish Twin Series 1967-1976

	Observed	Expected	RR
Males	10[a]	10.3	0.97
Females	3[b]	3.25	0.92

[a]Six pairs fully concordant: 1 prostate–prostate, 5 lung–lung.
[b]One pair fully concordant: breast–breast.

stomach and lung, and one case with cancers of the colon and lung, and colon and pancreas; in women one case with cancers of the peripheral nerves and stomach, and one case with cancers of the breast and bladder.

The number of cancers among cotwins of cancer probands was 13, whereas 13.6 were expected (Table 6). Seven site-concordant pairs were found; among these there were five lung cancer concordant male pairs. In two pairs, one of the twins had multiple primary cancers.

DISCUSSION

The main result of this study was that cancer morbidity in this twin series is less than that of the general Finnish population. The cancer morbidity of the singleton controls corresponded to that expected. Based on a series of 1,603 elderly twin pairs, Jarvik and Falek [4] concluded that cancer may be a less common cause of death among twins than in the general population. Harvald and Hauge [3] found that cancer mortality of twins did not differ from the general mortality either absolutely or relatively to all deaths. Incidence was, however, not analyzed. In the

Swedish Twin Registry with about 11,000 same-sexed twin pairs born between 1886 and 1925 and belonging to unbroken pairs in 1961, proportional cancer mortality between 1961 and 1968 was close to that expected [1].

In this study, the ratio of the observed to expected cancer morbidity closely reflected the standardized (total) mortality ratios for the same calendar years, suggesting that the lower-than-expected cancer morbidity may have a background in common with the lower-than-expected mortality. There was also a sex difference, in that the SMR for men remained rather unchanged, whereas that for women increased and was clearly higher than the relative risk of cancer toward the end of the follow-up period.

The lower-than-expected morbidity may be due to the fact that to be included in the study series, both members of a twin pair had to be alive, which excludes death-discordant pairs. The twin series was therefore probably selected as a healthier part of the population. The effect of this selection appears to diminish with time.

The observed concordance rate did not differ from that expected, which is in agreement with Harvald and Hauge's [3] result, whereas in the Swedish study [1] the observed to expected ratio was 2.06 in both MZ and DZ pairs. In children, however, MacMahon and Levy [6] estimated a concordance rate as high as 25% for leukemia in the identical twins. Draper et al [2] found that same-sexed twin pairs concordant for cancer were also site-concordant (excluding leukemias), whereas opposite-sexed pairs were always site-discordant. The Danish series [3] included only pairs in which both twins had survived beyond the age of 5, and only three cases out of 1,038 were diagnosed under the age of 20. The effect of genetic and familial factors on etiology of cancer in general may thus differ in children and adults. The low concordance rate found in this study suggests that it may be fruitful to study the environmental exposure of cancer-discordant MZ and DZ twins, whereas the cases of concordant pairs, in particular those with multiple primary cancers, can serve as index cases for genetic and family studies.

ACKNOWLEDGMENTS

This study was supported by the Council for Tobacco Research, U.S.A., and the Finnish Medical Research Council.

REFERENCES

1. Cederlöf R, Floderus B, Friberg L: Cancer in MZ and DZ Twins. Acta Genet Med Gemellol 19:69–74, 1970.
2. Draper GJ, Heaf MN, Kinnier Wilson LM: Occurrence of childhood cancers among sibs and estimation of familial risks. J Med Genet 14:81–90, 1977.
3. Harvald B, Hauge M: Heredity of cancer elucidated by a study of unselected twins. JAMA 186:749–753, 1963
4. Jarvik LF, Falek A: Cancer rates in aging twins. Am J Hum Genet 13:413–422, 1961
5. Lynch HT, Brodkey FD, Lynch P, et al: Familial risk and cancer control. JAMA 236: 384, 528, 1976.
6. MacMahon B, Levy MA: Prenatal origin of childhood leukemia: Evidence from twins. N Engl J Med 270:1082–1085, 1964.

7. McKusick VA (ed): "Mendelian Inheritance in Man: Catalogs of Autosomal Dominant, Autosomal Recessive and X-Linked Phenotypes," Ed 4. Baltimore: Johns Hopkins University Press, 1975.

8. Nance WE: The role of twin studies in human quantitative genetics. Prog Med Genet 3:73–107, 1979.

9. Purtilo DT, Paquin L, Gindhart T: Genetics of neoplasia — Impact of ecogenetics on oncogenesis. Am J Pathol 91:607–688, 1978

10. Rice J, Cloninger CR, Reich TH: Multifactorial inheritance with cultural transmission and assortative mating. I. Description and basic properties of the unitary models. Am J Hum Genet 30:618–643, 1978

11. Sarna S, Kaprio J, Sistonen P, Koskenvuo M: Diagnosis of twin zygosity by mailed questionnaire. Hum Hered 28:241–254, 1978.

12. Spranger J, von Verschuer O: Studies on the problem of the hereditary nature of cancer. Follow-up studies on the unselected twin series of v. Verschuer and Kober. Z Menschl Vererb v Konstitutionsl 37:549–571, 1969

13. Strong LC: Genetic and environmental interactions. Cancer 40:1861–1866, 1977.

14. Teppo L, Hakama M, Hakulinen T, Lehtonon M, Saxen E: Cancer in Finland 1953–1970: Incidence, mortality, prevalence. Acta Path Microbiol Scand Sect A, Suppl 252, 1975.

Twin Research 3: Epidemiological
and Clinical Studies, pages 225—230
© 1981 Alan R. Liss, Inc., 150 Fifth Avenue, New York, NY 10011

The Variations of Heritability as a Function of Parental Age

F.A. Lints and P. Parisi

*Department of Genetics, University of Louvain, Louvain-la-Neuve, Belgium
(F.A.L.), and The Mendel Institute, Rome (P.P.)*

In 1975 one of us (F.A.L.) devised an experiment in order to see whether the heritability of sternopleural bristle number in Drosophila melanogaster, a small fly, was or not a constant as a function of parental age [1, 13]. The purpose of the experiment was to determine whether, in animal breeding, the efficiency of selection could be increased by choosing parents at a particular moment of their life cycle. In fact, the heritability of sternopleural bristle number was found to change as a function of parental age. For instance, the heritability was 0.279 for offspring issued from parents aged 3 days, whereas it almost doubled for offspring issued from parents aged 28 days (Table 1).

Beardmore, who was associated in that first experiment, then decided to look at the same phenomenon in a fish, the guppy fish, Poecilia reticulata. There again, the results he obtained with one of his students, Shami, were quite clear (Fig. 1): The heritability of caudal fin rays number increased quite regularly as a function of the aging of the parental fish population [2, 18].

Later on, F.A.L. suggested one of his students, Stockhem, to investigate further the phenomenon in a mammalian species, namely, the cow, Bos taurus. Heritability was studied for both milk production and fat content of the milk. The problem was somewhat more complicated than in the cases of Drosophila or Poecilia. Indeed, raw data for milk production and milk fat content are not directly usable; they have to be corrected for different variables: for instance, the interval of time between calvings, the calving season, the year of calving, the average temperature and rainfall, the type of farm breeding, and so on. Furthermore, milk production and milk fat content are very generally negatively correlated. Whatever it is, heritability of these two traits varied significantly with parental age, but in opposite directions, decreasing for milk production and increasing for milk fat content (Fig. 2A and B) [19].

More recently, Lints and Baeten investigated the problem in the plant kingdom and studied 16 different traits in young seedlings of a pine tree, Pinus

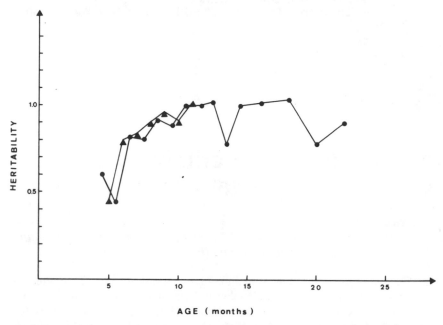

Fig. 1. Heritability of caudal fin rays number in the guppy fish, Poecilia reticulata as a function of parental age. Heritability is calculated from the offspring mid-parent regression. ● First experiment. ▲ Repetition made a year later. (Redrawn from Beardmore and Shami [2].)

TABLE 1. Heritability of Sternopleural Bristle Number in Drosophila melanogaster as a Function of Parental Age

Age of parents (in days)	3	14	28	42	56	70
Heritability	0.279	0.485	0.522	0.518	0.429	0.479

Parental flies are randomly mated. The heritability is calculated from the offspring mid-parent regression. (Modified from Table 4 in Beardmore et al [1].)

laricio. Some erratic variations were discovered, but on the average it may be said that, in Pinus laricio, heritability does not vary with parental age [11, 12].

A priori it might be supposed that, if heritability were to change with age, it would be more likely to decrease than to increase. This is because it has been argued that there is an accumulation of mutational, translational, or transcriptional errors with age in aging cells [4, 6, 15, 20]. If so, the resemblance between parents and offspring for a phenotypic trait with a value fixed at a point early in life—as with bristle number in flies or caudal fin rays number in fishes—should diminish with age. And this is not the case.

The phenomenon is, however, obviously related to age. But aging, in that light, should not be considered as a stochastic process, but as an event linked to the development of the individual, aging being simply one aspect of that de-

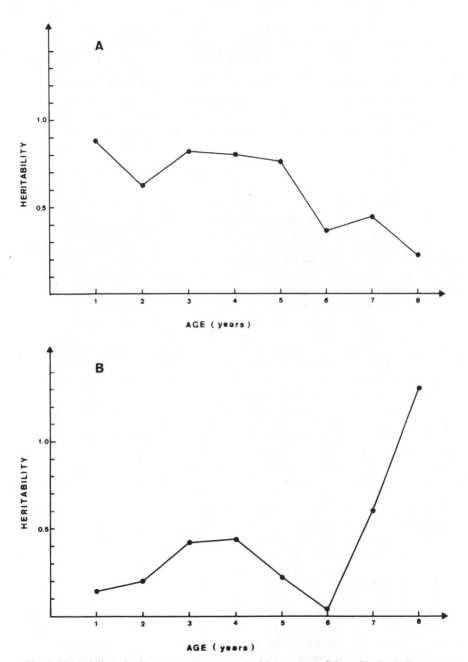

Fig. 2. Heritability of milk production (A) and of fat content of the milk (B) in Bos taurus as a function of parental age. Heritability is calculated from half-sib analysis. (Redrawn from Stockhem [19].)

velopment. (For a complete discussion on that topic, see Lints [10].) Further-more, the fact that variations of heritability could not be found among a popu-lation of trees—which, according to the available evidence, probably do not age in the true sense of the word [12, 21]—is another good piece of indirect evi-dence along that line.

In order to explain the variations of heritability with increasing parental age, and summarizing, variations in the amount of recombination in parental flies, variations in meiotic drive or affinity, variations of the quality of genetic mate-rial passing into the gametes were suggested as possible hypotheses [1]. Other alternative explanations will be discussed later.

An important objection could however be moved against the experiments made with Drosophila, Poecilia, Bos, or Pinus. Indeed, the analysis of the vari-ations of heritability in these experiments had been based on data obtained from aging populations. This means essentially that the heritability variations discovered could be due to two different factors, either the age of the individ-uals tested, or (and?) the changing genetic structure of the aging population. In other words, it may be asked whether the variations of heritability are a pure age effect, or are due to the fact that heritability is measured on populations with different genetic structures. The genetic structure of a population, as de-fined by a system of gene and genotype frequencies, may influence the esti-mates of heritability. Indeed, heritability, which expresses the proportion of the total phenotypic variance which is genetic in origin, will increase with a de-creasing environmental component of variance or with an increasing genetic component of variance. It may thus be argued that heritability will increase in an aging population when, in that population, the amount of heterozygotes in-creases at the expense of the homozygotes. It is highly probable that the amount of heterozygotes in a population increases when that population ages. This appears clearly from numerous studies, for instance, those of Dobzhansky and Wallace [7] in various species of Drosophila. In that same respect Shami [18], in his Poecilia study, has shown that his aging fish population was char-acterized by a significant reduction in the total phenotypic variance of the traits that he measured and by an increase of the number of heterozygotes at four polymorphic enzyme loci.

To discriminate between these two possibilities, one should measure both the phenotypic expression and the heritability of a given trait in progenies obtained at different ages from identical individuals. This is not easy. Another way of attacking the problem is through the study of twins. The analysis of the vari-ations in heritability and in the expression of a quantitative trait in twins should allow us to ascertain whether the variations in heritability are due to variations in the genotypic constitution of the population or to a pure age effect.

A dermatoglyphic study on twins associated with the Gregor Mendel Institute for Medical Genetics and Twin Studies in Rome was carried out. The quantita-tive trait, total finger ridge count (TFRC), was selected because it is relatively easy to evaluate and is known to undergo practically complete genetic condi-tioning [8]. Prints of all ten fingers were taken and analyzed on a total of 530 pairs of twins, 234 monozygotic (MZ) and 296 dizygotic (DZ). Fingerprints were taken, patterns defined, and TFRC measured according to standard procedures. Zygosity determination was based on a combination of criteria, including direct examination, identicalness and equivocalness, blood group tests, and, when available and reliable, fetal membrane information. These and other methodological details were explained in previous twin studies of dermatoglyphics by Parisi and Di Bacco [16, 17].

As we made already clear in a preliminary communication [14], within-pair differences in TFRC were found to decrease in MZ twins, and to increase in DZ twins, so that correlation coefficients increased in MZ twins and decreased in DZ twins, as a function of maternal age at conception. Therefore, and similarly to what had been found in previous studies, heritability appeared to increase with increasing maternal age (Table 2). Because of the very high positive correlation between paternal and maternal age, the actual role of the former is uneasy to determine. It may be noted that the question of the reliability of heritability estimates from twin studies and of what formula should be used does not seem to be relevant in this context, the point being that heritability, whatever its value, increases with increasing maternal age at conception. Even so, however, in the summary of results presented in Table 2, two different formulas have been used to derive heritability estimates, the classic one proposed by Holzinger [9] and a more recent one proposed by Cavalli-Sforza and Bodmer [5:573].

The study of heritability of total finger ridge count in man may give some ground to the hypotheses that consider the age effect on heritability either in terms of gene control or in terms of modifications of the genetic information transmitted by aging parents. Indeed, it is not only heritability that varies with age; the phenotypic expression of the trait varies also. Because MZ twins resemble each other more and more, while DZ twins differ phenotypically more from each other as parental age increases, any explanation based on an increase of the number of heterozygotes at the expense of homozygotes as the parental population ages is not plausible. In fact, in that case, the within-pair resemblance or dissimilarity should vary in the same direction both in MZ and DZ twins. Which is not the case.

TABLE 2. Twin Resemblance in Total Finger Ridge Count and Heritability Estimate by Maternal Age at Conception

Maternal age at conception	Within-pair differences				Within-pair correlation		Heritability[a]	
	MZ			DZ	MZ	DZ	1	2
	M	F	M+F					
< 28 years	10.2	13.2	11.5	32.2	0.934	0.610	0.831	0.872
28–33	7.6	9.0	8.4	35.2	0.978	0.512	0.915	0.943
> 33 years	5.2	8.7	7.4	32.5	0.979	0.571	0.951	0.948

[a]Heritability has been calculated (1) according to Holzinger [9] and (2) according to Cavalli-Sforza and Bodmer [5].

The age effect on heritability could thus be considered in terms of gene control. If this is so, it may mean two things. First, the information related to genetic control systems varies with the age of the parents in such a way that the older the parents, the better in the offspring the phenotypic expression of a given set of polygenes; ie, the phenotypic expression is less influenced by non-genetic factors. Second, it could be assumed that the additivity of action of a given set of polygenes responsible for a quantitative trait is increased when transmitted by older parents. Finally, it may also be more drastically hypothesized that genes are rearranged as a function of parental age. Gene rearrangement, produced by somatic recombination, was recently observed in mouse immunoglobulin genes and is suspected to play a role during normal cell differentiation [3]. Although the evidence has not been extended to cells undergoing meiosis to form gametes, it seems not unreasonable to assume that, if such rearrangements do occur, they may occur in these cells too.

REFERENCES

1. Beardmore JA, Lints FA, Al-Baldawi ALF: Parental age and heritability of sterno-pleural chaeta number in Drosophila melanogaster. Heredity 34:71–82, 1975.
2. Beardmore JA, Shami SA: Parental age, genetic variation and selection. In Karlin and Nevo (eds): "Population Genetics and Ecology." New York: Academic Press, 1976, pp 3–22.
3. Brack C, Hirama M, Lenhard-Schuller R, Tonegawa S. A complete immunoglobulin gene is created by somatic recombination. Cell 15:1–14, 1978.
4. Burnet M: "Intrinsic Mutagenesis." Lancaster: Medical and Technical Publishing Co., 1974.
5. Cavalli-Sforza LL, Bodmer WF: The genetics of human populations. San Francisco: Freeman, 1971.
6. Curtis HJ: Biological mechanisms of aging. Springfield, Illinois: CC Thomas, 1966.
7. Dobzhansky T, Wallace B: The genetics of homeostasis in Drosophila. Proc Natl Acad Sci USA, 39:162–171, 1953.
8. Holt SB: The genetics of dermal ridges. Springfield, Illinois: CC Thomas, 1968.
9. Holzinger KJ: The relative effect of nature and nurture on twin differences. J Ed Psychol 20:241–248, 1929.
10. Lints FA: Genetics and Ageing." Basel: Karger, 1978.
11. Lints FA, Baeten S: Etude de la descendance de quatre peuplements de pins de Koekalaere. I. Caractères très précoces. Bull Soc R For Belg 86:254–272, 1979.
12. Lints FA, Baeten S: Etude de la descendance de quatre peuplements de pins de Koekelaere. II. Heritability as a function of parental age. Gerontology 27:20–31, 1981.
13. Lints FA, Beardmore JA: Variation of heritability as a function of parental age in Drosophila melanogaster. Proc 10th Int Cong Gerontol 2:22, 1975.
14. Lints FA, Parisi P: Heritability and parental age. A twin study on finger ridge counts. Abstracts, Second International Congress on Twin Studies, Washington, 1977.
15. Orgel, LE: The maintenance of the accuracy of protein synthesis and its relevance to ageing. Proc Natl Acad Sci USA 49:517–521, 1963.
16. Parisi P, Di Bacco M: Le impronte digitali nei gemelli. Acta Genet Med Gemellol 16:71–100, 1967.
17. Parisi P, Di Bacco M: Fingerprints and the diagnosis of zygosity in twins. Acta Genet Med Gemellol 17:333–358, 1968.
18. Shami SA: Stabilizing selection, heterozygosity and parental age effects in Poecilia reticulata and Drosophila melanogaster. PhD thesis, Swansea, 1977.
19. Stockhem B: Influence de l'âge maternel sur l'héritabilité des caractères quantitatifs chez les bovins. Mémoire de fin d'études. U.C.L. Louvain-la-Neuve, 1977.
20. Szilard, L: On the nature of the aging process. Proc Natl Acad Sci USA 45:30–45, 1959.
21. Woolhouse HW: Longevity and senescence in plants. Sci Progr 61:123–147, 1974.

Twin Research 3: Epidemiological
and Clinical Studies, pages 231—238
© 1981 Alan R. Liss, Inc., 150 Fifth Avenue, New York, NY 10011

Genetics of Quantitative Variation of Human Scalp Hair Diameter

A. B. Das-Chaudhuri

Institute of Anthropology, University of Hamburg, Federal Republic of Germany

Works of Browne [4] and Oesterlen [14] marked the beginning of utilization of quantitative histomorphological characteristics of human scalp hair in racial classification. Since then, the diameter of human scalp hair has been studied mainly to establish its relationship with incidence of medullation [8, 10, 19], age [8. 10. 19], hair form and individual variability [1], population variability [11], and cuticular scales [9]. Genetic aspects of the hair diameter have apparently not been investigated, however.

On the other hand, Vernall [18], Das-Chaudhuri [5], Hrdy [11], and others have observed a very large amount of quantitative variability in the human scalp hair, which had previously gone unnoticed and such that would make it questionable to use this trait for anthropological classification. Therefore, a twin study has been carried out in order to shed more light on the extent of the variability of human hair diameter and its genetic basis.

MATERIAL AND METHODS

Hair samples of 48 pairs of German twins (Table 1) have been analyzed. Zygosity determination was based on the similarity method and on genetic markers (ABO, Rh, MNS, P, Kell, haptoglobin and transferrin) analyzed at the Institut für Humangenetik, University of Münster, Federal Republic of Germany. Hair samples were cut close to the scalp in the region of the vertex [15]. They were cleaned with equal parts of ether and absolute alcohol for 30 minutes. Starting from the proximal end, the diameter of each strand was measured randomly at 5–10 different places by 7× ocular calibrated with a micrometer and 0.65 mm objectives; each division of the micrometer being equal to 4 micrometers. As 100 strands from each individual were measured, the total number of strands studied was 9,600. The age range of the male and female twins was 2.50–20.25 and 6.50–44.50 years respectively, the mean age being 12.86 ± 1.21 and 13.30 ± 2.20 years.

TABLE 1. Number of Twin Pairs and (in parentheses) of Hair Strands Studied

	MM	FF	MF	Total
MZ pairs	8 (1,600)	9 (1,800)	–	17 (3,400)
DZ pairs	17 (3,400)	6 (1,200)	8 (1,600)	31 (6,200)
Total	25 (5,000)	15 (3,000)	8 (1,600)	48 (9,600)

STATISTICAL ANALYSIS

It should first be noted that the advanced methods of twin data analysis introduced by Kempthorne and Osborne [12], Vandenberg [16, 17] and Bock and Vandenberg [3] could not be used for the present data. In hair diameter, in fact, for each individual a set of n observations are obtained on each of the n number of randomly selected strands, so that the following variance components are expected to be present: 1) within-hair strand; 2) within-individual, between-hair strands; 3) between individuals in the populations of first and second individuals; and 4) between two individuals of any twin pair.

The Model and the ANOVA Table

We denote by $x^{(i)}_{jj'\lambda}$ the recorded λth observation on the j'th strand arising out of the ith pair of individuals and of the jth member of the ith twin pair:

$$i = 1, 2, \ldots M$$
$$j = 1, 2 \text{ (designated in the ANOVA Table as groups 1 and 2)}$$
$$j' = 1, 2, \ldots K$$
$$\lambda = 1, 2, \ldots n_{ij}$$

We take up the following model (random effects model):

$$x^{(i)}_{jj'\lambda} = \mu_J + \delta^{(i)}_j + \gamma^{(i)}_{jj'} + \epsilon^{(i)}_{jj'\lambda}$$

where μ_J = true value (of the character under study) on the jth member in the population of all such twin pairs, $\delta^{(i)}_j$ = excess effect of the jth member in the ith selected pair, $\gamma^{(i)}_{jj'}$ = excess effect of the j'th strand on the jth member of the ith selected pair, and $\epsilon^{(i)}_{jj'\lambda}$ = residual error attached to the λth observation on the j'th strand of the jth member of the ith selected pair.

We assume further that:

$$E(\delta^{(i)}_j) = E(\gamma^{(i)}_{jj'}) = E(\epsilon^{(i)}_{jj'\lambda}) = 0 \text{ for all } i, j, j', \lambda$$

Further, $V(\delta^{(i)}_j) = s^{*2}$

$$\begin{aligned} \text{Cov}(\delta^{(i)}_1, \delta^{(i)}_2) &= \varrho s^{*2} \\ V(\gamma^{(i)}_{jj'}) &= s_o^2 \\ V(\epsilon^{(i)}_{jj'\lambda}) &= s^2 \end{aligned} \qquad \text{for all } i, j, j', \lambda$$

and for all possible covariances equal to zero.

The analysis of variance table along with the expected values of different sum of squares is shown in Table 2.

Estimation of Variance Components

Monozygotic twin pairs. Here we have $n_{i1} = n_{i2} = n_i$ (say) and $\mu_1 = \mu_2$.

Hence $\quad E(s_e^2) = s^2 \qquad\qquad\qquad\qquad\qquad\qquad\qquad\qquad (2.1)$

$$E(s_r^2) = s^2 + s_o^2/M(\Sigma\eta_i) \qquad\qquad\qquad\qquad (2.2)$$

$$E(s_w^2) = s^2 + \frac{(xs^{*2} + s_o^2)}{M-1}\left(\sum_i \eta_i - \frac{\sum_i \eta_i^2}{\sum_i \eta_i}\right) \qquad (2.3)$$

and $\quad E(s_b^2) = s^2 + \left[s_o^2 + xs^{*2}(1-\varrho^*)\right]\dfrac{\sum_i \eta_i^2}{\sum_i \eta_i} \qquad (2.4)$

Here s_e^2, s_r^2, s_w^2, and s_b^2 all refer to corresponding mean squares in the ANOVA Table.

From the above, we get easily estimate of s^2, s_o^2, s^{*2}, and ϱ^*. Finally, the intrapair variance may be estimated as

$$\hat{V}(\delta_1 - \delta_2) = 2\widehat{s}^{*2}(1 - \widehat{\varrho}^*)$$

Dizygotic same-sex twin pairs or dizygotic opposite sex twin pairs. Here we have fundamentally $\mu_1 \neq \mu_2$; consequently, with reference to the ANOVA Table, the results (2.1), (2.2), and (2.3) still continue to hold, but, instead of (2.4), we have now $E(s_b^2) = E(s_B^2) = E(S.S.)$ corresponding to "between groups variation." As such, it essentially involves the quantity $(\mu_1 + \mu_2)^2$ besides the unknown parameter ϱ^*. Being so, it does not provide an estimate of ϱ^* (combined with (2.1), (2.2), and (2.3)). Instead, one can make use of so-called "covariance between groups" to seek an estimate of ϱ^*.

This we do below.

We adopt the following definition:

Covariance between groups $=$
$$SP_B = K\Sigma_i \sqrt{\eta_{i1}\eta_{i2}}\,(\bar{x}_1^{(i)} - \bar{x}_1)(\bar{x}_2^{(i)} - \bar{x}_2) \qquad (2.5)$$

From the model, we derive $\bar{x}_1^{(i)} - \bar{x}_1 = (\delta_1^{(i)} - \bar{\delta}_1) + (\bar{\gamma}_1^{(i)} - \bar{\gamma}_1) + (\bar{\epsilon}_1^{(i)} - \bar{\epsilon}_1)$

and similarly, $\bar{x}_2^{(i)} - \bar{x}_2 = (\delta_2^{(i)} - \bar{\delta}_2) + (\bar{\gamma}_2^{(i)} - \bar{\gamma}_2) + (\bar{\epsilon}_2^{(i)} - \bar{\epsilon}_2)$

TABLE 2. ANOVA Table

Sources of variation	d.f.	S.S.	E(S.S.)
Between groups	1	S_B^2	$\left[\dfrac{KN_1N_2}{N}(\mu_1-\mu_2)^2 + s^{*2} + \dfrac{s_o^2}{K}\left(\Sigma_i\eta_{ij}{}^2/(\Sigma_i\eta_{ij})^2\right) + \dfrac{s^2}{K}\sum_j\sum_i\dfrac{1}{\Sigma_i\eta_{ij}}\right]\left(\dfrac{\sum_i\eta_{i2}^2}{N_1^2} + \dfrac{\sum_i\eta_{i2}^2}{N_2^2} - 2\dfrac{\sum_i\eta_{i1}\eta_{i2}Q^*}{N_1,N_2}\right)$
Between individuals within groups	2(M−1)	S_W^2	$2(M-1)\,s^2 + (Ks^{*2}+s_o^2)\sum_j\sum_i\eta_{ij}\left(\dfrac{\sum_i\eta_{ij}{}^2}{\Sigma_i\eta_{ij}} - \dfrac{1}{\Sigma_i\eta_{ij}}\right)$
Between individuals	2M−1	S_I^2	$S_I^2 = S_B^2 + S_W^2$
Between strands within individuals	2M(K-1)	S_S^2	$(K-1)\,[s_o^2\,(\Sigma\Sigma\eta_{ij}) + s^2\,2M]$
Residual error	$K\sum_i\sum_j(\nu_{ij}-1)$	S_E^2	s^2 multiplied by d.f.
Total	$K\sum_i\sum_j \nu_{ij}-1$	S_T^2	

Consequently, $E(\bar{x}'^{(i)}_1 - \bar{x}_1)(\bar{x}'^{(i)}_2 - \bar{x}_2) = \text{Cov}(\delta'^{(i)}_1 - \bar{\delta}_1, \delta'^{(i)}_2 - \bar{\delta}_2)$

$$= s^{*2}\varrho^*\left(1 - \frac{\eta_{i2}}{N_2} - \frac{\eta_{i1}}{N_1} + \frac{\sum_\iota \eta_{i1}\,\eta_{i2}}{N_1\,N_2}\right)$$

and hence

$$E(SP_B) = Ks^{*2}\varrho^*\left(\sum_\iota \sqrt{\eta_{i1}\,\eta_{i2}} - \frac{\sum_\iota \sqrt{\eta_{i1}\,\eta_{i2}}\;\eta_{i2}}{N_2} - \frac{\sum_\iota \sqrt{\eta_{i1}\,\eta_{i2}}\;\eta_{i2}}{N_1}\right.$$

$$\left. + \frac{\sum_\iota \sqrt{\eta_{i1}\,\eta_{i2}}\;\sum_\iota \sqrt{\eta_{i1}\,\eta_{i2}}}{N_1\,N_2}\right) \tag{2.4$'$}$$

This (2.4)$'$ along with (2.1), (2.2), and (2.3) may be used to get estimation of s^2, s^2_o, s^{*2}, and ϱ^*.

Finally, the intrapair variance may be estimated as

$$\hat{V}(\delta_1 - \delta_2) = 2\hat{s}^{*2}(1 - \hat{\varrho}^*)$$

RESULTS AND DISCUSSION

In the present study on the effect of age on hair diameter, the mean hair diameter from the first member of each twin pair was used, constituting a sample of 48 individuals of different ages. The regression of hair diameter on age is $Y = 80.5980 + 0.2131$; the regression coefficient, 0.2131, is not statistically significant. This indicates that the hair diameter is age-independent in the present twin sample.

Estimates of error variance, correlation coefficient, and heritability estimate of hair diameter at different zygosity levels have been tabulated in Table 3. Results tabulated here were obtained from the computation of data on hair diameter.* The statistical analysis was based on the analysis of variance model. It will be evident from Table 3 that the within-strand variance, s^2, and the within-individual, between-strand variance, s^2_o, maintained almost a uniform value in all the pairs, irrespective of their sex and zygosity, which conforms with the assumption. The magnitude of within-strand variance is sufficiently smaller than that of the within-individual, between-strand variance. The smaller intrapair variances of hair diameter in both sexes of MZ twins in comparison to higher intrapair variance in their DZ counterparts suggest the presence of a genetic basis for the character under study.

Table 3 reveals that the intrapair variances of the twins are not greater than their respective within-individual, between-strand variances, although they are sufficiently greater than the respective within-strand variance. A genetic interpretation of this finding is difficult at this stage, as the intrapair variance is expected to be greater than within-individual, between-strand variance.

---

*Basic data collected on 9,600 strands of scalp hair diameter of different categories of twins are available upon request.

TABLE 3. Estimate of Error Variance, Correlation Coefficient, and the Heritability Estimate of Hair Diameter at Different Zygosity Levels

	Within-strand variance s^2	Within-individual, between-strand variance s_o^2	Variance between individuals in the populations of first and second individuals s^{*2}	Intrapair variance	Coefficient of correlation s^*	Heritability estimate
Monozygotic males	1.5818	14.4242	3.3730	0.1032	0.9847	0.9606
Dizygotic same-sex males	1.7407	15.7187	3.6091	4.6774	0.3520	
Monozygotic females	1.7040	12.6691	10.0637	0.5797	0.9712	0.9585
Dizygotic same-sex females	1.8130	13.0535	5.4240	13.9614	-0.2870	
Dizygotic opposite sex	1.4736	14.3023	9.7142	6.4658	0.6672	

In order to find a possible explanation, it should be recalled that in the present work the experimental setting is basically different from a conventional one: Instead of taking one measurement from each member of a twin pair, 100 strands were measured and from each strand 5–10 measurements were taken. So there might be high intraindividual variability, but that should not necessarily rule out the possibility of a high within-pair correlation. The finding of a high correlation in MZ pairs and of a low one in DZ pairs (and even a negative one in DZ female pairs) stands in support of this assumption. In the case of opposite-sex twin pairs, the correlation coefficient was found to be 0.6672, which appears to be very high in comparison to same-sex DZ twins. This finding is difficult to interpret at this stage, and further work will be necessary.

Finally, heritability estimate has been calculated using Kempthorne and Osborne's [12] modification of Newman, Freeman and Holzinger's formula [13]. From Table 3, it can be seen that about 96% of the variance of hair diameter would appear to be genetically determined.

The genetic basis of shaft diameter has to be further substantiated by family studies [6] as well as by the simultaneous analysis of twin and family data with respect to the possible mode of inheritance. It may be added that the present analysis revealed similar quantitative variations in the diameter of scalp hair as found by neutron activation analysis (NAA) of hair trace elements [2].

ACKNOWLEDGMENTS

I am indebted to Dr. A. R. Banerjee, Department of Anthropology, Calcutta University, for his invaluable research guidance and for supplying hair samples of zygosity-determined German twins, and to Drs. B. K. Sinha, Department of Statistics, Calcutta University, and B. K. Sinha, Indian Statistical Institute, for their statistical assistance.

This work was supported by the Council of Scientific and Industrial Research, Government of India. The main work was conducted in the Department of Anthropology, Calcutta University, and the manuscript was prepared during the tenure of a Humboldt Fellowship (1980) from Alexander von Humboldt-Stiftung at the Anthropologisches Institut, Universität Hamburg, Federal Republic of Germany. The author acknowledges thankfully Prof. Dr. R. Knussmann, Director of the Institute, for extension of all possible help during the preparation of the manuscript.

REFERENCES

1. Banerjee AR: Variation in the medullary structure of human head hair. Proc Natl Inst Sci India 29B:306–316, 1963.
2. Bate LC, Dyer FF: Trace elements in human hair. Nucleonics 23:74–78, 80–81, 1965.
3. Bock RD, Vandenberg SG: Components of heritable variation in mental test score. In Vandenberg SG (ed): "Progress in Human Behavior Genetics." Baltimore, John Hopkins Press, 1968, pp 233–260.
4. Browne PA: Trichologia mammalium, or a treatise on the properties and uses of hair wool, etc. Philadelphia: JH Jones, 1953.

5. Das-Chaudhuri AB: Genetics of quantitative variation of human head hair. PhD dissertation (unpublished), University of Calcutta, 1971.
6. Das-Chaudhuri AB: A study on genetics of quantitative variation of human head hair. DSc thesis (unpublished), submitted to the University of Calcutta, 1979.
7. Duggins OH, Trotter M: Age changes in head hair from birth to maturity. II. Medullation in hair of children. Am J Phys Anthropol 8:399–415, 1950.
8. Hausman LA: Further studies of the relationship of the structural characters of mammalium hair. Am Nat 58:544–557, 1924.
9. Hausman LA: The relationship of microscopical structural characters of human head hair. Am J Phys Anthropol 8:173–177, 1925.
10. Hausman LA: Recent studies of hair structure relationships. Sci Mon 30:258–277, 1930.
11. Hrdy D: Quantitative hair form variation in seven populations. Am J Phys Anthropol 39:7–18, 1973.
12. Kempthorne O, Osborne RH: The interpretation of twin data. Am J Hum Genet 13:320–339, 1961.
13. Newman HH, Freeman FN, Holzinger KJ: "A Study of Heredity and Environment." Chicago: The University of Chicago Press, 1937.
14. Oesterlan O: Das menschliche Haar und seine gerichtsartzliche Bedeutung. Tubingen, 1874.
15. Pinkus F: Die Normale Anatomie der Haut. Hanbuch der Haut-und Geschlechtskrankheiten, Vol. 1, 1927.
16. Vandenberg SG: Innate abilities, one or many? A new method and some results. Acta Genet Med Gemellol 16:41–47, 1965a.
17. Vandenberg SG: Multivariate analysis of twin differences. In Vandenberg SG (ed): "Methods and Goals in Human Behavior Genetics." New York: Academic Press, 1965b, pp 29–43.
18. Vernall DG: A study of size and shape of cross sections of hair from four races of men. Am J Phys Anthrop 19:345–350, 1961.
19. Wynkoop E: A study of the age correlations of the cuticular scales, medullas, and shaft diameter of human scalp hair. Am J Phys Anthropol 13:177–188, 1929.

Twin Research 3: Epidemiological
and Clinical Studies, pages 239—246
© 1981 Alan R. Liss, Inc., 150 Fifth Avenue, New York, NY 10011

Are Distances Between DZ Twins for Polygenes and for Major Genes Correlated?

Elisabeth Defrise-Gussenhoven, Charles Susanne, Yvette Michotte, Joseph Brocteur, and Bernadette Hoste
Centrum of Biomathematics, Free University of Brussels (E.D.-G., C.S., Y.M.), and Laboratory of Blood Groups and Transfusion, University of Liege (J.B., B.H.), Belgium

INTRODUCTION

For obvious reasons the localization of polygenes in man has not often been attempted. For one thing, experimentation is excluded and it is never known how many genes contribute to the size of a quantitative character. However, twin and family studies have repeatedly shown that many measurable characters are more or less in accordance with Fisher's model of polygenic inheritance [4].

We present a method enabling us, if not to locate polygenes, at least to lend them more reality; we look for correlation between distances for quantitative characters and distances for blood groups in a sample of 37 same-sexed dizygotic (DZ) twin pairs. The argument is as follows: When DZ twins have the same pheno- or genotype for a given blood group, the probability that they share one or two identical genes from their parents is larger (at least 75% and much more for polyallelic loci) than the probability that they possess no identical genes in common at the given locus (which is at most 25%). Now, when two sibs share an identical gene at one locus, they will also share identical genes for other characters at the neighboring loci, the chances of linkage being greater than the chances of crossing over. These neighboring identical genes might happen to be polygenes for one or several quantitative characters resulting in physical resemblance. Therefore it is not unreasonable to expect that same-sexed DZ pairs, differing for only a few blood groups, will be more alike biometrically than DZ pairs with many different blood groups. If this reasoning is correct, we can expect a positive correlation between the twin pair distances for the blood groups and the generalized distances for groups of body measurements.

This study was supported by a research grant from the Free University of Brussels.

MATERIALS AND METHODS

We use the preliminary results of an unfinished study of Belgian same-sexed twin pairs aged 18–25, 20 male and 17 female DZ pairs, and 25 male and 32 female MZ pairs. The zygosity diagnosis is based on at least 22 and at most 26 blood groups specified at the University of Liége [1] and summarized in Table 1. The probability of dizygosity for blood-concordant pairs has a mean of 0.00022, the extreme values being 0.00003 and 0.00091. Four measurements of the head (length, breadth, height, and frontal diameter), five of the body (standing and sitting height, arm length, breadth of shoulders, and pelvis), eleven of the face (frontal diameter, bizygomatic and bigonial breadth, face length, nasion–chin and nasion–stomion length, nasal height, nasal breadth, interocular breadth, lip height, mouth breadth) yield three generalized distances, denoted by Δ, for each DZ pair. The distances Δ are then correlated with the dissimilarity index D for all the blood groups.

Generalized Distance Δ for Groups of Measurements

For each sex and each separate group of measurements (head, body, face), let x_1 and y_1 be the standardized vectors for a given DZ pair x, y, and R the common correlation matrix calculated with the standardized measurements of the 188 twins.

$$\Delta(x,y) = \{(x_1 - y_1)'\ R^{-1}\ (x_1 - y_1)\}^{1/2} \tag{1}$$

is the generalized distance between the twins x and y defined by Defrise-Gussenhoven [2] and used in family studies by Susanne [5].

Minkowski Distance for Red Blood Cell Antigens

For the reactions with each of the 19 antisera summarized in Table 1, the DZ twins x and y are given scores 1 or 0 according to whether the reaction with the ith antiserum is positive or negative. The scores are denoted by x_i and y_i, and the Minkowski distance between the DZ twins x and y for all the red blood cell antigens is

$$d(x,y) = \Sigma\ |x_i - y_i| \qquad i = 1,2,\ldots,19 \tag{2}$$

This distance has been discussed by Defrise-Gussenhoven and Susanne [3] in the problem of uniovular dispermatic twins. In Table 2, d(x,y) is calculated for the case of twins x and y having all phenotypes equal except those of the ABO and the rhesus groups. This example shows that d(x,y) depends on the number of antisera that are used.

Minkowski Distance for the Plasmatic, Enzymatic, and HLA Systems

In these systems the general rule is: The distance per locus is equal to the number of genes possessed by one of the twins and not by the other. Denoting by the symbols L,M,N,P the allelic genes of a locus, the possible cases and their distances are given in Table 3. Table 4 indicates the scores to be used as

x_i and y_i in the Minkowski distance in the case of the plasmatic and the enzymatic systems. For the HLA phenotypes, the rule of Table 3 is used.

For example, let x possess: $AcP_1(A)$, $Km(1)$, $HLA(A_1A_2)$, $HLA(B_5B_5)$; and y: $AcP_1(BC)$, $Km(0)$, $HLA(A_{13}A_{14})$, $HLA(B_{37}B_{40})$. The distance $d(x,y)$ is then $3 + 1 + 4 + 3 = 11$.

When only one factor is detected as in $Km(1)$ and $Km(0)$, the distance between the two phenotypes is 1, because they differ by at least one gene.

The Minkowski distances for all the blood groups, including the red blood cell antigens, are added up. The sum is denoted by $d(x,y)$, a measure of the difference for all the blood systems in a DZ pair which we call the total Minkowski distance.

Dissimilarity Index D for the Blood Groups

We denote by M the total number of factors detected in the blood analysis (Table 1). M is also the largest possible distance between twins. In our study, M is not the same for all pairs and varies from 49 to 63; all pairs were tested for the 22 systems numbered 1–14 and 16–23 in Table 1. But in order not to lose the extra information yielded by the HLA system for 26 pairs, we use, instead of the distance $d(x,y)$, a dissimilarity index D, equal to $D = d(x,y)/M$ with $0 \leq D \leq 1$, where $d(x,y)$ is the total Minkowski distance and M the largest possible distance for the given pair. D is a measure of the twin difference for blood groups.

RESULTS

Table 5 summarizes the correlation coefficients between the dissimilarity index D for the blood groups and the three generalized distances for head, body and face (Δh, Δb, Δf). We have taken the male and female pairs together since there is no significant difference for sex between D, Δh, Δb and Δf. The correlations between the generalized distances are not significant. The dissimilarity index is positively correlated with Δf at the 3.8% level; it is also positively correlated with Δh and Δb though not significantly so.

DISCUSSION

The main part of our study is the search for positive correlation between dissimilarity for blood groups and distance in head, body, or face measurements for DZ twins. Table 5 shows an increasing correlation with D as more measurements are used to calculate the generalized distances; this fact seems to support the hypothesis that DZ pairs, alike for many blood groups, tend also to be alike for groups of measurements, the probability of positive correlation increasing as more measurements are used (4 for head, 5 for body, 11 for face). The significance of the correlation between D and Δf suggests that some polygenes for the face might be located in the neighborhood of some of the genes of the blood systems. The correlations between the generalized distances are not significant. The largest one is between Δh and Δf and can be explained by the presence, in both head and face measurements, of the frontal breadth.

TABLE 1. Blood Groups[a]

Red blood cell antigens	Antisera	Factors detected	Phenotypes
1. ABO	anti-A, anti-A$_1$, anti-B	3	6
2. Rhesus	anti-CC^w, anti-C^w, anti-c, anti-D, anti-E, anti-e	6	30
3. MNSs	anti-M, anti-N, anti-S, anti-s	4	9
4. P	anti-P$_1$	1	2
5. Kell	anti-K, anti-k	2	3
6. Lewis	anti-Le(a)	1	2
7. Duffy	anti-Fy(a)	1	2
8. Kidd	anti-Jk(a)	1	2
Plasmatic systems	**Method**		
9. Hp haptoglobin	starch gel electrophoresis	2	3
10. Gc group specific component	immunoelectrophoresis	2	3
11. Gm antigens of the γ chains of immunoglobulins	hemagglutination inhibition	3	5
12. Km (formerly Inv) antigens of the κ chains of immunoglobulins	hemagglutination inhibition	1	2
13. C3 third component of complement	agarose electrophoresis	2	3
14. Tf transferrin	agarose electrophoresis	3	6
15. Bf^b glycin-rich-β-glycoprotein complement C3 proactivator	agarose electrophoresis with immunofixation	2	3

Enzymatic systems	Method		
16. Acp₁ erythrocyte acid phosphatase	cellogel electrophoresis	3	6
17. PGM₁ phosphoglucomutase	cellogel electrophoresis	2	3
18. AK adenylate kinase	cellulose acetate electrophoresis	2	3
19. ADA adenosine deaminase	cellulose acetate electrophoresis	2	3
20. GPT glutamic pyruvic transaminase	starch electrophoresis	2	3
21. PGD 6-phosphogluconate dehydrogenase	cellulose acetate electrophoresis	2	3
22. EsD esterase D	cellogel electrophoresis	2	3
23. GLO glyoxylase I	cellogel electrophoresis	2	3
HLA[b] specifities recognized by WHO (1980):			
24. locus A: A1 A2 A3 A11 AW23(9) AW24(9) A25(10) A26(10) A28 A29 AW30(19) AW31(19) AW32(19)		13	91
25. locus B: B5 B7 B8 B13 B14 B15 B17 B18 BW21 BW22 B27 BW35 B37 BW38(W16) BW39(W16) B40 BW41 BW44(12) BW45(12)		19	190
26. locus C: CW1 CW2 CW3 CW4 CW5 CW6		6	21

[a] Blood of the twins was analyzed in the laboratoire Universitaire de Groupes Sanguins et de Transfusion, Liége (Directeur: Prof. André).
[b] Bf and HLA not specified for all the twin pairs.

TABLE 2. Example of Calculation of d(x,y)

Twin x is A_1, $C^w cDE$, MS, P_1, K+k+, Le (a+), Fy(a−), Jk(a−).
Cotwin y is A_2, CDe, MS, P_1, K+k+, Le(a+), Fy(a−), Jk(a−).

	ABO				Rhesus				
	anti-A	anti-A_1	anti-B		anti-CC^w	anti-C^w	anti-c	anti-D	anti-E	anti-e
x_i	1	1	0		1	1	1	1	1	0
y_i	1	0	0		1	0	0	1	0	1
d(x,y) =	0 +	1 +	0	+	0 +	1 +	1 +	0 +	1 +	1 = 5

TABLE 3. Rule for Calculation of d(x,y) With Codominant Genes L, M, N, P at One Locus

	Case 1	Case 2	Case 3	Case 4	Case 5	Case 6	Case 7
Twin x	LL	LM	LL	LL	LM	LL	LM
Cotwin y	LL	LM	LM	MM	LN	MN	NP
d(x,y)	0	0	1	2	2	3	4

CONCLUSION

The result of our study is such that we think it worth while to renew it with more DZ cotwins as soon as the study of Belgian twins is completed. Our twins form a group homogeneous for age and geographical origin. They were brought up together; 25 pairs still live together, and 10 pairs are separated since less than 5 years ago.

If it is true that some polygenes for quantitative characters are located in the neighborhood of some genes for blood groups, the homogeneity of our twin sample and the fact that the dissimilarity coefficient D is based on so many blood groups certainly increase the chances of positive correlations between D and the generalized distances Δh, Δb, Δf.

We also intend to correlate D with the distance for each separate measurement and to arrange them in ascending order for the correlation coefficients. We are still far from localization of one or more of the minor genes coding for a quantitative character, but, if positive correlations are found in our completed twin sample and in twin samples of other investigators, we think that a little progress will be made in the study of polygenic characters.

TABLE 4. Scores for the Phenotypes of Plasmatic and Enzymatic Systems (Maximum Distance per Blood System)

Plasmatic systems	Scores	Maximum distance
Hp[1]	11	
Hp[2−1]	01	2
Hp[2]	00	
Gc[1]	11	
Gc[2−1]	01	2
Gc[2]	00	
Gm(1, 2, 10)	111	
Gm(1, 2, −10)	110	
Gm(1, −2, 10)	101	3
Gm(1, −2, −10)	100	
Gm(−1, −2, 10)	001	
Km(1)	1	
Km(0)	0	1
C3(SS)	11	
C3(SF)	01	2
C3(FF)	·00	
AcP$_1$ (A)	100	
AcP$_1$ (B)	010	
AcP$_1$ (C)	001	3
AcP$_1$ (AB)	110	
AcP$_1$ (AC)	101	
AcP$_1$ (BC)	011	
PGM$_1^1$	11	
PGM$_1^{2−1}$	01	2
PGM$_1^2$	00	
AK[1]	11	
AK[2−1]	01	2
AK[2]	00	
ADA[1]	11	
ADA[2−1]	01	2
ADA[2]	00	
Tf(B)	100	
Tf(C)	010	
Tf(D)	001	3
Tf(BC)	110	
Tf(BD)	101	
Tf(CD)	011	
Bf(SS)	11	
Bf(SF)	01	2
Bf(FF)	00	
GPT[1]	11	
GPT[2−1]	01	2
GPT[2]	00	
PGD[A]	11	
PGD[AC]	01	2
PGD[C]	00	
EsD[1]	11	
EsD[2−1]	01	2
EsD[2]	00	
GLO[1]	11	
GLO[2−1]	01	2
GLO[2]	00	

TABLE 5. Correlation Coefficients for 37 DZ Cotwins

	D	Δh	Δb	Δf
D	1	0.0646 NS	0.2270 P = 0.089	0.2942 P = 0.039
Δh		1	0.0059 NS	0.1854 P = 0.138
Δb			1	0.0283 NS
Δf				1

P: Significance level for one-sided test.
NS: Nonsignificant.
D: Dissimilarity index for blood groups.
Δh, Δb, Δf: Generalized distances respectively for head, body, and face.

REFERENCES

1. Brocteur J, Hoste B, André A: Plasma protein and enzyme polymorphisms in Belgium. Hum Hered 4:221–224, 1980.
2. Defrise-Gussenhoven E: Generalized distance in genetic studies. Acta Genet 17:275–288, 1967.
3. Defrise-Gussenhoven E, Susanne C: Multivariate analysis in twin studies. In Nance WE, Allen G, Parisi P (eds): "Twin Research: Part A, Psychology and Methodology." New York: Alan R. Liss, 1978, pp 237–243.
4. Fisher RA: The correlation between relatives on the supposition of Mendelian inheritance. Trans R Soc Edinb 52:399–433, 1918.
5. Susanne C: Multivariate analysis in genetic studies. Acta Genet Med Gemellol 21:204–210, 1972.

Twin Research 3: Epidemiological
and Clinical Studies, pages 247—248
© 1981 Alan R. Liss, Inc., 150 Fifth Avenue, New York, NY 10011

Studies of Mutability in MZ Twins

L. Gedda, G. Brenci, C. Di Fusco, A. Noto, and E. Roselli
*The Gregor Mendel Institute of Medical Genetics and Twin Studies, Rome,
Italy*

The exchanges between sister chromatids represent a sensitive technique for the identification of chromosomal damage factors and more generally of mutagenic agents [2, 4, 5]. The correlation between exchange frequency and intensity of the mutagenic factor was shown for many chemicals (such as nitric mustards, quinacrine, acriflavin, proflavin) as well as for a physical factor, ultraviolet radiation. Furthermore, the frequency of exchange increases with respect to normal values also in some hereditary diseases like Xeroderma pigmentosum, Bloom's syndrome [1], and others. These two types of findings pose the problem of the relation between mutagenicity of the environment and the mutability of genes in the sense that, if an increase in sister chromatid exchanges can be obtained both through the variation of mutagenic factors and through a hereditary variation of the genome, then we are probably dealing with a single system with two variables: the mutagenicity of the environment and the mutability of the genome.

The mutability can be described more exactly taking into consideration its opposite, that is, the stability of a given gene with respect to the mutagenic capacity of a given environment. In order to verify whether the hypothesis of a system with two quasi-continuous variables could be valid (apart from considerations of the normal:pathological ratio) among normal individuals as well, and thus to determine whether mutability and therefore "stability" are also variable amongst clinically healthy individuals, we compared the chromatid-exchange frequency in MZ cotwins of three male pairs, 22 years of age.

Zygosity determination was based on the usual criteria, including the analysis of genetic markers, the probability of error being lower than 1%. The sister chromatid exchanges were studied in lymphocyte cultures of peripheral blood, stimulated with phytohemoagglutinine. At the beginning of culture, bromodeoxiuridine was added at a concentration of 10^{-4} M. The slides obtained by the usual techniques were colored with modified Giemsa [3].

The sister chromatid exchanges were evaluated on ten metaphasic slides for each individual. Mean values and standard deviations are shown in the upper part of Table 1. Student's t-test was then used as a method of analysis for small samples. In order to determine the variability between pairs, we compared the

TABLE 1. Sister Chromatid Exchanges in MZ Twins

	Number of exchanges					
	Pair A		Pair B		Pair C	
	1	2	1	2	1	2
$\bar{x}$	14.8	14.7	16.2	16.4	17.1	16.9
s	0.92	0.94	1.13	0.97	1.29	1.10
Variability within pairs						
$\bar{x}_1 - \bar{x}_2 = \triangle\bar{x}$		t		df		p
$1_A \rightarrow 2_A$ {14.8 - 14.7} = 0.1		0.239		18		$\simeq 0.80$
$1_B \rightarrow 2_B$ {16.2 - 16.4} = −0.2		0.424		18		$\simeq 0.70$
$1_C \rightarrow 2_C$ {17.1 - 16.9} = 0.2		0.373		18		$\simeq 0.75$
Variability between pairs						
$\bar{x}_1 - \bar{x}_2 = \triangle\bar{x}$		t		df		p
A → B {14.7 − 16.3} = −1.6		5.030		38		< 0.001
A → C {14.7 − 17.0} = −2.3		6.781		38		< 0.001
B → C {16.3 − 17.0} = −0.7		2.007		38		$\simeq 0.05$

mean values of pairs, and in order to identify the variability within pairs, we compared the mean values of cotwins.

The results (lower part of Table 1) indicate the existence of significant between-pair, but no within-pair variability. This is in agreement with the existence of an individual mutability associated to a differential stability of the corresponding genes.

REFERENCES

1. Chaganti RSK, Schonberg S, German J: A manyfold increase in sister chromatid exchanges in Bloom's syndrome lymphocytes. Proc Natl Acad Sci USA 71:4508–4512, 1974.
2. Perry P, Evans HJ: Cytological detection of mutagen-carcinogen exposure by sister chromatid exchange. Nature (Lond) 258:121–125, 1975.
3. Perry P, Wolff S: New Giemsa method for the differential staining of sister chromatids. Nature (Lond) 251:156–158, 1974.
4. Siminovitch L: On the nature of heritable variation in cultured somatic cells. Cell 7:1–11, 1976.
5. Wolff S: Sister chromatid exchanges. Ann Rev Genet 11:183–201, 1977.

Twin Research 3: Epidemiological
and Clinical Studies, pages 249—258
© 1981 Alan R. Liss, Inc., 150 Fifth Avenue, New York, NY 10011

Results of a Monozygotic Cotwin Control Study on a Treatment for Myopia

J. Theodore Schwartz
Bureau of Medical Services, Health Services Administration, USPHS, West Hyattsville, Maryland

This is a report on the outcome of a therapeutic trial on myopia originally described at the First International Congress on Twin Studies as an example of an ongoing prospective investigation employing monozygotic (MZ) cotwin controls. Descriptions of the study design and methods used were published in the proceedings of that congress [23]; accordingly, the current introduction will be limited as needed to place the findings and discussion in perspective.

Myopia is often classified into two main categories. The most common "simple" type is characterized as having an uncomplicated course showing progress during the growing years which stabilizes upon reaching maturity. Spectacle-corrected visual acuity remains normal. The other main category progresses through high levels of myopia, shows degenerative changes having potentially blinding complications, and is sometimes called degenerative or pathologic myopia. Although both the causes and management of myopia have excited immense interest over the past century, the extent to which either category represents an "etiologically pure" entity remains unsettled, as does the extent to which myopia is determined by hereditary and/or environmental factors.

Among environmental factors of suggested etiologic importance in simple myopia, one widely held theme, recurrent through the literature, relates progression of this common myopia to prolonged use of the eyes for reading or other close work. This is sometimes called the "use-abuse" theory. Some more widely employed attempts at the prophylaxis or retardation of myopia have been directed toward limiting or relaxing accommodation of the eye through the aid of bifocal spectacles or the use of cycloplegic medications. The latter is a category of pharmacologic agents that induces relaxation of the ciliary muscles of accommodation.

When this investigation was planned, promising prospective data were available [4, 5] in support of at least a temporary retardation of myopia by extended full-time cycloplegia attained through the use of atropine, a deep-acting and long-lasting cycloplegic agent. Earlier reports on the use of cycloplegic agents and/or bifocal spectacles [1, 2, 6–14, 19–22, 26–30] were generally based on retrospective observations drawn from clinical records. There were no other findings from long-term, prospective, randomized, single-masked, well-matched control studies on the prophylaxis or management of myopia.

This study was undertaken to test the effectiveness of a treatment that would induce relaxation of accommodation in an amount less than that which might interfere with daytime ocular function or appearance. Such a regimen, if effective, would seem readily acceptable to both patients and clinicians. The treatment regimen consisted of a combination of two drops of 1% tropicamide, a short-acting cycloplegic ophthalmic solution applied to each eye at bedtime, and the daytime use of bifocal spectacles having a reading addition of +1.25 diopters. The control twins received a standard single vision spectacle correction for myopia. The use of tropicamide had been reported [1, 2]; the combination with bifocals had not.

We set out to examine the general hypothesis that among the specially treated sample of twins, the average progression of myopia after 3 years would be less than their cotwin controls. From published descriptions of the rate of increase of myopia, an average expected increase during childhood and adolescence was estimated to be 0.58 diopters per year, and on this basis the present study was designed to detect a treatment benefit of 1 diopter in 3 years. Based on this and other considerations, the calculated number of required pairs was 22. (References, parameters, and calculations are given in the original article.)

To enter the study, the MZ twin pairs were required to be similarly myopic age 7–13 (one pair age 14), well within the age range of expected myopic progression. Treatment or control status was randomly assigned only after the twin pair and the parents expressed willingness to accept the rigorous requirements and the desire to participate. During the prospective observation period, the cohort was reexamined at approximately 6-month intervals at which time cycloplegic refractions were made under 1% cyclogel. All refractions were performed by the author, who was unaware of the treatment or control status of the examinees.

Each treated twin maintained a nightly record of medication adherence, generally with parental assistance. One parent, usually the mother, maintained general surveillance of the spectacle wearing patterns of each twin. Both of these monitored activities were reported and carefully reviewed at the 6-month visits.

RESULTS

Of the 26 pairs entered in the study, 25 participated through the full observation period, which was extended to 3½ years. Average entering age was 11.2 years; there were 13 male and 12 female pairs. Tabular distributions by age and sex were given in the original report.

A two-way summary of reported compliance to the regimen of drops and bifocal wear by treated members of the twinships is given in Table 1, which is oriented to show better compliance toward the lower left. Upon considering that 20 missed drops are equivalent to only 11% of the prescribed regimen, the overall medication compliance seems satisfactory. The twins were encouraged to wear their spectacles during school, study, and other close work, but a full-time spectacle wearing schedule was not required. Indeed, there is a scattering of mediocre performances for wearing time. For both activities, the need for accuracy in reporting was repeatedly stressed in preference to exemplary performance. Spectacle wearing history for the cotwin controls is not indicated in the table; however, within-pair wearing patterns were highly concordant.

Figure 1 shows the frequency distributions of spherical equivalent cycloplegic refraction (eyes averaged) for the treatment and control twin samples upon entry into the study. It might be mentioned that the existence of larger amounts

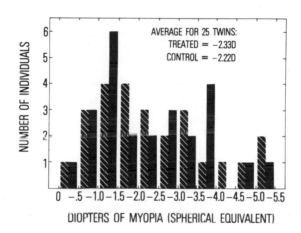

Fig. 1. Frequency distribution of cyclopegic refractions at baseline examination for 25 treated twins (crosshatch bars) and 25 control twins (solid bars). Each twin represented by average refraction for both eyes.

TABLE 1. Compliance With Treatment Regimen by 25 Treated Twins

Average hours of daily use of glasses	Average number of nights drops missed per (6-month) follow-up interval					
	<5	5–9	10–14	15–19	≤20 (value)	Total
<1	0	0	0	0	0	0
1–3	1	0	1	0	0	2
4–7	0	1	2	1	1 (46)	5
8–11	5	1	0	0	1 (21)	7
≤12	6	2	1	1	1 (62)	11
Total	12	4	4	2	3	25

of myopia in young children is generally regarded as a predictor of greater progression. No lower limit was established for entrance into the study, and there were a number of instances of low grade or marginal myopia. The average beginning refraction for the treated twins was –2.33 diopters and for the controls –2.22 diopters.

Figure 2 shows the average refraction at the baseline and successive follow-up examinations for the treated and control twin subsets. The dotted line portrays the anticipated trend increase for myopia, based on the literature. Clearly, neither twin subset achieved this amount of progression. It is also seen that the overall difference between the treated and control groups was small. To examine more effectively this main issue of relative progression, the differences exhibited between twin pairs are reflected in Figure 3. In preparing this graph, the change in refraction following the baseline observation was determined for each successive visit. The differences between treated and control members of each twin pair were determined and averaged, and are represented by the solid line. The dotted straight line was fitted to the same data using the

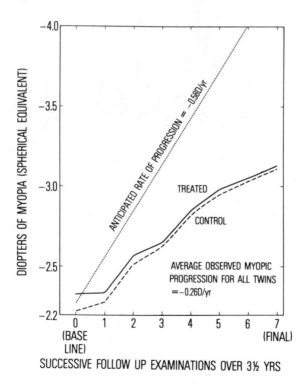

Fig. 2. Average cycloplegic refraction (spheric equivalent) at successive examinations for 25 treated and 25 control twins.

method of least squares assuming a zero baseline value. The sign convention for intrapair differences was selected to portray a treatment benefit as positive on the ordinate scale. (Intrapair difference = [–Diopters Myopic Progress of Treated Twin] — [–Diopters Myopic Progress of Control Twin].) The observed trend was directionally consistant with a treatment benefit, ie, there was on the average, less myopic progression among the specially treated members of the twin pairs. To lend a quantitative perspective to the amount of intrapair difference between treated and control members, however, a dashed line is shown which represents average successive refractions for all twins when superimposed using the same dioptic ordinate scale. The difference between treated and control twins was not statistically significant (paired "t-test" of the mean and sign test) and, by estimate based on the linear fit, it amounted to about 13% of the average myopic progression for the sample.

Because the total twin sample showed less overall myopic progression than anticipated, the data were reexamined for only those twin pairs in which at least one member, either the treated or control, progressed by ½ diopter or more during the period of observation. This truncation was an attempt toward elimination of those twinships destined to show little change with or without treatment.

The solid line in Figure 4 shows the average intrapair difference in refraction for the subset of 15 twinships exhibiting progression of ½ diopter or more. A dashed line representing average myopic progression for this sample of 15 is

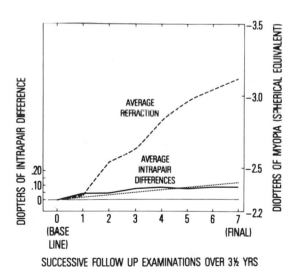

Fig. 3.   Average intrapair differences (treated minus control) in myopic progression from baseline at successive examinations for 25 total pairs. Average spheric equivalent refraction for total sample is shown for comparison.

again superimposed for perspective. A directional trend favoring treatment is
evident as before, but the difference is not statistically significant. The average
difference between treated and control members is equivalent to approximately
16% of the average myopic progress for this subset.

DISCUSSION

The Clinical Issue

This study was designed to detect an average treatment benefit of 1 diopter,
based on an expected overall rate of myopic progression substantially higher
than observed among the twin study sample. If the differences between treated
and control twins observed here were universally representative, about twice
the present sample size would be required in order to demonstrate statistical
significance. In view of the evident nonrepresentativeness of the present sample with respect to overall myopic progression, the author is reluctant to reject
the hypothesis of a treatment effect on the basis of the present findings. On
balance, the findings might be viewed as supportive of a more vigorous definitive clinical trial among singletons, studying, perhaps, a somewhat stronger yet
still acceptable clinical regimen.

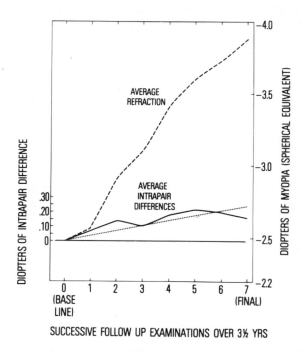

Fig. 4. Average intrapair differences (treated minus control) in myopic progression from
baseline at successive examinations for 15 subset pairs. Average spheric equivalent refraction of subset is shown for comparison.

Reports on the therapeutic use of cycloplegic agents available prior to this investigation were cited earlier [23]. Since this study was undertaken, an additional prospective trial of bifocal wear among singletons has appeared [18]. Using overall reading addition power comparable to that employed here, the authors reported a substantially lower annual rate of myopic progression among the bifocal wearers. The report indicates that the treated and comparison groups of subjects were similar for beginning refraction, sex and beginning age, but their treatment and nontreatment status were neither obscured from the examiner nor randomly assigned. Ending ages for some of the study groups were not the same suggesting also a disparity in duration of follow-up. A study based on the exacting design considerations required for a definitive answer to this question still does not appear to be available.

Twin Study Considerations

The usual presentation of detailed study critique seems superfluous to this report since the findings are already limited by the fundamental problem of relatively low myopic progression among the study sample and the relatively small numbers of pairs studied, given the finding of low progression. However, one potential criticism seems worthy of mention at this congress because it may point up a potential flaw in the cotwin control design of studies. Brief mention of selected aspects of our understanding of myopia will provide background for the use of myopia as the theoretical example for this potential flaw.

Figure 5 presents a list of most of the measurable ocular dimensions that contribute to the ocular refraction. The existence of substantial biologic variation of the individual components of refraction has been recognized for well over a century. In myopia, the combined configuration of the components of refraction is such that the net light-converging power of the curved refracting surfaces is too great in relation to length of the eye, causing parallel rays of light to come to a focus in front of the retina and a blurred image to fall upon the retina. A variety of possible component configurations can lead to the same myopic refractive error. For example, as shown to the right in diagram B, the net converging power of the corneal and/or lenticular configurations can produce excess convergence of light in an eye of ordinary length, a situation sometimes called curvature myopia. Conversely, as seen in diagram C, overall refractive power of an ordinary amount can coexist with myopia in an eye that is too long, a condition sometimes called axial myopia.

Since ultrasound measurement techniques were introduced, two major studies have been undertaken on inheritance of components of ocular refraction using twin heritability study methods [15–17, 24, 25]. Both investigators found an inconstant pattern of heritability among the batteries of individual components they studied. It is also of paranthetical interest that, although both investigators found high heritability for refractive error and for total axial length of the eye, their heritability findings were in direct opposition with respect to anterior lens curvature, lens thickness, and anterior chamber depth.

To return to the potential flaw in the cotwin control design of studies, the points to be emphasized from the foregoing are that the myopic refraction can be subclassified according to a variety of underlying causal configurations, ie,

MEASURABLE COMPONENTS OF REFRACTION

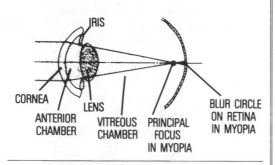

- FRONT CURVATURE OF CORNEA
- ASPHERICITY OF CORNEA
- BACK CURVATURE OF CORNEA
- ANTERIOR CHAMBER DEPTH
- FRONT CURVATURE OF LENS
- THICKNESS OF LENS
- BACK CURVATURE OF LENS
- LENGTH OF VITREOUS CHAMBER
- AXIAL LENGTH
- REFRACTIVE ERROR

EMMETROPIA AND TWO MYOPIC CONFIGURATIONS

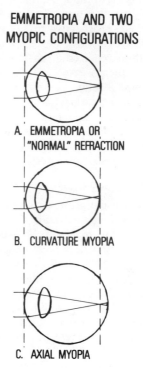

Fig. 5. Components of refraction and example of diagrams of component configurations in myopia.

the myopia observed clinically is actually a "common pathway" expression of a variety of component configurations. Suppose for this discussion that the relative roles of inheritance and environment differ among the various causal configurations of myopia, a supposition not inconsistent, perhaps, with the reports just cited [15–17, 24, 25], of dissimilar patterns of inheritance among the component elements of refraction. Given these conditions, a monozygotic cotwin control study requiring concordant pairs would favor entry of those twin pairs exhibiting the gene sensitive moiety(ies) and would be biased accordingly. If the inherited and environmentally determined forms were to have different responsiveness to the particular treatment under investigation, the generalizability of findings of the cotwin control study would be limited. Such potential source of bias might warrant consideration in other chronic disease applications of the MZ cotwin control design of studies. It could be assessed by including discordant pairs in the study to see if they respond to treatment as do the concordant pairs.

Much information needed for the understanding of myopia and its clinical management is potentially available through further applications of twin study methods. To mention a few immediate needs, a comparison of intrapair differences in refraction between MZ pairs reared apart and those reared together could greatly assist the interpretation of existing twin heritability data on myopia with respect to the "twin environmental assumption" [3] discussed at the first congress [23]. Furthermore, twin heritability studies on components of refraction warrant careful repetition using newly improved examination techniques (adequately pretested for validity and reliability), preferably based on relatively "representative" twin samples. In addition to new information on the existing disparate findings on heritability of the individual components and, perhaps, the more prevalent patterns of component configuration, such restudy would also permit the comparison of component elements and configurations between concordant and discordant MZ twin pairs to aid further in identifying and/or confirming those relatively heritable or nonheritable forms that might exist. With respect to future therapeutic trials among twin or singletons, the inclusion of adequate measurements of components of refraction could serve to identify myopic configurations that might be amenable to therapy by comparing components among those who respond to therapy with those who do not.

ACKNOWLEDGMENTS

Ophthalmic solution 1% mydriacyl (tropicamide) was supplied by Alcon Laboratories, Inc., Fort Worth, Texas.

REFERENCES

1. Abraham SV: A preliminary report on the use of bis-tropicamide in the control of myopia. J Ped Ophthalmol 1:39–48, 1964.
2. Abraham SV: Control of myopia with tropicamide. J Ped Ophthalmol 3:10–22, 1966.
3. Allen G: Scope and methodology of twin studies. Acta Genet Med Gemellol 25:79–85, 1976.
4. Bedrossian RH: The effect of atropine on myopia. Ann Ophthalmol 3:10–22, 1971.
5. Bedrossian RH: Treatment of progressive myopia with atropine XX. Concilium Ophthalmologicum Germania 1966. Int Cong Ser 146, Excerpta Medica Foundation. Acta Pars II pp 612–617.
6. Betz JN: Letter to Editor. Opt J Rev Optom 86:21–42, 1949.
7. Donders FC: "On the Anomalies of Accommodation and Refraction of the EYE." London: The New Sydenham Society, 1864.
8. Eggers H: The cause and treatment of school myopia. EENT Monthly 42:50–55, 1953.
9. Gamble JD: Considerations in myopia. Opt J Rev Optom 86:18–37, 1949.
10. Gostin SB: Prophylactic management of progressive myopia. South Med J 55:916–920, 1962.
11. Lancaster WB: "Refraction and Motility." Springfield, Illinois: C Thomas, 1953, p 152.

12. Leudde WH: Monocular cycloplegia for the control of myopia. Am J Ophthalmol 15:603–610, 1932.
13. Miles PW: A study of heterophoria and myopia in children (some of whom wore bifocal lenses). Am J Ophthalmol 54:111–114, 1962.
14. Miles PW: Children with increasing myopia treated with bifocal lenses. Missouri Med 54:1152–1155, 1957.
15. Nakajima A: Quantitative genetics in ophthalmology. Proc XX Int Cong Ophthal, Excerpta Med Int Cong Ser 146:1111–113, 1966.
16. Nakajima A, Kimura T, Kitamura K, Vesugi M, Handa Y: Studies on the heritability of some metric tratis of the eye and the body. Jpn J Hum Genet 13:1:20–39, 1968.
17. Nakajima A: The heritability estimates of the optical components of the eye and their mutual relationship by a new method of measurement on twins. Proc Second Int Cong Hum Genet G Mendel Inst Rome, pp 280–287, 1961.
18. Oakley KH, Young FA: Bifocal control of myopia. Am J Optom Physiol Optics 52:758–764, 1975.
19. Otsuka J: Research on the etiology and treatment of myopia. Acta Soc Ophthalmol Jpn 71:1–212, 1967.
20. Parker MW: Protective-corrective program for young myopes. Optom Weekly 49:681–683, 1958.
21. Parsons J: "Diseases of the Eye," 19th Ed, 1924, p 479.
22. Pascal JI: "Studies in Visual Optics." St. Louis: Mosby, 1952, p 287.
23. Schwartz JT: A monozygotic cotwin control study of a treatment for myopia. Acta Genet Med Gemellol 25:133–136, 1976.
24. Sorby A, Fraser GR: Statistical note on the components of ocular refraction in twins. J Med Genet 1:1:47–49, 1964.
25. Sorsby A, Sheridan M, Leary GA: Refraction and its components in twins. Privy Council Medical Research Council Special Report Series No. 303. Her Majesty's Stationery Office, London, 1962.
26. Tait EF: "Textbook of Refraction." Philadelphia: WS Saunders, 1951, pp 60–61.
27. Takano J: Treatment of myopia by the installation of tropicamide. Jpn J Clin Ophthalmol 18:45–50, 1964.
28. Takaro T, Kabe S: Treatment of myopia and changes in optical components. Report 1: Topical application of neosynephrine and tropicamide. Acta Soc Ophthalmol Jpn 68:1958–1961, 1964.
29. Toki T: Treatment of myopia with local use of neosynephrine hydrochloride. Jpn J Ophthalmol 4:213–219, 1960.
30. Warren GR: Myopia control and abatement. Opt J Rev Optom, 92:33–34, 1955.

Twin Research 3: Epidemiological
and Clinical Studies, pages 259—269
© 1981 Alan R. Liss, Inc., 150 Fifth Avenue, New York, NY 10011

Basic Survey on Atomic-Bomb-Exposed and Nonexposed Twin Pairs: Pilot Case Study From a Sociohistorical Viewpoint

Shoji Watanabe, Hiroshi Ueoka, Masaki Munaka, Naomasa Okamoto
Departments of Epidemiology and Social Medicine (S.W.), Biometrics (H.U., M.M.), and Geneticopathology (N.O.), Research Institute for Nuclear Medicine and Biology, University of Hiroshima, Japan

INTRODUCTION

The atomic bombing of Hiroshima brought many casualties on human society, and many follow-up studies have been made, especially on the effects of radiation, which so far have revealed such findings as increased incidence of leukemia among the survivors and high incidence of microcephaly in children born to women exposed in pregnancy, but few sociopsychohistorical investigations of the aftermath of the A-Bomb disaster have been made [1, 5, 6, 8]. At the authors' research institute, a research project concerning "A-bomb-exposed twins" was established several years ago, and preparations have been made for its conduct. The purpose of this study is to make, mainly on pairs of monozygotic (MZ) twins one of whom was exposed to the bomb and the other was not, a general sociopsychohistorical and medical investigation through a twin control study [11] to find whether the bombing, which can be considered to cause major environmental changes, has had any psychological effect on the individuals. The purpose is also to investigate what psychological effects and environmental factors including atomic bomb exposure have had on MZ twins who both were exposed by studying the same process of changes occurring in such twins by the difference of similarity of their post-A-bomb environment [4].

This study was supported by the Fund of the Welfare Ministry, and the Radiation effects association of Japan.

SAMPLING OF SUBJECTS

Considerable difficulty was involved in the collection of data because, owing to the bombing, basic data on the subjects of study and investigation were lost by fire, the community had collapsed, and study of the basic population given in the data was difficult to confirm. Under such circumstances, collection of multiple births based on information science was made from the following data by the following method insofar as possible: A) basic survey of A-bomb survivors (conducted in 1965); B) survey of family casualties in 1946; C) research on casualties near the hypocenter by mapping (conducted between 1969 and 1975); and D) survey of families (1973–1975).

Excepting the basic data, all are data from detailed investigations made through reconstruction of families as they were at the time of the bombing. As a result, 174,931 persons were examined from survey A, 127,674 from B, 42,002 from C, and 322,718 from D, of whom 587 pairs of multiple births were sampled by computer. Excluding from this number duplication sampling resulting from the data sampling method, 470 pairs of twins were selected. Among these 470 pairs of twins, survival of both twins was ascertained for 220; 48 pairs of opposite-sex and 172 pairs of same-sex dizygotic (DZ) twins were identified among them (Table 1 and 2).

TABLE 1. Collation Data Source of Multible Births Among A-Bomb Survivors

Research subject	A Basic research data	B Research data of 1946	C Casualties near the hypocenter	D Survey of families
Character of data	Exact No. of survivors	Family members and conditions of A-bomb	No. of residents before A-bomb	Family members at A-bomb
Time of research	Nov. 1, 1965	Aug. 10, 1946	1969–1975	1973–1975
Object	All of survivors on research	All of families in Hiroshima at bomb	All of families in 114 St. near hypocenter	All of survivors at research
Item	Age, sex, name, etc	Age, sex, name, residence, etc	Age, sex, name, residence, family relation, etc	Age, sex, name, residence, family relation, etc
No. of family or person	277,955 person	34,928 family	9,522 family	168,145 person
No. of research person	174,931	134,491	45,539	350,350
Basic research population	174,931	127,674	42,002	322,718

TABLE 2. Numbers of Pair of Twins, Collation of Data Sources

Source of data	A Basic research, 1965	B 1946 Research	C Casualties near hypocenter 1969–1975	D Family survey 1973–1975	No. of pair (%)
1	○				31 (6.6)
2	○			○	16 (3.4)
3	○	○			5 (1.1)
4	○		○		1 (0.2)
5	○	○		○	8 (1.7)
6	○		○	○	2 (0.4)
7	○	○	○		1 (0.2)
8	○	○	○	○	1 (0.2)
9				○	207 (44.0)
10		○		○	45 (9.6)
11		○	○	○	8 (1.7)
12			○	○	8 (1.7)
13		○			105 (22.3)
14		○	○		1 (0.2)
15			○		31 (6.6)
Pair of collation No. Total (%)	65 (11.1)	174 (29.6)	53 (9.0) 587 (100.0)	295 (50.3)	470 (100.0)

METHOD OF CASE STUDY

For the very limited sample of atomic-bomb-exposed twins, in number available for study, it is necessary to have an understanding of the living consciousness and identity they have developed [3] from the numerous mental stresses they suffered and the sociohistorical changes they experienced, including the changes in life from birth until the atomic bombing and from after the atomic to the present and the A-bomb disaster. With the above in mind, the following methods have been adopted:

1) Depth Interview Research

In order to determine as fully as possible the full particulars of the changes in their life history, the subjects were interviewed to gain knowledge of the psychological and social effects they incurred in the course of their lives, including the effects of the A-bomb disaster. Each individual subject was interviewed once or twice, for over an hour each time.

2) Projective Psychological Research

To supplement the interview research of 1), the Rorshach test as adapted and simplified by Hiroshi Motoaki et al has been carried out. (At the stage when understanding of the subject was obtained for the study, CMI was forwarded and knowledge of his or her physical status was obtained.) Also, a part of the Thematic Apperception Test (TAT) was used to determine the family relationship.

SUMMARY OF CASES

Case 1: Female MZ Twins, 50 Years of Age

A was exposed, B nonexposed. Shortly after their birth their mother died of adverse postpartal course. A was healthy at birth, but B, weighing only 2 kg at birth, was infirm. As the twins were far apart in age from their elder brother and sisters, they naturally always played by themselves. A was assigned the part of the younger of the twins by others around her and placed in the position of the youngest child of a rural family. For such reasons, she acted more freely than B, was more spoiled and selfish, and disposed to want to have her own way. She was extrovert and desired to assume an active way of life. B, given the role of the elder sister and nursed by her grandparents, on many occasions during her childhood because she was weak, developed an obedient and prudent personality.

At the time of the bomb. A was sent into Hiroshima City on the day following the bombing from a girls' high school in a suburb on a farming village to clear up the debris after the fire caused by the bomb and to extend care to the victims. She stayed and engaged in this labor service for a week at the site of a school near the hypocenter. During this time, she saw burnt dead bodies lying scattered all around and floating on the river, and she saw soldiers stacking and

TABLE 3. Case 1, ♀♀, Age, 50 MZ (November 1979)

	At birth	Younger years	Time of Bomb	Adulthood
Personal history				
A	Healthy	Personality: active, extrovert, A-B relation good	Early entrance and stay 1 week	Personality: bright, achievement desire (+) Anxiety: health after ovariosteresis, marriage of children
B	B. weight ↓ retardation	Personality: mild, obedient	Not exposed	Personality: bright, mild, achievement desire (+) Anxiety: marriage of children
Social family history				
A		Mother died Born (Farmer's home middle class)	Married	Children Ovariosteresis Poverty line*
B		Mother died Born (Same as A)	Married Live with father and mother-in-law	Children Father-in-law died Poverty line*

1920   '30   '40   '50   '60   '70   '80

*Level of Japanese public assistance. The curved line illustrates the economic level of the household, as in Rowntree [10].

burning dead bodies like sardines, which has remained strongly impressed on her mind. She had no acute symptoms, but after she was bedridden with fatigue for about a month, she returned home. She recovered thanks to sufficient nutrition in spite of the destitution after the war because food was produced by her family, and the living of the family was stable.

Post-A-bomb life. Both *A* and *B* grew up in a middle-class agricultural family in a rural community and have led a relatively stable life after marriage, with not too many ups and downs economically. They have lived a common married life, their homes not too far away from their parents' home.

Case 2: Male MZ Twins, 56 Years of Age

A was exposed and *B* was not. The twins were born in a family of a dealer of marine products in a suburb of Hiroshima. During their infancy their family had been well off. Many employees lived with the family, and they had been brought up indulgently. Following their father's death when they were 2 years of age, the family business was closed and the mother moved with the twins to her parents' home. Subsequently, the mother reared the twins with stern discipline as she was a strong-minded woman.

At the time of the bomb. Immediately after the A-bomb was dropped, *A* reported for work at a steel-making company in the suburbs of Hiroshima where he was employed. He went in search of relatives from his company and walked around the city, going as far as the vicinity of the hypocenter. For a week, he searched daily until evening. However, his efforts were fruitless, because the faces and bodies of persons who suffered burns and the dead bodies on the roadside were so burnt and bloated that they defied identification. At that time, *A* had no acute symptoms and worked as usual at his company. *B* was in military service and was not exposed to the atomic bomb because he had been dispatched to Taiwan.

Post-A-bomb life. *B* was repatriated 1 year after the war, and he and *A* went back to work in the same company they had worked for before. As *B* was of an unyielding spirit and of such a personality that it was difficult for him to hold in check his desires, he was at one time a leader of labor strikes which frequently occurred after the war, and then quit the company. In contrast, *A*, as the second son, had been allotted a smaller portion of his parents' estate under the provisions of the old Civil Law, and he had developed a persevering character that enabled him to tolerate grievances to some extent. He continued working at his company and retired as a skilled worker at mandatory retirement age. He has been employed by an affiliate company of his former company.

Case 3: Male MZ Twins, 53 Years of Age

A was exposed and *B* was not. The twins were born to a middle-class family of a rice dealer in a small city in Hiroshima prefecture. Both *A* and *B* volunteered for military service part way through middle school. They grew up in a

TABLE 4. Case 2, ♂♂ , Age 55, MZ (June 1980)

	At birth	Younger years	Time of bomb	Adulthood
Personal history				

A	Healthy	Father died
		Personality:
		  inferior complex to cousin
		  A-B relation good
			Acute radiation
			symptom (−)
			Early entrance and
			stay 1 week.
				Personality:
				  Mild. Social relation—good
				Anxiety: Growing old. Expense of
				  child education

B	Healthy	Personality:
		  Same as A
			not exposed
			went Army
				Personality:
				  Depressive. Unyielding
				Anxiety:
				  Trouble with business. Growing old

Social family history

*Level of Japanese public assistance. The curved line illustrates the economic level of the household, as in Rowntree [10].

TABLE 5. Case 3, ♂♂, Age 52, MZ (February 1980)

	At birth	Younger years	Time of bomb	Adulthood
Personal history				
A	B. weight ↓ retardation	Personality: extrovert A-B relation good	Acute symptom (++) exposed 1.5 km bed 3 month	Personality: Mild. Social relation—good Anxiety: psychological fear of the Bomb, problem of aging
B	Healthy	Personality: Same as A	Not exposed	Personality: mild Achievement desire (+) Anxiety: no problem
Social family history				
A	Born (rice dealer's home middle class)		Engaged as sanitary engineer	Married
B	Born (Same as A)		Engaged in clerical work	Married Children

*The level of Japanese public assistance. The curved line illustrates the economic level of the household, as in Rowntree [10].

family in favorable economic circumstances. During World War II, when his family business was merged with others under the wartime national food control system, the father decided to quit his business, entered a school of acupuncture and moxibustion in which he had an innate interest, graduated, and opened business.

At the time of the bomb. B was in military service elsewhere in Japan. A was serving in Hiroshima. He was marching in a small unit in the street 1.5 km northeast of the hypocenter and was exposed to radiation from behind. He fainted and was unconscious for a while. After regaining consciousness, he extricated himself from under a collapsed building and made his escape. At that time he sustained burns on his back and both arms and also developed such symptoms as diarrhea and epilation. Only several of his comrades escaped, but within a period of 1 year they either died or their whereabouts became unknown. On the day following the A-bomb, he was taken back to his parental home about 40 km away, where he was bedridden for 4 months. Physically, he recovered in a year. Mentally, his phobia against smoke persisted for several years.

Post-A-bomb life. B, after his demobilization, and A, after his recovery a year after the bomb, found employment and worked in Hiroshima (A—medical technologist, B—clerk-accountant). Their finances steadily improved with the recovery of the economy of Japan. Neither of them had financial worries, and they accommodated themselves well to society. However, because he has no children, A has a faint sense of uneasiness about the mental blow sustained from the A-bomb and the eschatological problem.

RESULT AND DISCUSSION

As a result of the projective psychological research, analysis based on the correlation among interviews, CMI, and clinical data was obtained on each case. Also, the Rorschach test and TAT were applied [2, 9] tentatively in order to clarify the psychology and human relationships of the exposed twin and nonexposed twin.

A Japanese version of TAT, and a version of Neugarten were used to clarify the familial relationship, but no remarkable difference in response was observed between them. It is desired to continue this study in the future on a larger number of cases. Next, regarding the response to the Rorschach test, the exposed one of the twins in all three cases, 1, 2, and 3, indicated psychological anxiety in his or her response to the Color Form (CF), particularly to the red and orange of cards 4 and 5; the responses were "bloody pus" (Picture 5), "elf fire," "bandage and blood," "dirty colors."

Compared with the exposed counterpart, this is a remarkable characteristic. Further, in regard to (4), the Color Form response shown at the time of investigation suggests a relationship to atomic bomb exposure.

TABLE 6. TAT Response

Case	Power	Affectiveness	Needs		Response				Result		
			Social approval	Belonging	Independent	Aggressive	Regressive	Fantastic	Happy	Unhappy	Indefinite
1 A	−	++	±	+	−		+				+
B	−	++	±	+	−		+		+		
2 A	−	++	+	+	+		+				+
B	+	+	+	±	+	++				+	
3 A	++	+	++	+		±			+		
B	+	+	++	+		±				±	

Degree of response: ++ strong, + fair, ± mild, − negative.

TABLE 7. Modified Rorschach Response

Case	Whole	Division	Form	Move.	Color*		Response No.**
					FC (Form C.)	CF (Color F.)	
1 A	±	+	+	±	±	±	+
B	±	∧	∧	±	±	−	+
2 A	+	++	+	++	±	+	++
B	±	+	±	±	±	reject	±
3 A	+	+	+	±	±	+	+
B	+	+	±	±	±	reject	±

*No. of response ++ 5–7, + 3–4, ± 1–2, − 0.
**No. of response ++ 30–, + 20–29, ± 10–19.

REFERENCES

1. Bolin R, Trainer P: Modes of family recovery following disaster: A cross-national study. In Quarantelli EL (ed): "Disasters Theory and Research." Beverly Hills: Sage Inc. 1978.
2. DeVos G: A comparison of the personality differences in two generations of Japanese Americans by means of the Rorschach test. Nagoya J Med Sci 17:153–265, 1954.
3. Erikson EH: "Identity and the Life Cycle: Selected Papers in Psychological Issues." New York: International Universities Press.
4. Inouye E: Modified method of Essen-Möller's zygosity diagnosis for Japanese Twin. In Uchimura H (ed): "Twin Research." Japan Society for the Promotion of Science, 1956, pp 9–13, (in Japanese).
5. Killian LM: The significance of multiple group membership in disaster. Am J Socio 57 (1952). In Wrenn RL (ed): "Basic Contributions to Psychology." 1966, pp 273–277.
6. Lifton RJ: "Death in Life—Survivors of Hiroshima." New York: Random House, 1967.
7. Munaka M, Watanabe T, Yamamoto H, Ueoka H, Watanabe M, Okamoto N: Vital statistics of A-bomb survivors in Hiroshima. Part 1. Trends in mortality of A-bomb survivors. Report of 15th annual meeting on the late effects of A-bomb detonation, 1975, pp 8–13, (in Japanese).
8. Nakano S: Genbaku Eikyo no Shakaigakuteki Chosa (Sociological study of the effects of A-bomb detonation). Daigakujinkai Kenkyuronshu, 1954, pp 29–39, (in Japanese).
9. Neugarten BL, Gutmann DL: Age sex roles and personality in middle age: A Thematic apperception study; in middle age and aging. In Neugarten BL (ed). Chicago: University of Chicago Press, 1968, pp 58–71.
10. Rowntree S: "Poverty: A Study of Town Life." 1901.
11. WHO: Report of a WHO meeting of investigations: The use of twin in epidemiological studies: Acta Genet Med Gemellol 15:110–128, 1966.

Twin Research 3: Epidemiological
and Clinical Studies, pages 271—276
© 1981 Alan R. Liss, Inc., 150 Fifth Avenue, New York, NY 10011

Pilot Case Study on the Natural History of Disease in Atomic-Bomb-Exposed Twins in Hiroshima

Yukio Satow, Hajime Okita, and Naomasa Okamoto

Departments of Geneticopathology (Y.S., N.O.), and Internal Medicine (H.O.), Research Institute for Nuclear Medicine and Biology, University of Hiroshima

INTRODUCTION

This is a twin control study on atomic-bomb-exposed twins. The purpose of this study is to make a general medical and sociological investigation on the exposed twins to look for any biological effect of atomic bomb exposure and provide data that are useful for the health management of atomic bomb survivors. Subjects are mainly pairs of monozygotic twins, one of whom was exposed to the atomic bomb and the other not exposed [7].

As for pairs who were both exposed, an investigation is also made to see how they have been affected by the difference of environmental conditions since they were exposed to the atomic bomb. They will be grouped with the similar findings to make clear the interrelation of environmental factors including atomic bomb exposure.

METHOD

Exposed twins were picked up by electronic computer from the master file of atomic bomb survivors in the data bank of our institute [6]. With their understanding and cooperation, clinical and physiological examinations and zygosity diagnosis of the twins were made. The natural history of their diseases was investigated to find out possible late effects of the atomic bomb. Among many check-up points the values of immunoglobulin M and A [1] and the height [2] are considered to be genetically controlled to a considerable extent. On the other hand, the values of immunoglobulin G [1], serum cholesterol, body weight, and blood pressure [3] are considered to be susceptible to both genetic and environmental effects. The concordance or discordance of these values may thus provide an indicator of the genetic and/or environmental effects.

This study was supported by the Fund of the Welfare Ministry, and the Radiation effects association of Japan.

A total of 470 pairs of exposed twins were picked up from the master file of atomic bomb survivors in the data bank of our institute. From this number, 220 pairs with both twins alive were extracted and 48 opposite-sex pairs and 172 pairs of the same sex were identified (Table 1). According to Weinberg's method [8] and considering that the MZ:DZ ratio is about 1.83:1 in the Japanese [5], about 112 pairs are assumed to be MZ and about 60 pairs DZ. Zygosity diagnosis was made according to the method of Inouye [4].

CASE REPORTS

So far three pairs of discordantly exposed and four pairs of concordantly exposed twins have been examined. These cases are summarized below.

Discordantly Exposed Pairs

Case 1: Female monozygotic twins, age 50 (Table 2). They have often been said to be as like as two peas since their childhood. When they were 16-year-old high school girls, one of them took care of the atomic bomb victims at a primary school close to the center of explosion for a week from the day following the bombing. She suffered from diarrhea. Both of them are almost in the same height but are slightly different in weight. Characteristics are accelerated blood sedimentation rate and a higher value of immunogloblin G, though there are no inflammatory findings. No specific effect of the discordant exposure is noticed.

Case 2: Male monozygotic twins, age 56 (Table 3). One of them, at the age of 21, entered Hiroshima immediately after the A-bomb was dropped to look for a fellow employee of his company and walked around the ruins every day for a week. He showed no acute symptoms. They have approximately equal height, body weight, and blood pressure. The value of immunoglobulin G is equal. Their x-ray pictures of chronic gastritis look like each other. Again, no specific effect of the discordant exposure is noticed.

Case 3: Male monozygotic twins, age 53 (Table 4). One of the pair, at the age of 18, was exposed to the A-bomb at 1.5 km from the center of explosion and he was burned and lost his senses. He also suffered from diarrhea. Both are almost the same in height but the exposed one is heavier than the other by 10 kg and shows higher blood pressure. The lighter of the pair works in a tobacco company and likes smoking. Both of them like drinking and are different in values of immunoglobulin G, A, and M. These findings show some effect of environmental factors, but the relationship to the A-bomb is not clear.

Concordantly Exposed Pairs

Case 1: Male monozygotic twins, age 35. Both were exposed at 1.5 km from the center of the explosion. After exposure they lived in different environments. There is a difference in their body weights. This difference seems to be due to environment. One of them suffered from gastric ulcer at the age of 24 and chronic hepatitis at the age of 29. As for the other twin, hepatitis and gas-

TABLE 1. Number of the A-bombed Twin Pairs

Birth (Age)	Total	Male-Male				Female-Female				Male-Female			
		Total	Both exposed	One, exposed	Unknown	Total	Both exposed	One, exposed	Unknown	Total	Both exposed	One, exposed	Unknown
Total	220	74	62	9	3	98	89	7	2	48	36	10	2
1945–46 (33–34)	13	4	4			8	8			1	1		
1940–44 (35–39)	60	20	20			22	22			18	16	2	
1935–39 (40–44)	35	15	12	2	1	14	13		1	6	5	1	
1930–34 (45–49)	30	11	10	1		15	13	2		4	4		
1925–29 (50–54)	53	19	12	5	2	20	17	3		14	6	6	2
1920–24 (55–59)	25	2	1	1		19	16	2	1	4	3	1	
1890–1919 (60–89)	4	3	3							1	1		

TABLE 2. Case 1 (♀♀ , 50 y, MZ)

	Exposed twin (next day entry)	Nonexposed twin
Acute symp.	Diarrhea (+)	—
Living in	Hiroshima	Hiroshima
	Two children	Two children
Alcohol	(–)	(±)
Tobacco	(–)	(–)
History	Ovarian cyst, 46 y.	Lumbago
	Housewife	Farmer
Height	145.4 cm	145.3
BW	47.9 kg ↑	39.3
BP	130 – 70	120 – 60
Hb	11.8g/dl ↓	12.8
Ht	34.0%	36.0
Total bilirubin	(0.5 – 1.0 mg /dl) 0.5	0.6
Direct bilirubin	(0 – 0.5 mg /dl) 0.3	0.4
GOT	(8 – 40 u) 30	34
GPT	(5 – 35 u) 15	14
LDH	(50 – 400 u) 338	525 ↑
Alkaline phos.	(4 – 12 u) 7.7	6.5
Blood sediment.	30 – 60mm/1 – 2h. ↑	35 – 65 ↑
ASLO	(–)	(–)
CRP	(–)	(–)
IgG	(1347 ± 299mg/dl) 2016 ↑	2016 ↑
IgA	(243 ± 97 mg/dl) 300	300
IgM	(♀207 ± 76 mg/dl) 234	332 ↑
HLA A Locus	2.11	2.11
B Locus	16.54	16.54
Diag.	Atrophia	Spondylosis
	uteri	deformans

TABLE 3. Case 2 (♂♂ , 56 y. MZ)

	Exposed twin (the day entry)	Nonexposed twin
Acute symp.	(–)	—
Living in	Hiroshima	Hiroshima
	Two children	Two children
Alcohol	(–)	(–)
Tobacco	(–)	(–)
History	np	np
Height	172.0	172.0
BW	60.0	64.0
BP	130 – 80	130 – 88
Hb	13.7	14.8
Ht	39.5	40.0
Total bilir.	0.6	0.7
Direct bilir.	0.3	0.3
GOT	24	26
GPT	15	19
IgG	1,554	1,554
IgA	296	360
IgM	152	214
HLA A locus	24	24
B Locus	52	52
Diag. Chronic	(+)	(+)
gastritis		

TABLE 4. Case 3 (♂♂ , 53 y. MZ)

	Exposed twin (1.5 km)	Nonexposed twin
Acute symp.	Burning (+) Diarrhea (+) Unconscious. (+)	—
Living in	Hiroshima No child	Hiroshima Two children
Alcohol	Sake 400 – 500 ml/day for 10 y.	Sake 400 – 500 ml/day for 30 y.
Tobacco	(–)	20/day
History	Appendectomy 46 y.	Hepatitis, Nephritis 29 y. Gastric ulcer 50 y.
Height	162.4	163.2
BW	70.0 ↑	60.2
BP	136–86	112–82
Hb	15.7	15.2
Ht	43.0	44.7
Total bilir.	0.9	1.0
Direct bilir.	0.4	0.5
GOT	33	25
GPT	45	13
LDH	305	306
IgG	1,134	1,386
IgA	380	292
IgM	154	140
HLA A Locus	24	24
B Locus	7, 22.1	7, 22.1
C Locus	4	4
Diag.	Nerve deafness of 1-ear	Chronic gastritis

tric ulcer were detected at the time of this examination; that is to say, he caught the same diseases about 10 years later.

Case 2: Male monozygotic twins, age 37. Both were exposed at 3 km away from the center of explosion. One was out of doors and was burned. He has not been married ever since. Except that he is heavier than the other by 13 kg and has higher blood pressure, there is no significant difference between the two.

Case 3: Male monozygotic twins, age 36. Both were taken to the ruined Hiroshima on the fifth day after the A-bomb was dropped. They are similar in height, body weight, and blood pressure. Although they live separately from each other, their characteristics suggest the similarity of their genetic background.

Case 4: Female monozygotic twins, age 53. Both were exposed at 2.3 km away from the center of the explosion. One of the twins had diarrhea and was infected. They live at remotely separated places. Considerable differences in height and body weight are observed. They are under medical care for hypertension, which was detected when they were 46 and 48 years old respectively.

CONCLUSION

From our preliminary observations, no special effect of the A-bomb exposure has been found. On the other hand, after a lapse of over 30 years since the atomic bombing, it is not easy to investigate its effects. As long as A-bomb survivors are alive, however, the work has to be continued. Whether the clinical data prove the relationship to the atomic bomb to be positive or negative, they will be useful for the health management of the survivors. We will continue to accumulate such cases as these over a long period of time.

REFERENCES

1. Escobar V, Corey LA, Nance WE, Bixler D, Biegel A: The inheritance of immunoglobulin levels. In Nance WE, Allen G, Parisi P (eds): "Twin Research: Part C, Clinical Studies." New York: Alan R. Liss, 1978, pp 171–176.
2. Furusho T: On the manifestation of genotypes responsible for stature. Hum Biol 40:437–455, 1968.
3. Hamilton M, et al: The aetiology of essential hypertension. 4. The role of inheritance. Clin Sci 13:593–601, 1954.
4. Inouye E: Modified method of Essen-Möller's zygosity diagnosis for Japanese twins. In Uchimura H (ed): "Twin Research." Japan Society for the Promotion of Science, 1956, pp 9–13 (in Japanese).
5. Inouye E: Pathological method for twin study. Jpn Clin 15:131–136, 1967. (in Japanese).
6. Munaka M, Watanabe T, Yamamoto H, Ueoka H, Watanabe M, Okamoto N: Vital statistics of A-Bomb survivors in Hiroshima. Part 1. Trends in mortality of A-Bomb survivors. Report of 15th annual meeting on the late effects of A-Bomb detonation, 1975, pp 8–13 (in Japanese).
7. Okamoto N: Outline of the research project on the A-bombed twin. Proc Hiroshima Univ RINMB 13:36–38, 1972 (in Japanese).
8. Weinberg W: Beiträge zur Physiologie und Pathologie der Mehrlingsgeburten beim Menschen. Arch ges Physiol 88:346–430, 1901.

Subject Index

PROGRESS IN CLINICAL AND BIOLOGICAL RESEARCH

DATE DUE

Demco, Inc. 38-293